Technology and Entrepreneurship Education

Denis Hyams-Ssekasi • Naveed Yasin
Editors

Technology and Entrepreneurship Education

Adopting Creative Digital Approaches to Learning and Teaching

Editors
Denis Hyams-Ssekasi
Institute of Management
University of Bolton
Bolton, UK

Naveed Yasin
Faculty of Management
Canadian University Dubai
Dubai, United Arab Emirates

ISBN 978-3-030-84291-8   ISBN 978-3-030-84292-5   (eBook)
https://doi.org/10.1007/978-3-030-84292-5

© The Editor(s) (if applicable) and The Author(s), under exclusive licence to Springer Nature Switzerland AG 2022
This work is subject to copyright. All rights are solely and exclusively licensed by the Publisher, whether the whole or part of the material is concerned, specifically the rights of translation, reprinting, reuse of illustrations, recitation, broadcasting, reproduction on microfilms or in any other physical way, and transmission or information storage and retrieval, electronic adaptation, computer software, or by similar or dissimilar methodology now known or hereafter developed.
The use of general descriptive names, registered names, trademarks, service marks, etc. in this publication does not imply, even in the absence of a specific statement, that such names are exempt from the relevant protective laws and regulations and therefore free for general use.
The publisher, the authors and the editors are safe to assume that the advice and information in this book are believed to be true and accurate at the date of publication. Neither the publisher nor the authors or the editors give a warranty, expressed or implied, with respect to the material contained herein or for any errors or omissions that may have been made. The publisher remains neutral with regard to jurisdictional claims in published maps and institutional affiliations.

This Palgrave Macmillan imprint is published by the registered company Springer Nature Switzerland AG.
The registered company address is: Gewerbestrasse 11, 6330 Cham, Switzerland

Foreword

The first course in entrepreneurship education is recognized to have been offered at Harvard University in 1947; taught by Miles Mace, it used a business plan method to teach 188 second-year MBA students the basics of venture creation (Katz, 2003). Since then, entrepreneurship education has grown into a worldwide phenomenon. It has expanded from individual classes to the establishment of concentrations, bachelor and graduate programs (Solomon et al., 1994). It has spread across universities, such that entrepreneurship education can be found in most academic disciplines (Pittaway & Hannon, 2008). It has even spread across educational systems and countries worldwide, and programs can now be found in elementary, secondary, and vocational schools (Morris et al., 2013). This spreading out of a new discipline across the educational landscape is unrivalled in the recent history of education. As practice has expanded, so the research of entrepreneurship education has followed. Early reviews indicate that research was focused on both programs 'for' entrepreneurs and 'in' universities (Dainow, 1986). As university efforts developed research expanded into discrete areas: training practices for small firms; education for new venture creation; and small business training for university students (Garavan & O'Cinneide, 1994a, 1994b). By the early 2000s research had further diversified and also considered student propensity and intentionality to become entrepreneurs, program design, and program evaluation (Henry et al., 2005a, 2005b) and included a focus on graduate outcomes, extracurricular activities, and assessment practice (Pittaway & Cope, 2007a). More recent reviews show that research has continued to mature and diversify (Mwasalwiba, 2010; Naia et al., 2014; Byrne et al., 2014).

This book is timely, given the growth of entrepreneurship education and the subsequent expansion of research. Many advocates of entrepreneurship education have maintained that practices in the topic benefit from an experiential approach (Gibb, 2002; Pittaway & Cope, 2007b). Students need to learn 'about' entrepreneurship but also acquire skills 'for' it, while engaging in opportunities to learn 'through' actual practice (Pittaway et al., 2009). Alongside these trends toward expansive practice in entrepreneurship education, a disruptor has materialized for education more generally. This is the growth and impact of technology in the educational domain and how it has changed the education business model. A trend that has been accelerated by the COVID pandemic. Examples are everywhere. One is the use of Massive Open Online Courses (MOOCs) and platforms like Coursera, Khan Academy, edX, and Udacity to deliver online learning. Another is the growth of Online Program Managers (OPMs) like Pearson, All Campus, Noodle, and 2U that manage online programs for universities, an industry that is now worth billions of dollars. Other examples include the expansion of technologies to improve engagement in online learning (e.g., VoiceThread; Zoom), the increasing availability of educational simulations, and the gamification of class designs (Fox et al., 2018). Such EdTech companies are becoming major players on exchanges worldwide. The next wave of innovation in learning technologies is also imminent, as augmented reality, virtual reality, and artificial intelligence (AI) begin to enter the fray. These disruptive innovations are starting to have an influence on the way in which education is provided and distributed, as well as beginning to impact pedagogy itself through blended, hybrid, and rotational models of learning design. All of these developments have accelerated noticeably in the last two years as a result of the pandemic and the social distancing requirements it has enforced upon educators and learners. Faced with the increasing shift to online delivery of education and the acceleration of new technology adoption, entrepreneurship educators must maintain their innovativeness and desire to encourage learning by doing, while utilizing these new methods of learning. The contribution of this book is to address this issue by presenting research that explores the use of technologies in entrepreneurship educational practice. It considers gamification, presents research on simulations, examines the creative use of digital learning, examines the role of MOOCs, and begins to consider how AI might impact learning.

Increasingly science, technology, engineering, and math (STEM) subjects are being asked to innovate to improve teaching methodologies and are using both new technologies and entrepreneurship education to address this need. Consequently, the second contribution of this book is to explore the expansion of entrepreneurship education into technology-based disciplines. Here it explores practices in digital marketing and considers experiential learning in science and technology. This is a particularly important contribution. As entrepreneurship educators begin to gain sway in these disciplines there is hope that more technologies derived from these subjects at universities worldwide will gain greater potential to be spun off and turned into new technology-based ventures. Equipping students in these disciplines with entrepreneurial mindsets and skills has the potential to improve entrepreneurial outcomes and impact economic development in a more general sense. Having entrepreneurial minded scientists and engineers may reap significant benefits for society, as was demonstrated during the nineteenth century and the industrial revolution.

Overall, this book will be influential. It is a collection of important essays and studies that advances our understanding of the role of technology in entrepreneurship educational practice. It highlights how these trends might impact educators and shows how technologies might be deployed to further enhance what educators do, in the classroom and in the online environment. Within the research domain, it advances understanding, beyond simply observing and reporting classes and/or reviewing student self-efficacy/intentionality, by going more deeply into the technological aspects of learning. This is a particularly important component as these aspects continue to accelerate in terms of their adoption within, and their disruption of, traditional educational models. Entrepreneurship educators should read this book because it will provide them with example practices and ideas about how to use new technologies to advance their courses, programs, and learning implementation. Educational researchers should read this book because it advances our understanding of key technological trends and explores how these trends have been researched in our subject, as well as providing detailed studies of the implementation of technologies within educational practice. In closing, the final chapter of this book provides insights into the future of technology in entrepreneurship education, as well as exploring entrepreneurship education in technology-based disciplines. It thus provides a sound basis for considering future research opportunities across these topics.

Centre for Entrepreneurship Luke Pittaway
Ohio University
Athens, OH, USA

References

Byrne, J., Fayolle, A., & Toutain, O. (2014). Entrepreneurship education: What we know and what we need to know. In C. Chell & M. Karataş-Özkan (Eds.), *The handbook of research on small business and entrepreneurship* (pp. 261–288). Edward Elgar Publishing.

Dainow, R. (1986). Training and education for entrepreneurs: The current state of the literature. *Journal of Small Business and Entrepreneurship, 3*(4), 10–23.

Fox, J., Pittaway, L., & Uzuegbunam, I. (2018). Simulations in entrepreneurship education: Serious games and learning through gameplay. *Entrepreneurship Education and Pedagogy, 1*(1), 61–89.

Garavan, T. N., & O'Cinneide, B. (1994a). Entrepreneurship education and training programmes: A review and evaluation—Part 1. *Journal of European Industrial Training, 18*(8), 3–12.

Garavan T. N., & O'Cinneide, B. (1994b). Entrepreneurship education and training programmes: A review and evaluation—Part 2. *Journal of European Industrial Training, 18*(8), 13–21.

Gibb, A. (2002). In pursuit of a new enterprise and entrepreneurship paradigm for learning: Creative destruction, new values, new ways of doing things and new combinations of knowledge. *International Journal of Management Reviews, 4*(3), 213–232.

Henry, C., Hill, F., & Leitch, C. (2005a). Entrepreneurship education and training: Can entrepreneurship be taught? Part I. *Education and Training, 47*(2), 98–111.

Henry, C., Hill, F., & Leitch, C. (2005b). Entrepreneurship education and training: Can entrepreneurship be taught? Part II. *Education and Training, 47*(2), 158–169.

Katz, J. A. (2003). The chronology and intellectual trajectory of American entrepreneurship education. *Journal of Business Venturing, 18*(2), 283–300.

Morris, M. H., Kuratko, D. F., & Cornwall, J. F. (2013). *Entrepreneurship programs and the modern university*. Edward Elgar.

Mwasalwiba, E. S. (2010). Entrepreneurship education: A review of its objectives, teaching methods, and impact indicators. *Education and Training, 52*(1), 20–47.

Naia, A., Baptista, R., Januário, C., & Trigo, V. (2014). A systematization of the literature on entrepreneurship education. *Industry and Higher Education, 28*(2), 79–96.

Pittaway, L., & Cope, J. (2007a). Entrepreneurship education: A systematic review of the evidence. *International Small Business Journal, 25*(5), 477–506.

Pittaway, L., & Cope, J. (2007b). Simulating entrepreneurial learning: Integrating experiential and collaborative approaches to learning. *Management Learning, 38*(2), 211–233.

Pittaway, L., & Hannon, P. (2008). Institutional strategies for developing enterprise education: A conceptual analysis. *Journal of Small Business and Enterprise Development, 15*(1), 202–226.

Pittaway, L., Hannon, P., Gibb, A., & Thompson, J. (2009). Assessment in enterprise education. *International Journal of Entrepreneurial Behavior and Research, 15*(1), 71–93.

Solomon, G. T., Weaver, K. M., & Fernald, L. W., Jr. (1994). Pedagogic methods of teaching entrepreneurship: A historical perspective. *Simulation & Gaming, 25*(3), 338–353.

Preface

Based on the UK Quality Assurance Agency's report (2012) it is reinforced that enterprise and entrepreneurship education continues to gain widespread interest for the wide range of benefits that it provides to universities and its stakeholders. Enterprise and entrepreneurship education has proven to encourage entrepreneurial endeavors and business start-ups among students while increasing inclusivity and wider participation, developing student's creativity, active citizenship, learning attainment, stakeholder engagement, demystify career opportunities, and enhancing employability (QAA, 2012).

Although the terms 'enterprise' and 'entrepreneurship' are used interchangeably, 'Enterprise is defined here as the generation and application of ideas, which are set within practical situations during a project or undertaking. This is a generic concept that can be applied across all areas of education and professional life' (QAA, 2012, p. 7). A range of concepts such as creativity, originality, idea generation, design thinking, and practical actions underpin this. On the other hand, 'Entrepreneurship' education implies the application of enterprise behaviors, attributes, and competencies into the creation of cultural, social, or economic value. This can, but does not exclusively, lead to venture creation as it can apply to both individuals and groups.

Agreed upon this is that enterprise educators would need to move beyond traditional teaching and assessment methods by adopting creative and innovative pedagogical approaches such as implementing technology, developing provisions for experiential learning, and simulation gaming approaches (Yasin & Hafeez, 2018). These approaches encourage students to 'learn from doing' whether that would be developing a business plan, pitch to investors, or even start up a company (Dickson et al., 2008; Fayolle et al., 2006; Stokes et al., 2010). Such educational practices in entrepreneurship also enable students to expand on their personal networks, academic success, and improve confidence levels (Csorba, 2014) while also increasing higher wage returns of participating students in the graduate labor market (Vestergaard et al., 2012).

Considering the numerous benefits that enterprise and entrepreneurship education offers to improve graduate prospects across higher education institutions globally, it is surprising there are relatively limited publications and knowledge-sharing platforms for enterprise educators that are the vehicle to mobilize such higher level objectives and translate such institutional and program goals into a tangible outcome.

Adopting contemporary technologies that promote experiential learning in enterprise education is widely encouraged as established in several studies (Yasin & Hafeez, 2018). Considering the impact of COVID-19 and an institutional shift toward online and blended learning methods would also reinforce the time of a dedicated book on technology and enterprise and entrepreneurship education to promote a dialogue between enterprise educators worldwide to implement and share effective practices. The explicit purpose of this book is to highlight the emerging technologies in enterprise education while also providing impetus for enterprise educators to engage in discourse to share their effective practices in teaching and learning which remain limited in the discourse of enterprise and entrepreneurship education.

In particular, this book addresses key questions: What are the effective practices enterprise educators utilize to develop digitally assisted enterprise and entrepreneurship education provisions for students in higher education institutions? Which types of digital technologies are effective to teach entrepreneurship to students in higher education in diverse educational contexts? Are there any international case studies that champion successful student engagement using digital technologies in the delivery of enterprise and entrepreneurship education?

We have divided this book into two parts, which examine entrepreneurship education and the use of technology in teaching and learning.

In Part I, the authors focus on teaching enterprise and entrepreneurship education. In Chap. 1, Hyams-Ssekasi and Taher provide a theoretical perspective of entrepreneurship education and the use of gamification in teaching and learning. In Chap. 2, Yasin, Gilani, and Contu provide an overview of simulation-based learning and its application specifically within entrepreneurship education. Followed by Al-Gindy, Yasin, Aerabe, and Omar (Chap. 3) further explore modern technology as an essential tool that enhances entrepreneurship education and skills development. Following these chapters are the measurements of the impact of simulation-based teaching on entrepreneurship skills and development at a higher level of learning (Salamzadeh, Tajpour, and Hosseini, Chap. 4). The empirical evidence follows, which unravels the factors that enhance learning and teaching with digital technology (Ahamat and Ai, Chap. 5).

Part II consists of five chapters that focus on collaboration in enterprise and entrepreneurship education considering the simulation-based teaching pedagogy. Bhullar and Aggarwal, Chap. 6, offer an account of entrepreneurship pedagogy adopted by higher education institutions placing more emphasis on simulation games. In Chap. 7, Ala, Robin, Rasul, and Wegner present a detailed framework for an effective instructor and integration of artificial intelligence in entrepreneurship education to promote an entrepreneurial learning experience, vision, and intentions. Chapter 8, Al Shaqsi and Syed, focuses on the massive open online courses (MOOCs) in entrepreneurship education pointing out the challenges as well the successful stories. The final two chapters focus on experiential learning and international entrepreneurship education. Smith, Roberts, Kole, and Campbell-Perry (Chap. 9) discuss the online entrepreneurial learning framework that enables students' engagement in collaborative projects with other students in other countries. Following this, the work of Blankesteijn and Houtkamp (Chap. 10) explores the digital tools used to enrich experiential learning in science-based entrepreneurship education. In the concluding Chap. 11, Hyams-Ssekasi and Yasin reflect on the key themes of this book and consider the future of technology in enterprise education teaching and learning.

We would like to thank the contributors of this book for writing their chapters. We are also thankful to all the reviewers who supported us (the editors) in the review process of each chapter. We would also like to thank

Liz Barlow for her support at every stage of this book and Saif MD, the Project Coordinator, as well as production team at Springer for their dedicated and professional work particularly in the production process.

Bolton, UK
Dubai, United Arab Emirates

Denis Hyams-Ssekasi
Naveed Yasin

References

Csorba, E. (2014, October 14). Why become a student entrepreneur? *The Telegraph*. Retrieved 10 June 2020, from http://www.telegraph.co.uk/education/universityeducation/student-life/11161134/Why-become-a-student-entrepreneur.html

Dickson, P. H., Solomon, G. T., & Weaver, K. M. (2008). Entrepreneurial selection and success: Does education matter? *Journal of Small Business and Enterprise Development, 15*(2), 239–258.

Fayolle, A., Gailly, B., & Lassas-Clerc, N. (2006). Assessing the impact of entrepreneurship education programmes: A new methodology, *Journal of European Industrial Training, 30*(9), 701–720.

QAA. (2012). *Enterprise and entrepreneurship education: Guidance for UK higher education providers*. The Quality Assurance Agency for Higher Education. Retrieved 22 August 2020, from http://www.qaa.ac.uk/en/Publications/Documents/enterprise-entrepreneurship-guidance.pdf

Stokes, D., Wilson, N., & Mador, M. (2010). *Entrepreneurship*. Cengage Learning EMEA, Andover.

Vestergaard, L., Moberg, K., & Jorgensen, C. (2012). *Impact of entrepreneurship education in Denmark–2011*. The Danish Foundation for Entrepreneurship—Young Enterprise.

Yasin, N., & Hafeez, K. (2018). Enterprise simulation gaming: Effective practices for assessing student learning with SimVenture Classic and VentureBlocks. In D. Hyams-Ssekasi & F. C. Caldwel, *Experiential learning for entrepreneurship* (pp. 51–69). Palgrave Macmillan.

Contents

Part I   Enterprise and Entrepreneurship Education   1

1   Re-assessing Entrepreneurship Education and
    Gamification as a Learning Process   3
    Denis Hyams-Ssekasi and Fatemeh Taheri

2   Simulation-based Learning in Business and
    Entrepreneurship in Higher Education: A Review of the
    Games Available   25
    *Naveed Yasin, Sayed Abdul Majid Gilani, Davide Contu, and
    Mohammad Jabar Fayaz*

3   Integrating Digital Technology in Enterprise and
    Entrepreneurship Education   53
    *Ahmed Al-Gindy, Naveed Yasin, Mariam Aerabe,
    and Aya Al-Chikh Omar*

4   Measuring the Impact of Simulation-Based Teaching on
    Entrepreneurial Skills of the MBA/DBA Students   77
    Aidin Salamzadeh, Mehdi Tajpour, and Elahe Hosseini

5 Teaching Digital Marketing: A Malaysian University Perspective 105
Amiruddin Ahamat and Jing Ai Pang

Part II Technology and Entrepreneurship Education 131

6 Simulation-based Teaching Pedagogy and Entrepreneurship Education: A Bibliometric Analysis 133
Pritpal Singh Bhullar and Monika Aggarwal

7 Understanding the Possibilities and Conditions for Instructor-AI Collaboration in Entrepreneurship Education 159
Mamun Ala, Mulyadi Robin, Tareq Rasul, and Danilo Wegner

8 Massive Open Online Courses and Entrepreneurship Education in Higher Education Institutions 187
Shamsa Al Shaqsi and Raihan Taqui Syed

9 A Case-based Transformative Framework for Online Collaborative and International Entrepreneurship Education 207
Anne M. J. Smith, Julie Roberts, Mindy S. Kole, and Sonya Campbell-Perry

10 Digital Tools and Experiential Learning in Science-Based Entrepreneurship Education 227
Marlous Blankesteijn and Jorick Houtkamp

11 The Future of Enterprise and Entrepreneurship Education in Relation to Technology 251
Denis Hyams-Ssekasi and Naveed Yasin

Index 261

Notes on Contributors[1]

Mariam Aerabe is a Research Assistant, STEMA Training and Development Center, Dubai, United Arab Emirates. She holds a bachelor's degree in computer engineering. Marian's experience includes teaching different technology topics such as artificial intelligence, virtual reality, coding, and robotics. She works as a mentor in supporting the learning of children through STEM education.

Monika Aggarwal is a Professor at the University Institute of Applied Management Sciences, Punjab University. Recipient of Dr. S Radhakrishnan Post-Doctoral Research Fellow, by UGC, she has authored and presented numerous research papers in conferences at the national and international level. Her Ph.D. was accepted by ICSSR, New Delhi, for a publication grant. She completed projects sponsored by UGC,

---

[1] We would like to thank all the below contributors to this book for their academic and professional input and all those who have supported us at the various stages in the text's developments. Our sincere thanks go also to the following reviewers for their time spent on reviewing the different chapters and the thoughtful comments that helped us to improve the book: Dr. Fatemeh Dekamini, University of Iran, Iran; Dr. Alvin Nadher Aldawod, University of Dahok, Iraq; Dr. Karren Denis, University of Surrey, UK; Dr. Dilnaz Muneeb, Abu Dhabi University, UAE; Dr. Nawaz Ahmad, Mehran University of Engineering & Technology, Pakistan; Dr. Gozde Inal, European University of Lefke, Cyprus; Dr. Mohammad Saud Khan, Victoria University of Wellington, New Zealand; Dr. Farooq Haq, Canadian University Dubai, UAE; Dr. Mahmoud Alajaty, University of Birmingham, UK; Dr. Amrinder Singh, LM Thapar University Patiala, India; and Dr. Pradeep Kumar Gupta, Thapar Institute of Engineering and Technology, India.

NABARD, and AICTE. She has also been awarded the ICSSR research program, and she is also part of CO-investigator in TIGR2ESS, University of Cambridge, and Global Challenges Research Fund Project. She has conducted training programs for educational institutions, banks, and mutual funds.

Amiruddin Ahamat is a Senior Lecturer at Universiti Teknikal Malaysia Melaka's Faculty of Technology Management and Technopreneurship (UTeM). He holds a Professional Certificate in Innovation and Entrepreneurship from the University of Maryland in the United States, as well as a Master of Business Administration (MBA) in Technology Entrepreneurship from the Universiti Teknologi Malaysia (UTM) in collaboration with Cranfield University in the UK. He received his doctorate in entrepreneurship from the University of Sheffield in the UK. His doctoral research looks into the biotechnology industry's entrepreneurial opportunities. He has been an active academic teaching entrepreneurship-related courses, earning him the Chartered Association of Management & Business Educator (ChAMB) designation from the Chartered Association of Business Schools in the UK. He has written over 50 peer-reviewed articles and publications on entrepreneurship, technology management, international business, and marketing.

Mamun Ala is Lecturer of Strategic Management and International Business at the Australian Institute of Business (AIB). He also taught at the University of South Australia (UniSA) and Flinders University for many years. His research focuses on international trade, innovation, industrial policy, and online learning and teaching. He has a Ph.D. in Applied Economics from the University of South Australia (UniSA), an MPhil in Management (NUB), and Graduate Certificate in Learning & Teaching from Swinburne University. He is a member of Australia and New Zealand International Business Academy (ANZIBA), Australia and New Zealand Academy of Management (ANZAM), and the Australian Human Resource Institute (AHRI).

Ahmed Al-Gindy is a Faculty Member at the Department of Electrical Engineering, Canadian University Dubai. He holds a Ph.D. in Electrical and Communication Engineering and obtained an M.Phil. Degree from Faculty of Engineering and Informatics, University of Bradford, UK, and a Bachelor of Engineering in Electrical and Computer Engineering from Faculty of Engineering & Engineering Technology, Maritime Academy for Science & Technology, Egypt. He is a Certified Academic Program Assessor in the association of Arab Universities, Department of Quality Assurance, and Quality Enhancement in Higher Education Institute. He is also certified in Business Process Management and Improvements from George Washington University, United States. He has developed several curriculum and instruction manuals on engineering and computing technologies. His research interests cover various signal and image processing algorithms, RFID technologies, and artificial intelligence.

Shamsa Al Shaqsi is an education technology enthusiast. Her research is focused on exploring existing technology that enhances the educational experience, specifically which enables inclusivity of individuals with special educational needs. She recently graduated with a bachelor's degree in management and organizational behaviour from the Modern College of Business & Science in Oman, affiliated with the University of Missouri-St Louis, USA. She has been able to explore her interests, develop knowledge in the areas of education technology as well as more technical skills in programming and data coding through MOOCs.

Pritpal Singh Bhullar is an Assistant Professor and Head, University Business School, MRSPTU Bathinda. He holds a Doctorate in Finance. His area of research is valuation, international finance, entrepreneurship, and IPOs. He has experience of more than one decade in teaching and research. He has published more than 25 research papers in the journals of national and international repute which are indexed in Web of Science, SCOPUS, and ABDC. He has authored four books in the field of finance. He is serving as Chairperson, Board of Studies, Faculty of Commerce and Management, MRSPTU Bathinda. He has got an ICSSSR-IMPACT sponsored project of Rs. 10 Lakh. He also has been awarded 'MRSPTU Budding Researcher Award'.

Marlous Blankesteijn, Ph.D. is an Assistant Professor in the Faculty of Science, VU University Amsterdam. Her research interests are the organization of knowledge infrastructures for science-based innovation, innovation in water management, science and innovation policy, and science-based entrepreneurship education. She has expansive experience in consulting in the private and public sectors. She has published academic papers in science as well as innovation science journals. She is a member of the editorial board of a professional journal for water managers. She teaches multiple courses on both bachelor's and master's levels within the SBI program and is the coordinator of the master's SBI.

Sonya Campbell-Perry is an experienced manager with 25 years in both public and private sectors. She recently joined GSBS as a full-time academic after nearly ten years of combining a management role with part-time teaching. She became a Senior Fellow of the Higher Education Academy in 2020 and teaches at all levels. Her doctoral research is in the field of customer service model development in HE, using phenomenographic approaches. She became the program leader for the Business Management program in September 2020. Previous research has reviewed the use of online tools.

Davide Contu is an Assistant Professor at the Canadian University Dubai, United Arab Emirates. He holds a Ph.D. in Environmental Economics from the London School of Economics and Political Science (UK). He also holds a Postgraduate Certificate in Higher Education from the London School of Economics and Political Science (UK), a Master of Science in Economics from the University of Cagliari (Italy), and a Bachelor of Science in Economics and European Policies from the University of Cagliari (Italy). He specializes in business research methods, stated preferences techniques, and structural equation modeling. He has published in leading journals in the field such as Applied Economics, Ecological Economics, and Energy Policy. Before joining CUD, he has worked as a consultant for market research, data, and digital transformation initiatives in the UAE.

Mohammad Jabar Fayaz is the Application Systems Manager at Canadian University Dubai (CUD) and currently managing the Oracle digital transformation project at CUD. He is also the architect of CUD's online learning platform. He has 15 years of experience in Application systems in different industries including Healthcare, Secure Logistics, and Higher Education in Canada. Mr. Mohammad Fayaz graduated from Ryerson University (Canada) in Computer Science and is a Certified Project Management Professional with PMI.

Sayed Abdul Majid Gilani is Senior Faculty at Westford University College, Sharjah (United Arab Emirates). He has experience of working in the UK delivering British curricula. He has a track record of working on impactful publications within entrepreneurship and business management journals and has also examined postgraduate and undergraduate dissertations at the University of Glasgow, Heriot-Watt University, Glasgow Caledonian University, Stirling University, Worcester University, and the University of Law. He graduated with a Ph.D. in Rural Entrepreneurship from Glasgow Caledonian University, a Master's in Corporate Strategy and Finance from Edinburgh Napier University, and a Postgraduate Certificate in Higher Education (PGCHE) from Falmouth University (UK). He is recognized as a Fellow of the Higher Education Academy (FHEA), a member of the Chartered Management Institute (CMI), and a member of the Society for Education and Training (MSET).

Elahe Hosseini is a Ph.D. candidate in Organizational Behavior and Human Resource Management, Yazd University. Her research interest is about organizational behavior, human resource management, and social and entrepreneurship activities to develop entrepreneurship in developing countries. Also, she has several publications in international journals and participated in several conferences in some countries. The title of her doctoral thesis is about the employee voice of knowledge-based companies in Iran.

Jorick Houtkamp is a junior teacher at the Faculty of Science, VU University Amsterdam. He holds a BSc in Physics and an MSc in Science, Business, and Innovation. His research interests are innovations in the health and life sciences and entrepreneurship education.

Denis Hyams-Ssekasi is a Research Coordinator and Lecturer in the Institute of Management at the University of Bolton, UK. He received his doctorate from the University of Huddersfield. He has a keen interest in entrepreneurship and enterprise. He has developed and delivered modules on entrepreneurship, ran several mentoring schemes, and offered consultancy to start-up businesses, especially in developing countries. He has also edited a book *Experiential Learning for Entrepreneurship: Theoretical and Practical Perspectives on Enterprise Education* and co-edited *Women Entrepreneurs and Strategic Decision Making in the Global Economy*. He is a Senior Fellow of the Higher Education Academy and a member of the Institute for Small Business and Entrepreneurship.

Mindy S. Kole is Assistant Professor of Business at SUNY Ulster in Stone Ridge, NY, teaching and developing a curriculum in entrepreneurship, marketing, management, leadership, and business ethics. She has presented her work, including the development of a student-run business, at NACCE (National Association of Community College Entrepreneurship), SUNY CIT, COIL, and other national conferences. She is an entrepreneur, founding and operating The Marketing Department, LLC, a marketing and advertising company that served small- and medium-sized businesses located throughout the Hudson Valley, from 1996 to 2016. She holds a Ph.D. in Organizational Management and Management Education from Capella University in 2016 and an MBA from the Stern School of Business at New York University.

Aya Al-Chikh Omar is a Research Assistant, STEMA Training and Development Center, Dubai, United Arab Emirates. She is a junior computer engineer with some working experience as a research assistant. She graduated in 2020 with a bachelor's degree in computer science and engineering. She is responsible for educating students about new technologies, robotics, programming, and artificial intelligence. She has managed some projects during her journey in the university and, as a capstone project, has built an autonomous car that works based on image processing techniques and machine learning using different software applications and hardware components.

Jing Ai Pang holds a Bachelor of Technology Management (High-Tech Marketing) degree from Universiti Teknikal Malaysia Melaka (UTeM). She is a well-rounded individual with a great desire to learn. Her study focuses on digital marketing and higher education.

Tareq Rasul is a Senior Lecturer at the Australian Institute of Business, Australia. He holds Doctorate in Marketing from the University of South Australia, Australia, and an MBA from the University of East London, UK. His research has been published in many international journals such as the *Journal of Knowledge Management, Tourism Recreation Research, Australasian Journal of Information Systems, International Journal of Web-Based Communities, Journal of Islamic Marketing,* and *Journal of Open Innovation: Technology, Market, and Complexity,* among others. He is also a Certified Practising Marketer (CPM) and a member of the Australian Marketing Institute (AMI) and Action Learning Action Research Association (ALARA).

Julie Roberts, Ph.D. is a Senior Lecturer of Innovation and Operations Management. She has multi-disciplinary expertise with a science background and has crossed disciplines into business management. She has industry experience, working in multiple roles in a medical diagnostic company before joining the higher education sector as a Knowledge Transfer Officer. She engages in pedagogical research, related to online international learning, student engagement, critical incidents impacting learning, and feedback literacy. Her research includes the impact of Brexit on supply chains and creative responses by businesses to COVID-19, and she leads a Knowledge Transfer Partnership supporting diversification of a company's business.

Mulyadi Robin is Associate Professor and Associate Dean (Teaching and Learning) at the Australian Institute of Business. He has previously held academic appointments at Monash University, the Centre for Workplace Leadership (The University of Melbourne), and Alphacrucis College. His research and research supervision predominantly focus on servant leadership and the unintended outcomes of good leadership practices. However, he has also researched the dark triad of personality, workplace deviant behaviors, high-performance work systems, international students, and the role of faith at work. His research has been published in outlets such as *The Leadership Quarterly, Journal of Business Ethics, Personnel Review,* and *The Conversation,* among others.

Aidin Salamzadeh is an Assistant Professor at the University of Tehran. His interests are startups, new venture creation, and entrepreneurship. He serves as an Associate Editor in *Revista de Gestão, Innovation & Management Review, Entrepreneurial Business and Economics Review, Journal of Women's Entrepreneurship and Education* as well as an editorial advisory in *The Bottom Line.* Besides, he is a reviewer in numerous distinguished international journals. He is the co-founder of the Innovation and Entrepreneurship Research Lab (UK) and a reviewer in numerous distinguished international journals. He is a member of the European SPES Forum, the Asian Academy of Management, and Ondokuz Mayis University.

Anne M. J. Smith research and publications are in entrepreneurship, rural entrepreneurship, entrepreneurial learning, and enterprise education. These research strands are interests derived from being a third-generation family business, and a business partner in a rural business. She is committed to developing rural communities with new knowledge and developing young people through entrepreneurship and professionalization. She lectures on entrepreneurship and innovation, has a passion for design and innovation of the broader curriculum, and has significant expertise in teaching design development, delivery, and accreditation. Most notable achievements are in teaching and learning through the delivery of entrepreneurship and employability programs using innovative, experimental learning designs, remote online collaborations, and global/business partnerships

Raihan Taqui Syed is passionate about building society-centric entrepreneurial higher educational institutions and assisting start-ups to strategize and internationalize, based on his international exposure, industry experience, and professional competencies. He is the founding director of *Center for Entrepreneurship & Business Incubation* and head of *Management Program* at Modern College of Business & Science, Muscat, Oman—affiliated to the University of Missouri, St Louis, USA. Also, he is on the Expert Panel of Arabian Research Bureau, Oman, as *Research Associate—Entrepreneurship*.

Fatemeh Taheri is Associate Professor (Teaching and Research) at the IAU of Iran. She has previously held the position of consultant and manager at several educational and business institutions. She has provided consultancy services to various organizations within different departments. She has the responsibility of supervising and advising numerous theses in the field of business and education at master's and Ph.D. levels. She has carried out researches over a wide range covering management and education in the Middle East. Her most important research areas are the use of digital technologies in teaching and learning, business, and services. She has an extensive range of publications in the field of e-learning, e-business, user experience of e-business, and e-governments.

Mehdi Tajpour is a Ph.D. in Corporate Entrepreneurship from the University of Tehran (Iran). Also, he is a research fellow at Ondokuz Mayıs University. His main areas of interest are innovation management, higher education, entrepreneurship, entrepreneurial university, academic spin-offs, internationalization of the university, and human resources management. He had published several academic manuscripts in international journals and contributed to some national and international conferences. Also, he serves as a reviewer for a series of distinguished international journals.

Danilo Wegner is Senior Lecturer in Finance (Education Focused) at The University of Sydney. He has previously held academic appointments at the University of Queensland and the Australian Institute of Business. In finance, his research predominantly focuses on financial crises and the impact of government intervention in financial markets; in education, his work has focused on effective feedback and the use of mind maps in the context of online learning. His research has been published in outlets such as *The International Review of Economics and Finance* and the *Journal of Financial Economic Policy*, among others.

Naveed Yasin is a (Full) Professor of Entrepreneurship at the Canadian University Dubai, United Arab Emirates. He is the award winner of the highly acclaimed 'Outstanding All-Round Academic Award' conferred by the Teaching and Learning Institute (UK) and Senior Fellow of the Higher Education Academy, Chartered Manager and Companion of CMi (UK), and CIM Chartered Manager (Canada). Yasin has published research in the leading journals and textbooks in entrepreneurship education and has examined Ph.D. and DBA programs in UK, Europe, Asia and Africa.

List of Figures

Fig. 1.1	Requirements for gamification. (Source: Hakak et al. (2019, p. 29))	13
Fig. 2.1	Graphical representation of key information from Table 2.3	45
Fig. 4.1	Theoretical framework. (Source: Authors' elaboration)	87
Fig. 4.2	T-values. (Source: Authors' elaboration)	91
Fig. 4.3	Factor loadings, and R2. (Source: Authors' elaboration)	92
Fig. 5.1	Conceptual framework of effectiveness of digital marketing teaching delivery	118
Fig. 6.1	Co-authorship analysis	143
Fig. 6.2	Co-occurrences keyword-wise	144
Fig. 6.3	Document-wise citation analysis	146
Fig. 6.4	Bibliographic coupling	146
Fig. 6.5	Co-citation analysis	147
Fig. 6.6	Entrepreneurship teaching pedagogy model	151
Fig. 7.1	A framework for instructor-AI collaboration in a student-centered entrepreneurship education	172
Fig. 8.1	Power of technology. (Source: (Thille, 2017) From Stanford Micro Lecture made available on YouTube)	194
Fig. 8.2	Virtuous cycle of using data collection in education. (Source: (Thille, 2017) From Stanford Micro Lecture made available on YouTube)	195
Fig. 9.1	Transformative learning framework for online collaborative global entrepreneurship projects	218

Fig. 10.1 The innovation chain (Berkhout et al., 2010) — 232
Fig. 10.2 Conceptualization of the underlying mechanisms in a case based on theory — 233

List of Tables

Table 1.1	Game based on learning contents	12
Table 2.1	Review of core gaming simulations	34
Table 2.2	Review of competing gaming simulations	38
Table 2.3	The simulation services in terms of their involvement in teaching the entrepreneurship subject area in higher education	44
Table 3.1	The roles of Technology and Entrepreneurial Educators	64
Table 3.2	Educational levels descriptions	65
Table 4.1	Summary of the results of previous research	83
Table 4.2	Variables, components, questions, and Cronbach's alpha	88
Table 4.3	Validity and reliability measures	90
Table 4.4	Divergent validity	90
Table 4.5	SRMR and NFI	93
Table 4.6	Hypothesis test results	93
Table 5.1	Pearson correlation coefficient analysis	121
Table 5.2	Summary of Pearson correlation coefficient result	122
Table 6.1	Acceptance criteria	140
Table 6.2	Year-wise documents published	141
Table 6.3	Source-wise publication	141
Table 6.4	Country-wise publications	142
Table 6.5	Document-wise citation analysis	145
Table 7.1	Evolution of pedagogy in research on entrepreneurship education	165

List of Tables

Table 10.1 Summary of design principle to enable implementation of university-industry technology transfer education   236
Table 10.2 Design principles of experiential learning in SBI bachelor's and master's program courses   239

Part I

Enterprise and Entrepreneurship Education

1

Re-assessing Entrepreneurship Education and Gamification as a Learning Process

Denis Hyams-Ssekasi and Fatemeh Taheri

Introduction

In the post-global economic crisis, the world is faced with new trends, ideas, and grand challenges. In these conditions, innovation and entrepreneurship have become all the more important unlike any other time (Díaz-García et al., 2015; Grivokostopoulou et al., 2019). The rise of entrepreneurship has provided opportunities to stimulate economic growth, move toward a sustainable economy, improve business, and has boosted the national and international markets. Entrepreneurship is linked to economic growth and fosters innovation and sustainability worldwide (Barba-Sánchez & Atienza-Sahuquillo, 2018; Zaman, 2013). Busenitz et al. (2003) argue that the prime mover behind a contemporary

---

D. Hyams-Ssekasi (✉)
Institute of Management, University of Bolton, Bolton, UK
e-mail: dh4@bolton.ac.uk

F. Taheri
Department of Educational Management, IAU, Babol, Iran

economy is entrepreneurship. It plays a vital role in the economic output as well as the employment in the industry.

In the post-economic crisis era, entrepreneurship has proven itself as a strategic and important means of reversing cyclic economic downturns as well as a driver for the development and creation of social capital. It is viewed as the process of creating a business plan and transforming that plan into a viable product or service for an intended market. Stevenson and Jarillo (1990, p. 23) perceive entrepreneurship as "a process by which individuals—either on their own or inside organizations—pursue opportunities without regard to the resources they currently control." As a process, entrepreneurship is something that many business-minded people seek to embrace, and governments around the world have promoted the creation of programs specifically to develop future entrepreneurs (Sanchez, 2013).

Several studies on entrepreneurship have demonstrated that although personal characteristics play a facilitator role, entrepreneurship can be learned and trained (Nabi et al., 2018; Martin & Iucu, 2014; Sirelkhatim & Gangi, 2015). The understanding that entrepreneurial mentality, knowledge, skills, and competencies can be learned has resulted in entrepreneurship education (EE) becoming a priority when it comes to policy making in many countries around the world (Galvão et al., 2018; Voogt & Roblin, 2010). Entrepreneurship education (EE) is based on the principle that entrepreneurship mentality "can" be developed and requires skills and key competencies in areas such as accounting, financial management, taxation regulations, credit management, and business projections (Winarno & Wijijayanti, 2018; Nabi et al., 2018; Martin & Iucu, 2014). The teaching of entrepreneurial skills and knowledge can start as early as childhood education and continue through to higher education (Olokundun et al., 2018; Winarno & Wijijayanti, 2018; Bahador & Haider, 2017).

Entrepreneurship has been seen by several governments as a promoter of economic growth and this has prompted investment in entrepreneurship education (Fayolle et al., 2006). The UK government has concentrated on entrepreneurship education and training. In this regard, the government has created a subsidiary funding to introduce entrepreneurship education in higher education institutions (HEIs), principally, to inspire universities to communicate and share the best practices of entrepreneurship with businesses and the community (Davies et al., 2002). To further encourage entrepreneurship education, resources have been offered which include the enterprise capital funds and the national council for graduates (Harding, 2004). But the question is why entrepreneurship education?

Entrepreneurship Education

Efforts have been made to define the term entrepreneurship education (EE). In general terms, EE is the teaching of entrepreneurship principles and the training of entrepreneurs. It is not restricted to entrepreneurship students; but also, anyone who is interested in setting up a venture or any socio-economic participation (Jones & English, 2004; International Labour Office, 2016). Education provides a positive influence on entrepreneurship and is not restrictive (Fayolle et al., 2006; Stokes et al., 2010). In their study Robinson and Sexton (1994) found that there is a correlation between entrepreneurship education and the possibility to become a successful entrepreneur.

Entrepreneurship education exposes students to a wide knowledge of the business. Because of this, EE includes activities that develop the learners' perception of themselves, their world, and others, and teaches management of resources to empower them with knowledge, capabilities, skills, and motivation in setting up a business or venture (Fayolle et al., 2006; Jones & English, 2004; Quality Assurance Agency, 2012). EE is a type of education where an individual develops entrepreneurship skills to run a business successfully, acquires the information, skills, and impetus to pursue a subject in a different learning environment (Ekankumo & Kemebaradikumo, 2011). Ultimately, the goal of EE is to develop an entrepreneurial mindset, skills, behaviors, and attitudes needed to analyze entrepreneurship opportunities, find resources, and create value from uncertainty (Davis et al., 2016; McGrath & MacMillan, 2000; Isabelle, 2020).

According to Okiti (2009), entrepreneurship education is a gateway to taking advantage of opportunities to set up a venture and constantly increases self-reliance and self-employment among graduates. Onu (2008) describes entrepreneurship education as an education that increases the self-reliance of an individual which leads to an increase in self-employment. Additionally, the work presented in Jones and English (2004) designates entrepreneurship education as a procedure aimed at providing learners with skills to analyze business opportunities, increase self-esteem, and increase knowledge and the ability to take advantage of all these. Fayolle and Klandt (2006) point out that entrepreneurship education is any educational program and training procedure that increase entrepreneurial skills and attitudes. Lastly, entrepreneurship education has also been defined as a type of education that seeks to help students with creative thinking to obtain knowledge for developing skills, self-reliance, and desirable attitudes (Fayolle & Klandt, 2006; Jacob & Ariya, 2015).

Entrepreneurship education programs are beneficial not only for future entrepreneurs but also for students analyzing entrepreneurship opportunities (Slavtchev et al., 2012, Kuckertz, 2013; Isabelle, 2020). Most entrepreneurship education programs are based on traditional methods such as lectures which have limitations such as lack of assistance to students in understanding the consequences of actions in setting up and running a business (Hytti & O'Gorman, 2004; Buzady & Almeida, 2019). Souitaris et al. (2007) are of a view that any introduction of entrepreneurship education programs requires a consideration of the "conventional wisdom" which is based on "how" to become an "entrepreneur." To gain insights into entrepreneurship programs, there is a need for students to first grasp the concept of entrepreneurship (Kourilsky & Walstad, 1998), and this might increase their aspirations to become entrepreneurs.

In 2013 the European Commission developed the "Entrepreneurship 2020 Action Plan," which was a roadmap to stimulate entrepreneurship in Europe and emphasized the importance of teaching and practicing entrepreneurship from an early age. The plan also encouraged future economic development and sustainability via an entrepreneurial culture (Galvão et al., 2018).

Throughout the years, entrepreneurship education has changed from traditional lectures on business basics, market analysis, financial statements, cost analysis by primary learning methods to analyzing entrepreneurial opportunities, business planning, integrating data to expound the current state, and the presupposed future of the business (Honig, 2004; Matlay, 2008; Honig, 2004; Isabelle, 2020). Recently entrepreneurship education has moved toward the recognition of business models (Osterwalder & Pigneur, 2010). Learning through case studies has equipped students with the knowledge to recognize, analyze, and formulate assumptions, seek alternatives, and provide recommendations. This type of learning helps increase analytical skills, but it does not provide them an opportunity to learn through implementation and study of the results (Osterwalder & Pigneur, 2010; Ganesh & Sun, 2015; Isabelle, 2020). Other advocates have noted different pedagogical approaches concerning entrepreneurship education which include project, problem, and service-based learning (Jones & English, 2004; Tan & Ng, 2006; Desplaces et al., 2009). Emphasis is also placed on other aspects of entrepreneurship education such as the exploitation of opportunities (Rae, 2007), innovativeness, value creation, building a successful relationship with external stakeholders (Shapero & Sokol, 1982; Bruyat & Julien, 2001). Such effective pedagogical approaches indicate the added value of entrepreneurship education, and how it can be embedded into the teaching and learning with a view of growing students' entrepreneurial motivation, engagement, and attitudes.

Predicting entrepreneurial intentions from merely entrepreneurship education is not straightforward. Hence, the theory of planned behavior (Ajzen, 1991) becomes an important tool for predicting student's entrepreneurship intentions and desirability. It is argued that entrepreneurial intention is not innate but can be developed and nurtured by education and training (Athayde, 2009). According to this theory, the intention of action can be predicted by controlled behavior, attitudes, and social norms. According to Zhang et al. (2015) self-efficacy and self-esteem are important determinants of controlled behavior and implementation of entrepreneurial tasks. It is also believed that self-efficacy increases entrepreneurial intentions which in turn is affected by entrepreneurship education (Zellweger et al., 2011; Zhao et al., 2005).

In their study, Bae et al. (2014) note the relationship between entrepreneurship education and entrepreneurship intentions. They argue that what might impact the linkage can be due to cultural differences which are assessed by high-institutional collectivism, low level of equality, and low uncertainty avoidance. Other studies have investigated the relationship between entrepreneurship attitudes, skills, competencies, and knowledge. They also demonstrate that people who attend an EE program have greater entrepreneurial intent, self-belief about their abilities to pursue an entrepreneurial career (Abou-Warda, 2016; Buzady & Almeida, 2019). Similarly, there are numerous studies on the relationship between the effectiveness of EE and the importance of an efficient EE program and career success (Elmuti et al., 2012; Stamboulis & Barlas, 2014; Askun & Yıldırım, 2011. As a result, it can be concluded that EE is essential and entrepreneurial skills are needed (Isabelle, 2020).

Entrepreneurship is a central part of any business and therefore needs to be studied at all levels. Some of the objectives of entrepreneurship education are (1) understanding the whole concept of entrepreneurship, (2) knowing how to perform jobs like an entrepreneur, and (3) finally becoming a successful entrepreneur (Heinonen & Poikkijoki, 2006). According to reports of the Global Entrepreneurship Monitor, four entrepreneurial stages are acknowledged. The first stage relates to "potential entrepreneurs" who are seeking to start a new venture; the second stage relates to "nascent entrepreneurs" who are presently involved with a business; the third stage relates to entrepreneurs who have started a venture; and finally, the last stage is related to experienced entrepreneurs who own an established venture (Kelley et al., 2012). The importance of the role of higher education in the first and second stages is apparent (Ploum et al., 2018).

The European Commission (2003) suggests that universities should include entrepreneurship as a branch of knowledge to be obtained at a higher level of learning. This requires providing programs relevant to the individual needs and not what suits the instructors. Liñán (2004) identifies four programs suitable for entrepreneurship education, however, fails to offer ways in which these programs can be delivered. The programs include (i) Entrepreneurship Awareness Education which is about the development of the know-how on the subject; (ii) Education for Start-Up which concentrates on the individual with some background on the subject matter and the need for gaining a practical understanding of how to set up a self-employed; (iii) Education for Entrepreneurial Dynamism which adds to the energetic attitude needed after the startup phase; (iv) Continuing Education for Entrepreneurs which emphasizes the on-going pursuit of knowledge and skills. Similarly, Béchard and Grégoire (2005) divide entrepreneurship education into four analysis paths which seem to blend with Liñán's (2005) programs. The first analysis path examines the influence of entrepreneurship education on the people and society; the second focuses on the structure of entrepreneurship education, concentrating on innovation, resilience, and system change; while the third dwells on the content of entrepreneurship and how it is delivered (a fundamental aspect in entrepreneurship education) and fourthly the analysis path places emphasis on the individual participant's needs in entrepreneurship education.

What seems to make entrepreneurship education stand out is because it considers the fundamental theories and practices which are evident in all types of businesses. More importantly, it alludes to educational strategies that appeal to different audiences. In this regard, entrepreneurship education is classified into three but distinct provisions: "for, about, and through" enterprise and entrepreneurship education (O'Connor, 2013; Heinonen & Hytti, 2010, Hoppe et al., 2017). Notably, knowledge provision "for" entrepreneurship is a task-oriented approach and aims at imparting entrepreneurs with the necessary knowledge and skill; knowledge "about" entrepreneurship is about content and theory and is aimed at overall understanding of the study, a generic approach in HEIs. Knowledge acquired "through" is based on experiential learning to develop knowledge and skills. Hoppe et al. (2017) argue that the three provisions "for, through, and about" lead to highly different pedagogical approaches for entrepreneurship education depending on their purpose. Hence, embedding these provisions in entrepreneurship education offers new avenues of opportunities to enhance student learning in higher education.

Gamification in Teaching

Designing an efficient and effective entrepreneurship education framework can be quite challenging. Like other areas of education, entrepreneurship education is striving to enhance its content and methods to formulate a more effective and efficient framework of teaching by using innovative methods such as gamification and virtual reality (Mason, 2011; Antonaci et al., 2015; Caponetto et al., 2014).

The notion of gamification as a technique for learning has been presented over the years, each emanating from different viewpoints from game scholars and practitioners. Generally, gamification is defined as the use of game design and principles for non-game applications (Deterding et al., 2011; Isabelle, 2020). According to Boskic and Hu (2015, p. 1) gamification is about "applying game mechanics and game design and game design techniques to the non-game environment to help people achieve their goals." On the other hand, gamification is viewed as the usage of video game elements to advance user's knowledge, experience, and engagement in non-game services and applications (Deterding et al., 2011; Isabelle, 2020; Hamari et al., 2014). Taking a motivation-based approach, Gamification is viewed as *a way of incorporating several game elements such as points, badges, levels, leaderboards, status, trophies, rewards, and progress bars* (Deterding et al., 2011; Seaborn & Fels, 2015; Isabelle, 2020) *to engage, motivate, and reward the target audience to learn new skills or change behaviors via active involvement* (Isabelle, 2020; Kapp, 2012; Iscenco & Li, 2014; Caponetto et al., 2014). As per the Motivational Affordance perspective, gamification is about *human beings seek out (and continue to engage in) activities if these promise (and succeed) to satisfy motivational needs, such as competence, autonomy, or relatedness* (Deterding et al., 2011, p. 2). In this respect, the context of self-determination theory conceptualizes gamification as *getting behavioral outcomes via Motivational Affordance* (Hamari et al., 2014; Isabelle, 2020). Regardless of which definition of gamification is adopted, when using gamification, it is of primary importance to understand the required level of engagement that stimulates learners to increase their learning interest, experience, and knowledge construction (Ruiz-Alba et al., 2019).

The use of gamification has become popular to the extent that it has penetrated education. Gamification is now used in various domains such as learning, customer engagement, and employee performance due to its ability to motivate learners and as a result enhances the overall outcome (Huotari & Hamari, 2012; Kapp, 2012). It enables students to engage in challenging situations, tasks, and quests to obtain the desired objectives within a short span of time. Furthermore, games offer more opportunities as they allow the game players to redo the failed task. Despite the dependency of education efficiency on students' soft skills, gamification has the potential to sustain entrepreneurship knowledge, skills, and competencies (Antonaci et al., 2015). It is argued that gamification methods designed for virtual reality environments and serious games can help to demonstrate and explain concepts that are impossible to explain using just words (Antonaci et al., 2015; Caponetto et al., 2014).)

In recent decades, especially with the evolution of the internet, entertainment has been the primary focus of games developers. Whilst some efforts have been made in the field of designing games for educational purposes, not enough has been done to develop educational games (Khalil et al., 2018). It can be said that of all the educational games that have been developed, the majority concentrate on a single specialist subject, mostly in medicine, computer science, engineering, and general science—a list of existing games based on learning content has been included in Table 1.1. As can be observed, there are still many challenges that must be overcome to achieve the aim of revolutionizing modern education by gamification (Hakak et al., 2019).

Given the above, Hakak et al. (2019) have proposed a comprehensive framework for gamification based on several research studies. They have also identified five key elements (see Fig. 1.1) which are fundamental as far as gamification is concerned. They further argue that if these requirements are implemented successfully in gamification, they can enhance the process of learning in education.

1. Motivation: This is considered to be one of the most important elements in education. As a learning tool, games can motivate learners to complete an assigned task.
2. Short-term tasks: Breaking a task in a game into smaller parts increases the student's ability to redo the failed task several times.
3. Reward system: A well-planned reward system for completing tasks consists of different tokens of appreciation such as points, trophies, or gift cards, and it can lead to making the learning process more efficient.
4. Task design: A well-designed task flow lowers anxiety levels and balances the terms of completing a task.

Table 1.1 Game based on learning contents

Name of the game	Purpose
RobotBASIC: A STEM-focused Programming Language	Most powerful educational game for learning programming languages.
The Blood Typing Game	Teaches the basics of human blood like the classification of blood and blood transfusion.
DNA—The Double Helix	Allows the user to match DNA molecules base pairs to their respective strands.
The Immune System	To teach the basics of the immune system where the user must protect the human body against bacteria by utilizing white blood cells through a finger wound.
Control of the Cell Cycle	Teaches the cell division process.
Lord of the Flies	Powerful memory-based game to improve analytical skills.
The Transistor	Physics-based course game to teach the basics of the transistor.
Dice: Fractions, Order of Operations, Adam Dream: Numbers Nightmare, Axiom, Champs of Numeria, Chima, Zeus vs Monsters, YodelOh Math Mountain, Door 24, Funbrain, Magnahigh	Enhancing mathematical capability in young kids.
BrainNook, Cackleberries, Clever Island, Cookie, DimensionU, Futaba, Fuel the Brain, Gadzookery, Game Classroom, Gamequarium, GameUp, Grading Game, Moody Monster Manor	To enhance the overall behavior of students by focusing on a variety of subjects like English language, arts, reading and help in refining their thinking skills.
Historia, Learning Games for Kids, Lure of the Labyrinth, Science Heroes, SimCityEDU	These games offer students to learn about history, nature, health, geography, adventure

Source: Hakak et al. (2019, p. 25)

5. Game identity: More applicable in multi-player games and requires the cooperation of team members. In groups of learners, such as a team, a specific status or identity can be given to the most efficient player who contributes the most toward the achievement of the common goal (Hakak et al., 2019).

1 Re-assessing Entrepreneurship Education and Gamification...

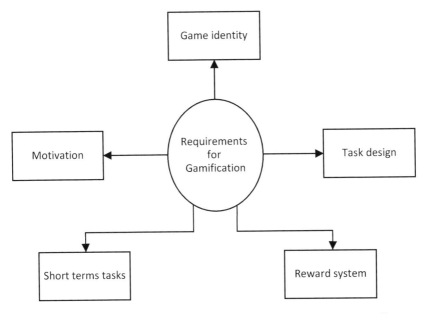

Fig. 1.1 Requirements for gamification. (Source: Hakak et al. (2019, p. 29))

Why Does Gamification Matter Entrepreneurship Education?

Gamification is viewed as a vital approach that optimizes learning. It has become a widely adopted pedagogical approach. Kapp (2012) gives an outline of the key elements of integrating a game into instructional environment. He identifies two types of gamifications, namely gamification of content, where content is altered to make it more game-like; and structural gamification where game elements are applied with a view to guiding the learner through the content without changing the content. It is noted that content and structural gamification can go well with each other and also used concurrently to create a more engaging and effective learning experience. In their study, Boskic and Hu (2015) noted that games designed specifically for students provide opportunities for students to examine and attempt different things and to appreciate their efforts. The ultimate goal of games in education is to increase student's motivation and participation in the learning as well as the ability to interact and communicate effectively with each other without technology negatively affecting students' learning. Advocates for well-designed educational games concur that such games engage students with the subject matter on a higher level, enable them to understand the new content better (Bransford & Schwartz, 1999), increase student's participation, give them the means to achieve something, enable them to make choices of what to learn, and control student's learning (Gee, 2003); students become more aware of their academic performance, progress, remember information, develop a grasp of concepts (Gee, 2003), and have the opportunity to receive immediate feedback for the tasks accomplished (Bogost, 2007; Juul, 2008; Kapp, 2012).

The study by Rosli et al. (2019) shows how game-based education can be taught in business courses such as accounting. In their view, the use of educational board games encourages students to excogitate and develop critical thinking skills through the power of play and completing the task. Other studies have shown the benefits of using gamification as a learning process. According to Fratto (2011) the use of gamification approach promotes students' interests, enthusiasm, determination, and analytical skills whilst for Nitkin (2012) it enhances learning, engagement, and encourages social interactions as students learn to collaborate effectively with other players doing similar assigned tasks. Gressick and Langston (2017) view games as a means to engage and motivate students whilst enabling them to demonstrate mastery of skills and content knowledge. Gamification has the potential for cognitive benefits especially when students are engrossed into the game-play. These include basic information, problems solving and comprehension of fundamental principles and concepts (Apostol et al., 2013), self-monitoring of own learning, keeping track of progress and performance via feedback to improve learning (Zimmerman, 1990). Undoubtedly, gamification approach has been embraced and it has been noted that it strengthens the teaching and learning. In this regard, students have added advantage of interacting face-to-face or online with fellow students and also tutors respectively. Shanklin and Ehlen (2007) argue that hands-on experience (learning by doing) especially in a simulation class, students tend to learn faster and have a keen interest in the subject matter.

Gamification impacts students' learning in a positive way. The study by Poole et al. (2014) found that students become more engaged in their learning and that the performance or ratings of individuals completing a test improved greatly with a gameshow style approach in undergraduate business students. It has been noted that some world's top universities and business schools have integrated games in their curriculum in order for the students to engage and to have fun. Davis (2016) has identified some business schools that are using gaming such as monopoly to stimulate learning in their programs. The Alliance Manchester Business School, Manchester University (UK), created an interactivity within the classroom through gamification. The results show that through the engagement in games, students enjoyed, took actions, and were inspired to modify their behavior to benefit the environment. Similarly, Fox School of Business and Management, Temple University (USA), implemented gamification through competition and leaderboards. The aim was to strengthen a particular skillset among first year students. Students who engaged most in the program were rewarded. Due to the competition and reward incentives, the results of the program improved greatly each year and more students got involved in the activities that were being offered. In the School of Business, Adolfo Ibanez University (Chile), a simulation-oriented digital game that enables students to make decisions in a simplified manner was used. The experiences of using such game developed an interconnection between technology and knowledge. Fundamentally, this game allowed students to learn the desired concepts and to get involved in the post-game discussion in which the players had the liberty to analyze their strategies and debate on what needed to be improved.

Conclusion

This chapter has re-assessed entrepreneurship education and noted that entrepreneurship is still important today. Entrepreneurship education is given top priority worldwide due to its capacity to enhance learning, instill engagement, promote economic success, and create job opportunities. Due to the nature of entrepreneurship, the urge to develop an efficient and effective entrepreneurship education in higher education institutions is paramount. It requires renewed effort from both the government and HEIs to ensure that it is desirable, motivational, maintained, and fully resourced.

Given that entrepreneurship education is here to stay, HEIs have a duty to keep it attractive. This necessitates a pedagogical approach that appeals to students. Innovative learning strategies for modern pedagogy, educational innovative practices, and innovative educational technologies make the teaching entrepreneurship more interesting. The benefits of game-based learning and in particular gamification are enormous. Gamification approach has the potential to boost and sustain entrepreneurship education. Educational institutions that have integrated gamification approach in their programs have increased students' interest, motivation, participation, perseverance, interactions, collaboration, and learning which are perceived as the main drivers for embracing gamification techniques. While gamification approaches are being encouraged to support entrepreneurship education, there is still need for HEIs to be innovative, creative, and attractive and to utilize technology in such a way that it becomes the norm for remote learning. Hence, gamification is an important technique, a learning process that should not be ignored in entrepreneurship education.

References

Abou-Warda, S. H. (2016). New educational services development: Framework for technology entrepreneurship education at universities in Egypt. *International Journal of Educational Management, 30*(5), 698–717.

Ajzen, I. (1991). The theory of planned behavior. *Organizational Behavior and Human Decision Processes, 50*(2), 179–211.

Antonaci, A., Dagnino, F. M., Ott, M., Bellotti, F., Berta, R., De Gloria, A., & Mayer, I. (2015). A gamified collaborative course in entrepreneurship: Focus on objectives and tools. *Computers in Human Behavior, 51*, 1276–1283.

Apostol, S., Zaharescu, L., & Alexe, I. (2013, April). Gamification of learning and educational games. *The 9th International Scientific Conference learning and Software for Education*. Bucharest, Romania.

Askun, B., & Yıldırım, N. (2011). Insights on entrepreneurship education in public universities in Turkey: Creating entrepreneurs or not? *Procedia Social and Behavioral Science, 24,* 663–676.

Athayde, R. (2009). Measuring enterprise potential in young people. *Entrepreneurship Theory and Practice, 33*(2), 481–500.

Bae, T. J., Qian, S., Miao, C., & Fiet, J. O. (2014). The relationship between entrepreneurship education and entrepreneurial intentions. A meta-analytic review. *Entrepreneurship: Theory & Practice, 38*(2), 217–254.

Bahador, K. M. K., & Haider, A. (2017). Incorporating information technology competencies in accounting curriculum: A case study in Malaysian higher education institutions. *Journal of Engineering and Applied Sciences, 12*(21), 5508–5513.

Barba-Sánchez, V., & Atienza-Sahuquillo, C. (2018). Entrepreneurial intention among engineering students: The role of entrepreneurship education. *European Research on Management and Business Economics, 24,* 53–61.

Béchard, J. P., & Grégoire, D. (2005). Entrepreneurship education research revisited: The case of higher education. *Academy of Management Learning & Education, 4,* 22–43.

Bogost, I. (2007). *Persuasive games: The expressive power of videogames.* MIT Press.

Boskic, N., & Hu, S. (2015). Gamification in higher education: How we changed roles. *European Conference on Games Based Learning.* Academic Conferences International Limited, p. 741.

Bransford, J. D., & Schwartz, D. L. (1999). Rethinking transfer: A simple proposal with multiple implications. In A. Iran-Nejad & P. D. Pearson (Eds.), *Review of research in education* (Vol. 24, pp. 61–101). American Educational Research Association. https://doi.org/10.3102/0091732X024001061

Bruyat, C., & Julien, P.-A. (2001). Defining the field of research in entrepreneurship. *Journal of Business Venturing, 16,* 165–180.

Busenitz, L. W., West, G. P., Shepherd, D., Nelson, T. E., Chandler, G. N., & Zacharakis, A. (2003). Entrepreneurship research in emergence: Past trends and future directions. *Journal of Management, 29*(3), 285–308.

Buzady, Z., & Almeida, F. (2019). FLIGBY—A serious game tool to enhance motivation and competencies in entrepreneurship. *Informatics, 6*(3), 27.

Caponetto, I., Earp, J., & Ott, M. (2014). Gamification and education: A literature review. *European Conference on Games Based Learning.* Academic Conferences International Limited.

Davies, J., Hides, M., & Powell, J. (2002). Defining the development needs of entrepreneurs of SMEs. *Education + Training, 44*(8/9), 406–413.

Davis, E. (2016). *Business school gamification-AACSB*. Retrieved 20 June 2020, from https://www.aacsb.edu/insights/2016/april/gamification-in-the-business-school

Davis, M. H., Hall, J. A., & Mayer, P. S. (2016). Developing a new measure of entrepreneurial mindset: Reliability, validity, and implications for practitioners. Consulting psychology. *Journal: Practice and Research, 68*(1), 21–48.

Desplaces, D. E., Wergeles, F., & Mcguigan, P. (2009). Economic gardening through entrepreneurship education: A service-learning approach. *Industry and Higher Education, 23*, 473–484.

Deterding, S., Dixon, D., Khaled, R., & Nacke, L. (2011, September 28–30). From game design elements to gamefulness: Defining gamification. *Proceedings of the 15th International Academic MindTrek Conference: Envisioning Future Media Environments*, New York, pp. 9–15.

Díaz-García, C., Sáez-Martínez, F., & Jiménez-Moreno, J. (2015). Assessing the impact of the "Entrepreneurs" education programme on participants' entrepreneurial intentions. *International Journal of Educational Technology in Higher Education, 12*, 17–31.

Ekankumo, B., & Kemebaradikumo, N. (2011). Entrepreneurship and entrepreneurial education (EE): Strategy for sustainable development. *Asian Journal of Business Management, 3*(3), 196–202.

Elmuti, D., Khoury, G., & Omran, O. (2012). Does entrepreneurship education have a role in developing entrepreneurial skills and ventures' effectiveness? *Journal of Entrepreneurship. Education, 15*, 83.

European Commission. (2003). *The commission's green paper: Entrepreneurship in Europe*. HMSO.

Fayolle, A., Gailly, B., & Lassas-Clerc, N. (2006). Assessing the impact of entrepreneurship education programmes: A new methodology. *Journal of European Industrial Training, 30*(9), 701–720. https://doi.org/10.1108/03090590610715022

Fayolle, A., & Klandt, H. (2006). *International entrepreneurship education: Issues and newness*. Edward Elgar Publishing.

Fratto, V. A. (2011). Enhance student learning with PowerPoint games: Using twenty questions to promote active earning in managerial accounting. *International Journal of Information and Communication Technology Education (IJICTE), 7*(2), 13–20.

Galvão, A., Ferreira, J. J., & Marques, C. (2018). Entrepreneurship education and training as facilitators of regional development: A systematic literature review. *Journal of Small Business Enterprise Development, 25*, 17–40.

Ganesh, G., & Sun, Q. (2015). Using simulations in the undergraduate marketing capstone case course. *Marketing Education Review, 19*(1), 7–16.

Gee, J. (2003). *What video games have to teach us about learning and literacy* (2nd ed.). Palgrave Macmillan.

Gressick, J., & Langston, J. B. (2017). The guided classroom: Using gamification to engage and motivate undergraduates. *Journal of Scholarship of Teaching and Learning, 17*(3), 109–123.

Grivokostopoulou, F., Kovas, K., & Perikos, I. (2019). Examining the impact of a gamified entrepreneurship education framework in higher education. *Sustainability, 11*, 5623.

Hakak, S., Noor, N. F. M., Ayub, M. N., Affal, H., Hussin, N., & Imran, M. (2019). Cloud-assisted gamification for education and learning–recent advances and challenges. *Computers & Electrical Engineering, 74*, 22–34.

Hamari, J., Koivisto, J., & Sarsa, H. (2014). Does gamification work? A literature review of empirical studies on gamification. *Proceedings of the 47th Hawaii International Conference on System Science*, pp. 3025–3034. https://doi.org/10.1109/HICSS.2014.377

Harding, R. (2004). Social enterprise: The new economic engine? *Business and Strategy Review, 15*(4), 39–43.

Heinonen, J., & Hytti, U. (2010). Back to basics: The role of teaching in developing the entrepreneurial university. *International Journal of Entrepreneurship and Innovation, 11*(4), 309–318.

Heinonen, J., & Poikkijoki, S. A. (2006). An entrepreneurial-directed approach to entrepreneurship education: mission impossible? *The Journal of Management Development, 25*(1), 80–94.

Honig, B. (2004). Entrepreneurship education: Toward a model of contingency based business planning. *Academy of Management Learning & Education, 3*(3), 258–273.

Hoppe, M., Westerberg, M., & Leffler, E. (2017). Educational approaches to entrepreneurship in higher education: A view from the Swedish horizon. *Education + Training, 59*(7/8), 751–767.

Huotari K., & Hamari, J. (2012, October 3–5). Defining gamification: A service marketing perspective. *Proceedings of the 16th International Academic MindTrek Conference*, Tampere, Finland. ACM Press.

Hytti, U., & O'Gorman, C. (2004). What is "enterprise education"? An analysis of the objectives and methods of enterprise education programmes in four European countries. *Education+Training, 46*, 11–23.

International Labour Office. (2016). *Towards an entrepreneurial culture for the twenty-first century: Stimulating entrepreneurial spirit through entrepreneurship education in secondary schools*. UNESCO.

Isabelle, D. A. (2020). Gamification of entrepreneurship education, decision sciences. *Journal of Innovative Education, 18*(2), 203–223.

Iscenco, A., & Li, J. (2014). The game with impact: Gamification in environmental education and entrepreneurship. Moldovan Environmental Governance Academy. Retrieved 26 June 2021, from https://www.changemakers.com/sites/default/files/competition_entry_form_files/alexandr_iscenco_johnathan_li_-_the_game_with_impact_-_full_0.pdf

Jacob, S., & Ariya, A. (2015). Teaching entrepreneurship education in tertiary institutions and the disposition of social studies students towards self-reliance in Plateau State, Nigeria. *International Journal of Educational Research, 3*, 95–108.

Jones, C., & English, J. (2004). A contemporary approach to entrepreneurship education. *Eduation+Training, 46*, 416–423.

Juul, J. (2008). Fear of failing: The many meanings of difficulty in Video Games. In M. J. P. Wolf & B. Perron (Eds.), *The video game theory reader*. Routledge.

Kapp, K. M. (2012). *The gamification of learning and instruction*. Wiley.

Kelley, D. J., Singer, S., & Herrington, M. (2012). *Global entrepreneurship monitor 2011 global report*. Global Entrepreneurship Research Association, London Business School.

Khalil, M., Wong, J., de Koning, B., Ebner, M., & Paas, F. (2018). Gamification in MOOCs: A review of the state of the art. *2018 IEEE Global Engineering Education Conference*. Santa Cruz de Tenerife, Canary Islands, Spain, pp. 1635–1644.

Kourilsky, M. L., & Walstad, W. B. (1998). Entrepreneurship and female youth: Knowledge, attitudes, gender differences, and educational practices. *Journal of Business Venturing, 13*(1), 77–88.

Kuckertz, A. (2013). Entrepreneurship education: Status quo and prospective developments. *Journal of Entrepreneurship Education, 16*, 59–71.

Liñán, F. (2004). Intention-based models of entrepreneurship education. *Piccola Impresa/Small Business, 3*, 11–35.

Liñán, F. (2005). Development and validation of an entrepreneurial intention questionnaire (EIQ). *15th Internationalizing Entrepreneurship Education and Training Conference*, Guildford.

Martin, C., & Iucu, R. (2014). Teaching entrepreneurship to educational sciences students. *Procedia Social Behavioral Science, 116*, 4397–4400.

Mason, C. (2011). Entrepreneurship education and research: Emerging trends and concerns. *Journal of Global Entrepreneurship, 1*(1), 13–25.

Matlay, H. (2008). The impact of entrepreneurship education on entrepreneurial outcomes. *Journal of Small Business and Enterprise Development, 15*(2), 382–396.

McGrath, R. G., & MacMillan, I. (2000). *The entrepreneurial mindset: Strategies for continuously creating opportunity in an age of uncertainty.* Harvard Business School Press.

Nabi, G., Walmsley, A., Liñán, F., Akhtar, I., & Neame, C. (2018). Does entrepreneurship education in the first year of higher education develop entrepreneurial intentions? The role of learning and inspiration. *Studies in Higher Education, 43*, 452–467.

Nitkin, M. R. (2012). Game of business: A game for use in introductory accounting. *The Accounting Educators Journal, 21*(1), 1–12.

O'Connor, A. (2013). A conceptual framework for entrepreneurship education policy: Meeting government and economic purposes. *Journal of Business Venturing, 28*(4), 546–563.

Okiti, A. F. (2009). University lecturers' perception of entrepreneurship education at the tertiary levels of education. *African Journal of Education Research Development, 3*, 79–85.

Olokundun, M. A., Moses, C. Y., Iyiola, O., Ogunaike, O., Ibidunni, A. S., Kehinde, O., & Motilewa, D. (2018). Experiential pedagogy and entrepreneurial intention: A focus on university entrepreneurship programmes. *Academy of Entrepreneurship Journal, 24*(2), 1–13.

Onu, V. C. (2008). Repositioning Nigerian youths for economic empowerment through entrepreneurship education. *Journal of Home Economics Research, 9*, 148–157.

Osterwalder, A., & Pigneur, Y. (2010). *Business model generation: A handbook for visionaries, game changers, and challengers.* Wiley.

Ploum, L., Blok, V., Lans, T., & Omta, O. (2018). Toward a validated competence framework for sustainable entrepreneurship. *Organisation and Environment, 31*, 113–132.

Poole, S. M., Kemp, E., Williams, K. H., & Patterson, L. (2014). Get your head in the game: Using gamification in business education to connect with Generation Y. *Journal for Excellence in Business Education, 3*(2), 1–9.

QAA. (2012). *Enterprise and entrepreneurship education: Guidance for UK higher education providers.* Quality Assurance Agency.

Rae, D. (2007). *Entrepreneurship: From opportunity to action.* Palgrave Macmillan.

Robinson, P. B., & Sexton, E. A. (1994). The effect of education and experience on self-employment success. *Journal of Business Venturing, 9*, 141–156.

Rosli, K., Khairudin, N., & Saat, R. M. (2019). Gamification in entrepreneurship and accounting education. *Academy of Entrepreneurship Journal, 25*(3), 1–6.

Ruiz-Alba, J., Soares, A., Rodríguez-Molina, M., & Banoun, A. (2019). Gamification and entrepreneurial intentions. *Journal of Small Business and Enterprise Development, 26*(5), 661–683.

Sanchez, J. C. (2013). The impact of entrepreneurship education program on entrepreneurial competencies and intention. *Journal of Small Business Management, 51*(3), 447–465. https://doi.org/10.1111/jsbm.12025

Seaborn, K., & Fels, D. I. (2015). Gamification in theory and action: A survey. *International Journal of Human-Computer Studies, 74*, 14–31.

Shanklin, S. B., & Ehlen, C. R. (2007). Using the Monopoly® board game as an in-class economic simulation in the introductory financial accounting course. *Journal of College Teaching & Learning, 4*(11), 65.

Shapero, A., & Sokol, L. (1982). The social dimensions of entrepreneurship. In *Encyclopedia of entrepreneurship* (pp. 72–90). Prentice-Hall.

Sirelkhatim, F., & Gangi, Y. (2015). Entrepreneurship education: A systematic literature review of curricula contents and teaching methods. *Cogent Business & Management, 2*(1), 1052034. https://doi.org/10.1080/23311975.2015.1052034

Slavtchev, V., Laspita, S., & Patzelt, H. (2012). Effects of entrepreneurship education at universities. *Jena Economic Research Papers 25*. Friedrich Schiller University and Max Planck Institute of Economics, pp. 1–33.

Souitaris, V., Zerbinati, S., & Al-Laham, A. (2007). Do entrepreneurship programmes raise entrepreneurial intention of science and engineering students? The effect of learning, inspiration and resources. *Journal of Business Venturing, 22*(4), 566–591.

Stamboulis, Y., & Barlas, A. (2014). Entrepreneurship education impact on student attitudes. *International Journal of Management Education, 12*, 365–373.

Stevenson, H. H., & Jarillo, J. C. (1990). A paradigm of entrepreneurship: Entrepreneurial management. *Strategic Management Journal, 11*, 17–27.

Stokes, D., Wilson, N., & Mador, M. (2010). *Entrepreneurship*. Cengage Learning EMEA, Andover.

Tan, S. S., & Ng, C. K. F. (2006). A problem-based learning approach to entrepreneurship education. *Education + Training, 48*(6), 416–428.

Voogt, J., & Roblin, N. P. (2010). *21st century skills discussion paper*. University Twente, 1–62. Retrieved 18 August 2020, from http://opite.pbworks.com/w/file/fetch/61995295/White%20Paper%2021stCS_Final_ENG_def2.pdf

Winarno, A., & Wijijayanti, T. (2018). Does entrepreneurial literacy correlate to the small-medium enterprises performance in Batu East Java? *Academy of Entrepreneurship Journal, 24*(1), 1–15.

Zaman, M. (2013). Entrepreneurial characteristics among university students: Implications for entrepreneurship education and training in Pakistan. *African Journal of Business Management, 7*(39), 4053–4058. https://doi.org/10.5897/AJBM10.290

Zellweger, T., Sieger, P., & Halter, F. (2011). Should I stay or should I go? Career choice intentions of students with family business background. *Journal of Business Venturing, 26*(5), 521–536. https://doi.org/10.1016/j.jbusvent.2010.04.001

Zhang, P., Wang, D.-D., & Owen, C.-L. (2015). A study of entrepreneurial Intention of University Students. *Entrepreneurship Research Journal, 5*, 61–82.

Zhao, H., Siebert, S. E., & Hills, G. E. (2005). The mediating role of self-efficacy in the development of entrepreneurial intentions. *Journal of Applied Psychology, 90*(6), 1265–1272.

Zimmerman, B. J. (1990). Self-regulated learning and academic achievement: An overview. *Educational Psychologist, 25*(1), 3–17. https://doi.org/10.1207/s15326985ep2501_2

2

Simulation-based Learning in Business and Entrepreneurship in Higher Education: A Review of the Games Available

Naveed Yasin, Sayed Abdul Majid Gilani, Davide Contu, and Mohammad Jabar Fayaz

Introduction

Challenges in teaching and learning differ depending on the discipline being taught (Sherin et al., 2007). A particular case is represented by the entrepreneurship discipline, where a recurring concern is whether the course would indeed drive students to become entrepreneurs (Yasin & Hafeez, 2018). Students need to be exposed to dealing with uncertainty, be flexible, focused, pay attention to the bigger picture as well as the

---

N. Yasin (✉)
Faculty of Management, Canadian University Dubai,
Dubai, United Arab Emirates
e-mail: naveed.yasin@cud.ac.ae

S. A. M. Gilani
Westford University College, Sharjah, United Arab Emirates
e-mail: sayed.g@westford.org.uk

© The Author(s), under exclusive license to Springer Nature Switzerland AG 2022
D. Hyams-Ssekasi, N. Yasin (eds.), *Technology and Entrepreneurship Education*,
https://doi.org/10.1007/978-3-030-84292-5_2

details (Khosla & Gupta, 2017). A fundamental measure to take in this regard is to foster experiential learning which allows the students to learn through trial and error. To this end, the delivery of content and learning experience can be enhanced with the aid of simulation games where learners can engage in real-life problem-solving tasks.

There are many examples of applications of simulation games from a wide range of disciplines, including nurse education (Cant & Cooper, 2009), medical education (Al-Elq, 2010; Lateef, 2010), STEM education (D'Angelo et al., 2014), engineering and management (Alfred & Chung, 2011; Brubacher et al., 2015). According to the systematic review of Chernikova et al. (2020), they do seem to significantly and postively impact the learning experience, facilitating learning of complex skills across different disciplines. However, there has been relatively little scholarly attention on the purpose, use, and effectiveness of simulation games in enterprise education as a whole (See, Yasin & Hafeez, 2018).

Simulation games can help students put into practice what they learn in class (Boocock & Schild, 1968). These can be, at the same time, a great tool for both students and instructors as the key aim of teaching is to help students learn. While they appear indeed fundamental tools for particular disciplines such as medicine, nursing, aircraft piloting, where the practice is necessary for learning, it does not seem to be investigated what is the impact of simulation games on enterprise education. So, to what extent does simulation gaming help to reach more effective learning in the context of business and enterprise education? In this chapter, we will assess the current offering in terms of simulation games for business and entrepreneurship, as well as whether there are published studies investigating their effectiveness. The next section describes the taxonomy of simulation tools and reviews available evidence of the impact of

---

D. Contu
Canadian University Dubai, Dubai, United Arab Emirates
e-mail: davide.contu@cud.ac.ae

M. J. Fayaz
Canadian University Dubai, Dubai, United Arab Emirates
e-mail: Mohammad.Fayaz@cud.ac.ae

simulation games on enterprise education; followed by a section "Simulation Games Focusing on Entrepreneurship: A Review", which assesses the current landscape of simulation games that can be adopted for enterprise education in higher education; finally, section "Conclusion" concludes the review of simulation games that are available for the delivery of entrepreneurship education.

Literature Review

Simulation Tools and the Learning Experience

Both the instructor and the students play a great role in learning. Teaching requires a solid understanding of the complex interactions in a classroom between teachers, students, and technology-including simulation games. Students are characterized by different cultural backgrounds, subject knowledge, motivations, expectations, and pre-conceptions. A lot of questions might pervade the minds of the instructor's conscious of the possible heterogeneity in the classroom. Which students in the class are interested in starting a business? Are they interested in assimilating an entrepreneurial approach to business? Can they be equipped to overcome financial and operational challenges usually faced by new businesses (Keat & Ahmad, 2012)? The delivery of relevant learning material is in this sense critical, as well as fostering critical thinking and ensuring student engagement. Challenges in teaching are amplified in an online delivery mode (Kebritchi et al., 2017) and greatly magnified during a pandemic (Daniel, 2020). This invites instructors to continually seek strategies, techniques, and tools to rise to the challenge of effective and engaging teaching.

One of these strategies pertains to the tailoring of the teaching style based on particular scenarios. For instance, different styles might be needed when comparing plenary sessions against smaller group classes. In plenary sessions, the approach might tend to be more teacher-centered; that is, the instructor acts as the key source of information and leader of the activities, directed toward the individual learners. Whereas, during smaller classes, the teaching style might be more student-centered. Students are encouraged to explore existing knowledge and to actively take part in the learning process, rather than passively assimilating concepts. This approach might foster collaborative efforts between students, enhancing learning, teamwork, and communication skills, which are crucial in a business and enterprise context. Besides the size of the class, specific learning styles of the students need to be taken into consideration to avoid a mismatch with the teaching style (Chetty et al., 2017).

Regardless of the teaching approach, either more teacher-centered or more student-centered, it seems key to include in the teaching style enthusiasm towards the subject and especially towards the teaching itself (Kunter et al., 2008; Kunter et al., 2011). Student engagement can be fostered through physical immediacy too (Bamaeeroo & Shokrpour, 2017). Passion for the subject and teaching is essential, but to stimulate active participation and build trust, simple yet crucial personal characteristics play a role, for example, eye contact, open body postures, positive reinforcement like smiling and respectful listening. All these, while delivering the teaching material in a convincing, knowledgeable, and fun manner. When it comes to business and entrepreneurship, it appears crucial to consider the following elements: inviting guest speakers, mentors provided specialized training, provide practical experience, site visiting, role-playing (Esmi et al., 2015), the latter being particularly relevant aspect of simulation games.

Above all, a good class or lecture necessitates the apt use of learning technologies. A lot of tools can be used to help the students. Key is the support offered by learning management systems, such as Moodle (Horvat et al., 2013) or Blackboard (Bradford et al., 2007). For instance, before the class, students can be asked to complete tasks shared through the university virtual learning portal, such as completing a survey, a quiz, or reading a case study. Other learning technologies that can be adopted include sharing the class slides on the virtual learning portal, so that they are easily accessible for reference before or after the class. When relevant and applicable, data sets should be available for students to practice on the selected software. Additionally, whiteboards (physical or digital) should be used to write down the formulas or main points as a visual aid. Students should be also exposed and incentivized to hold meetings to catch up on tasks related to group projects, which can be conducted with the aid of conferencing tools. Finally, in face-to-face delivery, handouts can be provided to structure group activities; the same should be uploaded in the virtual learning portal following the classes. A combination of these various learning technologies can help both the instructor and the students in being efficient and staying alert.

Learning technologies need to be powered by enthusiastic teachers, who need to be continuous learners, the attitude that is also vital in business and for entrepreneurs (Herms, 2015). Instructors must keep improving their teaching style and delivery. Instructors need to pay attention to student feedback (Leckey & Neill, 2010), both explicit—for instance, utilizing course evaluation surveys—and implicit—for instance, by observing the behavior of the students. Some students, although a relatively small number, might fail to participate and engage in the readings or other pre-class tasks. One way of dealing with this is to break the structure of the class and come up with effective group activities to involve them in the learning process. However, some students could remain disinterested in the course material, even failing to be present in some of the classes. Such uncooperative behavior could be futile and time-consuming as well as dissuasive towards other students. Therefore, the instructor needs to remain focused on delivering the material and not deviate from the learning objective of the lesson and consider innovative solutions. Are simulation games the answer to the need for innovative solutions?

A Taxonomy of Simulation Tools

Simulations are needed to help individuals practice specific scenarios, regular operations and tasks, and how to deal with unlikely events and emergencies. This is greatly important in fields such as medicine, the military, and the airline industry, where high stakes are at play (Herrington et al., 2007). When in this work we refer to simulations, we include role-playing, games, gaming, computer simulations (Feinstein et al., 2002). Different types of simulation games can be distinguished. A key distinction is between a virtual simulation environment and human simulation. In both cases, there is a link with experiential learning; that is, where learning is fostered through direct experience (Yasin & Hafeez, 2018).

However, in the latter, there is a focus on simulations happening in a physical space and interactions with other human beings as well as tools, as opposed to a virtual, digital, or computerized environment. Furthermore, we can differentiate between simulations that aim to replicate operations or simulate specific scenarios that can be experienced at work, versus simulations instead designed to test and/or train specific skills of students or employees indirectly associated with the tasks they would need to perform on the job, such as dynamic decision making (Rosa et al., 2020).

Simulation-based learning can be conducted via immersive learning technologies to foster realism. While this can be quite costly, there are industries where it appears a necessity, for instance, for astronauts and aircraft pilots. Yet, unless strictly needed given the industry or context considered, a great deal of realism might not be the key feature to develop a successful simulation experience: there has to be engagement with the learner, and to this end, learners' preferences have to be taken into account (Herrington et al., 2007). In this sense, simulations which are not delivered via a virtual environment might be able to complement efficiently and effectively the education journey of the learner.

Assessments of human-simulation-based learning have been extensively conducted in the field of medicine, where a key interest is that of reducing medical errors. Drawing from a systematic review, Sarfati et al. (2019) conclude that while learning, human simulation can be considered as additional support in education for healthcare, it does not seem to substantially help prevent medical errors. In the systematic review of Cant and Cooper (2009), improvement in self-efficacy, knowledge acquisition, and strong student satisfaction with simulation education were found. In line with this, as far as midwifery education is concerned, increased confidence and competence, improved communication skills, and self-efficacy were found (Cooper et al., 2012). Scant is however the evidence of studies reporting tangible quantitative improvements, except for Ford et al. (2010) who reported a reduction of medication administration error rates from 30% to 4%.

Escape rooms are a particular case of human simulations. A scenario is described to the participants who need to complete a set of tasks to progress in the game. This particular type of simulation can foster teamwork, besides fostering confidence and critical thinking. For example, Morrel and Eukel (2020) describe the implementation of a nursing cardiovascular escape room, where students worked in a team to solve a series of puzzles and activities such as drug dosage calculation. An additional example is provided by Sarage et al. (2021), who prepared an escape room with a patient manikin, individuals acting as family members and health care providers, and tasks including puzzles and riddles.

The Impact of Simulation Games in Enterprise Education

Among scant research on the matter, a study that has carried out an in-depth assessment of the impact of simulation games in enterprise education was conducted by Fox et al. (2018). In this assessment, they considered the level of fidelity (i.e., the amount of realism), verification (the quality of the game's technical design), and validation (the game's adherence with the tasks that are being attempted to be simulated). While finding that simulation games foster experiential learning, they highlight that the reality simulated appears rather superficial and tends to focus on small business management scenarios. Additionally, it emerged that the interactions between players were quite limited; this is particularly concerning as it seems quite important, in enterprise education, to allow for team-based learning (Bailey et al., 2021). Finally, common elements of entrepreneurship were missing, such as ambiguity and uncertainty.

Simulation gaming tools can then be complemented by activities that replicate work that would be conducted in a real situation. For instance, a student side hustle as documented by Forster-Holt (2020). Furthermore, when applicable, the software that would be used in real settings could be used as part of the simulation task. For instance, in a business where reporting is conducted via dashboards, tools such as Microsoft BI, Tableau and Qlik View can be considered (Carlisle, 2018; Hoelscher & Mortimer, 2018; Reddy et al., 2018). Additional examples of tools that can be used to simulate business operations are Salesforce Marketing and

Oracle Eloqua in the field of marketing; Qualtrics, QuestionPro, Google Forms for survey preparation (Evans & Mathur, 2018); Salesforce Sales Cloud for managing sales and leads; Salesforce Service cloud to manage customer service operations (Manchar & Chouhan, 2017); Synthesio or Spriklr for social media management (Kane, 2015); Dataiuku for data analytics and management operations.

Simulation Games Focusing on Entrepreneurship: A Review

In terms of research methodology, a secondary research approach has been adopted which has involved manual searches/online website searches through Google and Google Scholar search engines. The key phrases/words inputted into the search engines were 'simulations', 'simulation games', 'simulation games for education', and 'simulation games for entrepreneurship'. The identified simulation games were separated into core simulation games and competing simulation games. The rationale behind this separation between the identified games was that the core simulation games represent programs that seem to be already established in higher education (HE); instead, the competing simulation games represent programs that appear to be new to HE. The results of the review of core simulation games employed in HE are presented in Table 2.1. For each game, the source, subject area, a brief explanation, function in HE, and, finally, a concluding remark are presented in Table 2.1.

Glo-bus and Edumundo seem to have been adopted in higher education. However, it is not clear whether they have been utilized in teaching within the area of entrepreneurship. On the other end, the following simulation games: The Startup Game, GoVenture: Entrepreneur, GoVenture World, Hipster CEO, Innovative Dutch, Interpretive solutions: Entrepreneur, SimVenture, Venture blocks, Venture Strategy, and VSL simulations have all been used in teaching related to the area of entrepreneurship in higher education.

2 Simulation-based Learning in Business and Entrepreneurship...

The competing simulation games have been reviewed in terms of whether they have been involved in teaching at the higher education level and what subject area have they been involved in. The results of the review are presented in Table 2.2. For each game, the source, subject area, a brief explanation, function in HE, and, finally, a concluding remark are presented in Table 2.2.

As shown in Table 2.2, Capsim, Cesim, Hubro Education, Marketplace, PriSim, Processim Labs, and Smart Sims have been adopted in teaching the business area in higher education, but it is unclear whether these simulations have been involved in the teaching of the entrepreneurship subject area. Despite being adopted for coaching/teaching the business area it is unclear whether the X Learning simulation has been adopted in the entrepreneurship area as well as in higher education. Barista Sim has been identified as a simulation that has been involved in coaching/teaching in the entrepreneurship area, however, like X Learning it is unclear whether it has been adopted in higher education. Unlike the other competing simulation services and like Venture blocks and VSL from the core simulations, Virtonomics has been adopted to support teaching within the area of entrepreneurship in higher education.

Finally, an illustration of the core and competing simulations in terms of whether they have been involved in teaching the entrepreneurship subject area at the higher education level is illustrated in Table 2.3. The color green represents a yes and the color red represents a no. Additionally, there is a confirmation (Yes/No) in Table 2.3 of whether there is a published study to assess the efficacy of each simulation game (Fig. 2.1).

As shown in Table 2.3, the core simulation services of the Entrepreneurship Simulation: The Startup Game, GoVenture: Entrepreneur, GoVenture World, Hipster CEO, Innovative Dutch, Interpretive solutions: Entrepreneur, SimVenture, Venture blocks, Venture Strategy, and VSL simulations along with the competing simulation service of Virtonomics have been identified as the only services that have been involved in the teaching of the entrepreneurship subject area at the higher education level.

Table 2.1 Review of core gaming simulations

Simulation game	Source	Subject area	What are the games?
Edumundo	Edumundo (2020)	Management, finance, strategy, and marketing	Edumundo has experience in e-learning and activating learning. Edumundo offers digital learning products in more than 25 countries. Edumundo's vision is to offer a digitized form of education where it is continually looking to develop creative and innovative solutions.
Entrepreneurship Simulation: The Start-up Game	Fox et al. (2018); Mollick (2014)	Business (entrepreneurship)	This simulation tracks players along with a variety of dimensions that lead to start-up success which includes the interaction between hiring and strategy, the trade-off between wealth and control, the skills that are required to run an organization, and valuations that start-up businesses receive.
Glo-bus	Mohsen et al. (2019); Thompson et al. (2019)	Business strategy	Glo-bus focuses on competitive business strategy. The simulation involves business owner-managers making decisions related to processes like component usage, camera performance, product line breadth, production operations, workforce compensation, outsourcing, pricing, sales and marketing, and finance. The challenge presented by the simulation is to craft and execute a competitive strategy that leads to a respected brand image, keeps the business in contention for global market leadership, and generates improved financial performance as measured by earnings per share, return on investment, stock price appreciation, and credit rating. Additionally, all features of the Glo-Bus business strategy game mirror/parallel the functioning of the real-world digital camera market, thus allowing users to (1) think rationally and logically in deciding what to do and (2) get valuable practice in making a variety of business decisions under circumstances that resemble competitive conditions in the real world

Their function in higher education	Concluding remark
Edumundo focuses on creating an interactive learning experience for students by bringing the latest in digital technology to, and beyond, the classroom.	Edumundo has been adopted in higher education but the literature does not clarify whether it has been involved in the area of entrepreneurship.
The simulation provides interactive scoreboards for lecturers to use during class debrief and includes video interviews with renowned business visionaries like Neil Blumenthal (Warby Parker). The Teaching Note in this simulation provides guidance on running effective lesson debriefs. This simulation is one of The Wharton School's most popular simulations adopted in daily teaching where the simulation can be used as an introduction to any entrepreneurship-related class.	Entrepreneurship Simulation: The Start-up Game has been involved in teaching related to the area of entrepreneurship in higher education where the simulation is only playable among groups of 20–86 students in a classroom.
Glo-bus is a completely online exercise where teams of students run a digital camera company in head-to-head competition against companies run by other class members. Just as in the real world, companies compete in a global market arena, selling digital cameras in four geographic regions—Europe-Africa, North America, Asia-Pacific, and Latin America.	From reviewing the literature, it appears that Glo-bus has been adopted in higher education, however, it is not clear whether it has been involved in the area of entrepreneurship.

(*continued*)

Table 2.1 (continued)

Simulation game	Source	Subject area	What are the games?
GoVenture: Entrepreneur	Fox et al. (2018); GoVenture (2021)	Business (entrepreneurship)	This simulation begins with the user having with them management over a lemonade stand which leads to opportunities for users to level up to a kiosk, food truck (basic/entry-level experience), and full business (advance level experience). This is then followed by an opportunity for users to build a regional franchise (advance level experience) from the ground up in the most realistic settings for a new/start-up business.
GoVenture: World	Fox et al. (2018); GoVenture World (2021)	Business (entrepreneurship)	The simulation is a global business game where players/users can run virtual businesses while competing and collaborating with other businesses from around the world. Here players can select either a retail or manufacturing business to run.
Hipster CEO	Fox et al. (2018); Hipster CEO (2021)	Business (entrepreneurship)	This simulation for the users attempts to simulate what it is like to launch and run their start-up. It is compared to being a Sim City for start-ups outside of the fun visuals.
Innovative Dutch	Fox et al. (2018); Innovative Dutch (2021)	Business (entrepreneurship)	It has been created to bridge the gap between education and industrial institutions.
Interpretive solutions: Entrepreneur	Fox et al. (2018); Interpretive Simulations (2021)	Business (entrepreneurship)	This is a retail entrepreneurship-based simulation where users can purchase and operate a retail clothing business.
Sim-venture	Venture Simulations Limited (2020); Williams (2015)	Business (entrepreneurship)	This online simulation lets people run a virtual company for up to ten simulated years while lecturers/ trainers/tutors observe and assess progress in class or remotely.

2 Simulation-based Learning in Business and Entrepreneurship...

Their function in higher education	Concluding remark
The simulation allows teachers to inspire students with an exciting way to teach and learn. The simulation learning enhances instructor-led and self-directed courses for youth and adults, online and offline participants.	The GoVenture: Entrepreneur simulation has been involved in teaching related to the area of entrepreneurship in higher education.
Lecturers/teachers adopt this simulation to deliver an engaging and realistic training environment that delivers real-time and authentic performance evaluations during lessons.	The GoVenture: World simulation has been involved in teaching related to the area of entrepreneurship in higher education.
The simulation can be adopted by lecturers/teachers in the lesson to create a start-up business environment for students where they can grow the business to a multi-national level. However, this simulation is not as common as other simulations in higher education.	The Hipster CEO simulation has been involved in teaching related to the area of entrepreneurship in higher education.
Innovative Dutch design advanced business simulations for universities and executive training to help users bridge the gap between education and professional settings in industry. It is offered as an add-on to existing courses, as a 6-module course package, or as half-day training modules.	The Innovative Dutch simulation has been involved in teaching related to the area of entrepreneurship in higher education.
Students are given the ability to evaluate financing, staffing, marketing, and inventory management options as start-up business owner-managers during classes. The students work as a team to compete against other teams during classes where they aim to maximize business profits through managing sales growth and other key operations.	The Interpretive solutions: Entrepreneur simulation has been involved in teaching related to the area of entrepreneurship in higher education.
This simulation allows users to manage and scale up an SME (small to medium enterprise) and learn about the challenges of leading a growing company in a competitive environment. Venture Simulation Limited (VSL) has a collaboration with ten partner universities throughout the design and build their simulator. Following its launch, VSL has been embedded into various undergraduate and postgraduate modules.	The VSL simulation has been involved in teaching related to the area of entrepreneurship in higher education.

(*continued*)

Table 2.1 (continued)

Simulation game	Source	Subject area	What are the games?
Venture blocks	Loon et al. (2015); Neck and Greene (2015); Venture Blocks (2020)	Business (entrepreneurship and marketing)	It adopts game-based simulations to achieve deep learning.
Venture Strategy	Fox et al. (2018); Marketplace Simulations (2021)	Business (entrepreneurship)	The Venture Strategy simulation provides users with a safe virtual environment where they can gain the experience of starting and running new businesses.

Table 2.2 Review of competing gaming simulations

Simulation game	Source	Subject area	What are the games?
Barista Sim	Barista Sim (2020)	Business and management, strategic management, entrepreneurship and hospitality management	Barista Sim provides an opportunity for users to practice their skills in marketing, operations, and finance in a business context, as well as allowing users to develop critical thinking and decision-making skills.
Capsim	Capsim Management Simulations Incorporated (2020)	Operations and supply chain management	This service offers simulation technology that helps educators engage, assess, and develop learners through real-world experiences
Cesim	Aguilera et al. (2019); Cesim Practice Makes Perfect (2020)	Business, management, strategy, and hospitality	Cesim uses the latest technology to help the user in improving their knowledge retention, business decision making, and teamwork skills of their students or employees.

Their function in higher education	Concluding remark
Missions, levels, and points guide students through the customer development process. They get instant feedback, so they can learn from their mistakes. The virtual environment makes the experience feel real.	The Venture blocks simulation has been involved in teaching related to the area of entrepreneurship in higher education.
As in the real business world, students have the opportunity to analyze markets and evaluate various business opportunities.	The Venture Strategy simulation has been involved in teaching related to the area of entrepreneurship in higher education.

Their function in higher education	Concluding remark
Not clarified	Barista Sim has been identified as a simulation that has been involved in the entrepreneurship area, however, it is unclear whether it has been used in higher education.
Capsim is adopted by over a thousand academic and corporate institutions from over 50 countries to use solutions generated by Capsim to prepare students for career success.	It has been confirmed that Capsim has been adopted in higher education, but it is unclear whether it has been involved in supporting teaching in the area of entrepreneurship.
The service allows teachers to ensure that students gain a real-life understanding of how business concepts are applied while undertaking the course. This is achieved through business simulation games for colleges and universities which enable the teacher to enlighten, challenge, and motivate students to become better decision makers, team players, and holistic thinkers in a business environment.	Cesim has been adopted in higher education, but the literature does not clarify whether it has been involved in the area of entrepreneurship.

(continued)

Table 2.2 (continued)

Simulation game	Source	Subject area	What are the games?
Hubro Education	Danske Bank (2020); Hubro Education (2020)	Business, marketing, and finance	Hubro Education is recognized as delivering engaging learning experiences and aha moments for universities, schools, and corporations.
Marketplace simulation	Marketplace Solutions (2020)	General business area	This simulation offers business education tools that engage and transform lives all around the world.
PriSim	PriSim Business Simulations (2020)	General business area	The service enables users to enhance business decision making and improve business performance
Processim Labs	Processim Labs (2020)	Business area	Processims develop college-level educational games. Simulations of complex processes designed specifically for mobile devices enable students' learning through putting their decision-making skills to practice, and exercise critical thinking in an engaging learning environment, e.g. perceived to be fun, entertaining, and dynamic. The simulation aims to transform smartphones into pocket-based simulators that college/university lecturers can adopt as effective and convenient teaching tools.

Their function in higher education	Concluding remark
They provide business simulations in a remote setting for university students. Hubro Education wants to create great learning experiences as accessible as possible. Hubro Education delivers simulation games that are enjoyable and innovative, with ease of use at the forefront of design. They also enable learners to go deeper and apply theory in realistic business situations. Hubro Education believes that educators should help learners learn, not worry about technical details. Therefore, they help educators in making simulations an integral piece of their course, quick and without worry.	Hubro Education has been adopted in higher education, but the literature does not clarify whether it has been involved in the area of entrepreneurship.
The purpose of Marketplace simulation is to equip teachers/lecturers with games for business that empower students to transform practice into skill. The service encourages students to experiment with ideas, evaluate the results, and adjust their approaches/methods.	It has been confirmed that Marketplace simulation has been adopted in higher education, but it is unclear whether it has been involved in supporting teaching in the area of entrepreneurship.
PriSim courses combine classroom lectures with computerized business simulations, allowing students to improve critical business skills, test new ideas, and practice business strategy in a risk-free environment. However, the role of PriSim in higher education is not clarified.	The role of PriSim in teaching the subject area of entrepreneurship in higher education is not clarified.
The simulation games can be played individually as well as in teams and can be easily run as both on-campus or online classes. The simulations are downloaded from players' app store onto their phones, therefore, allowing them to absorb the learning experience and take it with them wherever they go. The teaching simulations provide an experiential learning tool for teachers/lecturers to adopt in their lectures. The simulations allow students to put classroom concepts into practice and gain hands-on experience in a risk-free environment. The teaching tools are mainly used by business students from undergraduate courses up to MBA courses.	Processim Labs has been adopted in higher education, but the literature does not clarify whether it has been involved in the area of entrepreneurship by identifying its adoption in the general business area.

(*continued*)

Table 2.2 (continued)

Simulation game	Source	Subject area	What are the games?
Smart Sims	Smart Sims Business Simulations (2020)	Business strategy and management concepts	Smart Sims provide educational business simulators that are adopted worldwide by students, teachers, and business professionals.
Virtonomics	Virtonomics (2020)	Business areas that also include entrepreneurship	This is a business simulation game that is fully populated by business owner-managers and university/college students as well as other overall smart individuals forming a friendly, business-oriented community. Virtonomics enables an environment where players share their knowledge and experience, explain how to implement successful business strategies, and grow their company exponentially.
X learning	X Learning Limited (2020)	Business in general	X Learning provides simulations that involve participants working in small teams, often in competition with each other, to run a business through dealing with a range of internal and external issues. The simulations typically last between one and three days, each one addressing different organizational and business challenges, and can be run in their vanilla format, or combined with additional content for a bespoke organizational solution.

Their function in higher education	Concluding remark
This service provides an experiential learning environment that enables students in understanding business strategy and management concepts at a deeper level while creating memorable learning experiences. Smart Sims prepares students for the workforce and increases their employability by giving participating students real-world skills, experience, and confidence.	Smart Sims has been adopted in higher education, but the literature does not clarify whether it has been involved in the area of entrepreneurship.
University students develop their understanding of business processes through participating in business simulation-based games and online training which gives them real-life experience as a business owner-manager through real-life simulation-based games.	The literature has confirmed that Virtonomics has been adopted to support teaching within the area of entrepreneurship in higher education.
Not clarified.	X Learning has been identified as a simulation that has been adopted in the business area, however, it is unclear whether it has been involved in the entrepreneurship area in higher education.

Table 2.3 The simulation services in terms of their involvement in teaching the entrepreneurship subject area in higher education

Simulation service	Core/Competing Simulation	Higher Education	Entrepreneurship	Is there a published study to assess the Simulation's efficacy?
Barista Sim	Competing			No
Capsim	Competing			Yes
Cesim	Competing			Yes
Edumundo	Core			No
Glo-bus	Core			Yes
GoVenture: Entrepreneur	Core			Yes
GoVenture World	Core			Yes
Hipster CEO	Core			Yes
Hubro Education	Competing			Yes
Innovative Dutch	Core			Yes
Interpretive solutions: Entrepreneur	Core			Yes
Marketplace	Competing			No
PriSim	Competing			Yes
Processim Labs	Competing			No
SimVenture				Yes
Smart Sims	Competing			No
The Entrepreneurship Simulation: The Startup Game				Yes
Venture Blocks	Core			No
Venture Strategy	Core			Yes
Virtonomics	Competing			Yes
VSL	Core			Yes
X Learning	Competing			No

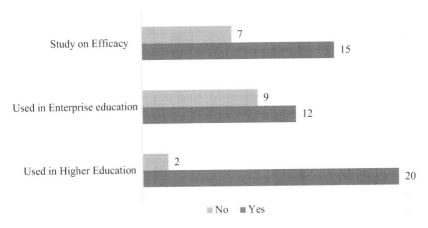

Fig. 2.1 Graphical representation of key information from Table 2.3

Conclusion

As there has been a rapid increase in the number of digital solutions to support enterprise and entrepreneurship education teaching in higher education, the purpose of this chapter was to review the nature of provisions for enterprise educators. The authors identified fourteen digital software (games) that are being used in higher education with a specific focus on whether such approaches are being used more generally in higher education or whether such approaches are being applied specifically within the discipline of enterprise, entrepreneurship, and business management education. This chapter illustrates the relevance of such approaches, which could inform the vibrancy in teaching and learning pedagogy for enterprise educators by offering multiple options to engage students through gamification (Yasin & Hafeez, 2018). Furthermore, the value of learning in this chapter supports the experiential learning and teamwork components for instructors to be able to engage their students through the use of technology-based learning.

The authors acknowledge that there are limitations associated with the web search conducted in relation to this chapter's development as a greater variety of keywords in the search engine may have led to the revelation of more simulation games/programs. Additionally, there is a possibility that the simulation games/programs have not been reviewed on their effectiveness but their visibility in studies resulting from online searches through a particular set of keywords.

References

Aguilera, A., Guerrero, M., Lozano, C., & Rios, W. (2019). *Simulations in business education: A case study of Cesim Global Challenge*. IGI Global.

Al-Elq, A. (2010). Simulation-based medical teaching and learning. *Journal of Family and Community Medicine, 17*(1), 35–40.

Alfred, M., & Chung, C. (2011). Design, development, and evaluation of a second-generation interactive Simulator for Engineering Ethics Education (SEEE2). *Science and Engineering Ethics, 18*(4), 689–697.

Bailey, J., Read, J., Linder, B., & Neeley, L. (2021). Interdisciplinary team-based learning: An integrated opportunity recognition and evaluation model for teaching business engineering and design students. *Entrepreneurship Education and Pedagogy, 4*(2), 143–168.

Bamaeeroo, F., & Shokrpour, N. (2017). The impact of the teachers' non-verbal communication on success in teaching. *Journal of Advances in Medical Education & Professionalism, 5*(2), 51–59.

Barista Sim. (2020). Glossary of terms used in Barista Sim. https://www.baristasim.com/education.html

Boocock, S. S., & Schild, E. O. (1968). *Simulation games in learning*. Sage Publications.

Bradford, P., Porciello, M., Balkon, N., & Backus, D. (2007). The Blackboard learning system: To be all and end all in educational instruction? *Journal of Educational Technology Systems, 35*(3), 301–314.

Brubacher, S. P., Powell, M., Skouteris, H., & Guadagno, B. (2015). The effects of e-simulation interview training on teachers' use of open-ended questions. *Child Abuse and Neglect, 43*(1), 95–103.

Cant, R. P., & Cooper, S. J. (2009). Simulation-based learning in nurse education: A systematic review. *Journal of Advanced Nursing, 66*(1), 3–15.

Capsim Management Simulations Incorporated. (2020). Bringing real-world experiences to any learning environment. https://www.capsim.com/about/

Carlisle, S. (2018). Software: Tableau and Microsoft Power BI. *Technology Architecture Design, 2,* 256–259.

Cesim Practice Makes Perfect. (2020). What is business simulation? https://www.cesim.com/

Chernikova, O., Heitzmann, S. M., Holzberger, D., Seidel, T., & Fischer, F. (2020). Simulation-based learning in higher education: A meta-analysis. *Review of Educational Research, 20*(10), 1–43.

Chetty, N. D. S., Handayani, L., Sahabudin, N. A., Ali, Z., Hamzah, N., Rahman, N. S. A., & Kasim, S. (2017). Learning styles and teaching styles determine students' academic performances. *International Journal of Evaluation and Research in Education, 8*(3), 610–615.

Cooper, S., Cant, R., Porter, J., Bogossian, F., McKenna, L., Brady, S., & Fox-Young, S. (2012). Simulation-based learning in midwifery education: A systematic review. *Women and Birth, 25,* 64–78.

D'Angelo, C., Rustein, D., Harris, C., Bernard, R., Borokhovski, E., & Haertel, G. (2014). *Simulations for STEM learning: Systematic review and meta-analysis.* SRI International.

Daniel, J. (2020). Education and the COVID-19 pandemic. *Prospects, 49,* 91–96.

Danske Bank. (2020). Hubro education. https://thehub.io/startups/hubro-education-1

Edumundo. (2020). About us. https://www.edumundo.com/en/home

Esmi, K., Marzoughi, R., & Torkzadeh, J. (2015). Teaching learning methods of an entrepreneurship curriculum. *Journal of Advances in Medical Education & Professionalism, 3*(4), 172–177.

Evans, J. R., & Mathur, A. (2018). The value of online surveys: A look back and a look ahead. *Internet Research, 28*(4), 854–887.

Feinstein, A. H., Mann, S., & Corsun, D. L. (2002). Charting the experiential territory. Clarifying definitions and uses of computer simulation, games, and role-play. *Journal of Management Development, 21*(10), 732–744.

Ford, D., Seybert, A., Smithburger, P., Kobulinsky, L., Samosky, J., & Kane-Gill, S. (2010). Impact of simulation-based learning on medication error rates in critically ill patients. *Intensive Care Medicine, 36*(9), 1526–1531. https://doi.org/10.1007/s00134-010-1860-2

Forster-Holt, N. (2020). Stimulation versus simulation: The student side hustle as a learning innovation. *Entrepreneurship Education and Pedagogy, 1*, 22.

Fox, J., Pittaway, L., & Uzuegbunam, I. (2018). Simulations in entrepreneurship education: Serious games and learning through play. *Entrepreneurship Education and Pedagogy, 1*(1), 61–89.

GoVenture. (2021). The most realistic small business startup and operations simulation-based learning in the world. https://www.goventure.net/en

GoVenture World. (2021). About GoVenture World. https://goventureworld.com/about.html

Herms, R. (2015). Self-regulated learning, team learning and project performance in entrepreneurship education: Learning in a lean startup environment. *Technological Forecasting and Social Change, 100*, 21–28.

Herrington, J., Reeves, T. C., & Oliver, R. (2007). Immersive learning technologies: Realism and online authentic learning. *Journal of Computing in Higher Education, 19*(1), 80–99.

Hipster CEO. (2021). Build your own tech start-up already. http://www.hipsterceo.com/

Hoelscher, J., & Mortimer, A. (2018). Using Tableau to visualize data and drive decision-making. *Journal of Accounting Education, 44*, 49–59.

Horvat, A., Dobrota, M., Krsmanovic, M., & Cudanov, M. (2013). Student perception of Moodle learning management system: a satisfaction and significance analysis. *Interactive Learning Environments, 23*(4), 515–527.

Hubro Education. (2020). How does it work? https://hubro.education/en/

Innovative Dutch. (2021). Our simulations. https://www.innovativedutch.com/

Interpretive Simulations. (2021). Getting to know Entrepreneur Retail Entrepreneurship Simulation. https://www.interpretive.com/business-simulations/entrepreneur/

Kane, G. C. (2015). Why social engagement may be more important than marketing. *MIT Sloan Management Review, 57*(1).

Keat, Y., & Ahmad, S. (2012). A study among university students in business start-ups in Malaysia: Motivations and obstacles to become entrepreneurs. *International Journal of Business and Social Science, 3*(19).

Kebritchi, M., Lipschuetz, A., & Santiague, L. (2017). Issues and challenges for teaching successful online courses in higher education: A literature review. *Journal of Educational Technology Systems, 46*(1), 4–29.

Khosla, A., & Gupta, P. (2017). Traits of successful entrepreneurs. *The Journal of Private Equity, 20*(3), 12–15.

Kunter, M., Frenzel, A., Nagy, G., Baumert, J., & Pekrun, R. (2011). Teacher enthusiasm: Dimensionality and context. *Contemporary Educational Psychology, 36*(4), 289–301.

Kunter, M., Tsai, Y.-M., Klusmann, U., Brunner, M., Krauss, S., & Baumert, J. (2008). Students' and mathematics teachers' perceptions of teacher enthusiasm and instruction. *Learning and Instruction, 18*(5), 468–482.

Lateef, F. (2010). Simulation-based learning: Just like the real thing. *Journal of Emergencies, Trauma, and Shock, 3*(4), 348–352.

Leckey, J., & Neill, N. (2010). Quantifying quality: The importance of student feedback. *Quality in Higher Education, 7*(1), 19–32.

Loon, M., Evans, J., & Kerridge, C. (2015). Learning with a strategic management simulation game: A case study. *The International Journal of Management Education, 13*(3), 227–236.

Manchar, A., & Chouhan, A. (2017). *Salesforce CRM: A new way of managing customer relationship in a cloud environment.* 2017 Second International Conference on Electrical, Computer and Communication Technologies (ICECCT).

Marketplace Simulations. (2021). Venture strategy. https://www.marketplace-simulation.com/venture-strategy#:~:text=The%20Venture%20Strategy%20simulation%20provides,and%20evaluate%20various%20business%20opportunities

Marketplace Solutions. (2020). Enhance the power of knowledge through active learning. https://www.marketplace-simulation.com/

Mohsen, K., Abdollahi, S., & Omar, S. (2019). Evaluating the educational value of simulation games: Learners' perspective. *Innovations in Education and Teaching International, 56*(4), 517–528.

Mollick, E. (2014). Entrepreneurship simulation: The startup game. https://hbsp.harvard.edu/product/WH0001-HTM-ENG

Morrel, B., & Eukel, H. N. (2020). Shocking escape: A cardiac escape room for undergraduate nursing students. *Simulation and Gaming, 52*(1), 72–78.

Neck, H., & Greene, P. (2015). Identifying business opportunities through the practice of play. https://www.babson.edu/academics/executive-education/babson-insight/entrepreneurship-education/identifying-business-opportunities-through-play/

PriSim Business Simulations. (2020). Business simulations that improve business performance. https://www.prisim.com/

Processim Labs. (2020). About us. https://www.processimlabs.com/about-us

Reddy, C. S., Sangam, R. S., & Rao, B. S. (2018). A survey on business intelligence tools for marketing, financial, and transportation services. In *Smart intelligent computing and applications* (pp. 495–504). Springer.

Rosa, E., Dahlstrom, N., Knez, I., Ljung, R., Cameron, M., & Willander, J. (2020). Dynamic decision-making of airline pilots in low-fidelity simulation. *Theoretical Issues in Ergonomics Science, 22*(1), 83–102.

Sarage, D., O'Neill, B., & Eaton, C. (2021). There is no I in Escape: Using an Escape Room Simulation to Enhance Teamwork and Medication Safety Behaviors in Nursing Students. *Simulation & Gaming, 52*(1), 40–53. https://doi.org/10.1177/1046878120976706

Sarfati, L., Ranchon, F., Vantard, N., Schwiertz, V., Larbre, V., Parat, S., Faudel, A., & Rioufol, C. (2019). Human-simulation-based learning to prevent medication error: A systematic review. *Journal of Evaluation in Clinical Practice, 25*(1), 11–20. https://doi.org/10.1111/jep.12883

Sherin, M. G., Mendez, E. P., & Louis, D. A. (2007). A discipline apart: The challenges of 'fostering a community of learners' in a mathematics classroom. *Journal of Curriculum Studies, 36*(2), 207–232.

Smart Sims Business Simulations. (2020). About us. https://www.smartsims.com/

Thompson, A., Stappenbeck, G., Reidenbach, M., Thrasher, I., & Harms, C. (2019). About the GLO-BUS business strategy simulation. https://www.glo-bus.com/help/users/WhatIs.html

Venture Blocks. (2020). VentureBlocks uses game-based simulation to achieve deep learning. https://ventureblocks.com/experience

Venture Simulations Limited. (2020). Business games that impact learning. https://simventure.com/business-games/

Virtonomics. (2020). Business simulation game. https://virtonomics.com/

Williams, D. (2015). The impact of SimVenture on the development of entrepreneurial skills in management students. *Industry and Higher Education, 29*(5), 379–395.

X Learning Limited. (2020). Business simulations. https://www.xlearning.co.uk/businesssimulations.html

Yasin, N., & Hafeez, K. (2018). Enterprise simulation gaming: Effective practices for assessing student learning with SimVenture Classic and VentureBlocks. In *Experiential learning for entrepreneurship* (pp. 51–69). Palgrave Macmillan.

3

Integrating Digital Technology in Enterprise and Entrepreneurship Education

Ahmed Al-Gindy, Naveed Yasin, Mariam Aerabe, and Aya Al-Chikh Omar

Introduction

Entrepreneurship has always been prevalent in human culture and is innate in it. It has been increasingly relevant in past decades because of the need to address persistent and growing economic challenges.

A. Al-Gindy (✉)
Canadian University Dubai, Dubai, United Arab Emirates
e-mail: agindy@cud.ac.ae

N. Yasin
Faculty of Management, Canadian University Dubai,
Dubai, United Arab Emirates
e-mail: naveed.yasin@cud.ac.ae

M. Aerabe
STEMA Training and Development Centre, Dubai, United Arab Emirates
e-mail: research@stema-center.com

A. A.-C. Omar
University of Sharjah, Sharjah, United Arab Emirates
e-mail: U21102801@sharjah.ac.ae

© The Author(s), under exclusive license to Springer Nature Switzerland AG 2022
D. Hyams-Ssekasi, N. Yasin (eds.), *Technology and Entrepreneurship Education*,
https://doi.org/10.1007/978-3-030-84292-5_3

Specialization in entrepreneurial competencies has become critical for adjusting modern labor markets. When discussing entrepreneurship education, it is essential to remember that it is consistently incorporated into the educational sector as a goal. Academic institutions were established to serve society. Three missions were developed to accomplish this goal: education by teaching, research, and the third, which is of particular importance to us, contribution to economic growth by business technology or the establishment of enterprises by students and teachers. The term "enterprise" expresses the generation and implementation of ideas in practical circumstances during a coordinated set of activities. This broad term can be generalized to any aspect of education or career pursuit. It incorporates problem recognition, problem-solving, imagination, language, communication, practical action with invention, originality, initiative, concept development, creative thinking, adaptability, and reflexivity. Enterprise education introduces new concepts and technologies to real-world environments, intending to develop individuals who have the mindset and capabilities to adapt to challenges, demands, and shortfalls, with core skills such as setting the pace, decision making, problem-solving, networking, seek opportunities, and personal effectiveness. Enterprise education is a reliable resource for preparing students for ever-changing worlds. Students would then be well-positioned throughout their lives to contribute meaningful social, cultural, and economic benefits to society through entrepreneurial activity. Entrepreneurship and enterprise learning may significantly affect the educational institution through graduation start-ups that improve the institution's reputation and new external partnerships with growth-oriented organizations. These events work together to promote the sector's delivery of various techniques, including teaching and learning, study and effect, and knowledge sharing and interaction. Entrepreneurship and enterprise education are essential aspects of the classroom setting, and its exemplary implementation is critical to the sector's overall growth (Sánchez García, 2017).

Review on Traditional Education

Education is in a constant state of change. The "traditional" teaching method is being questioned, and a "modern" method is being advocated to take its place. The standard teaching approach, also known as back-to-basics education, is still commonly practiced in schools and universities. The traditional teaching method was based entirely on recitation; for example, students would remain silent while one student after another took turns reading aloud the lesson before they had been called upon (Stephen Perse Foundation, 2017). Traditional teaching methods ensured that students were praised for their achievements, and class times were used effectively, adding simple guidelines to control students' actions. They were based on long-standing practices used successfully in schools for many years. Teachers conveyed information and upheld behavioral standards.

Education from Traditional to Modern

Knowledge is now taught from a radically different perspective due to modern educational changes. Instead of believing that all students are at the same degree of learning, the progressive teaching approach relies on particular students' interests. This modern approach to teaching is more activity-based, using methods such as different technologies, challenges, problem-based practices, demonstrations, presentations, and teamwork. The traditional education system was primarily concerned with providing knowledge through books and statistics. Students may be well-versed in theoretical aspects of learning but cannot apply what they have learned in the real world. The modern educational method balances theoretical and practical learning with more focus on student skills. Modern educational processes help students to learn more in less time. The importance remains on sparking a passion for practical learning and cultivating an inquisitive mindset. It contributes to developing a curious and imaginative mind capable of comprehending ambiguity from all angles (Miller, 2020).

With its well-defined laws and regulations, the old school system may have been ideal for creating equivalent minds with robotic personalities. This method, in which everything is described in terms of being right or wrong, leaves no space for imagination, ingenuity, or experimenting. On the other hand, the new educational system prepares the mind for cognitive development by allowing students to ask questions and discover appropriate responses by experimentation and using modern technologies that act as learning assets. Both the old and contemporary education programs use progressive teaching. The standard educational structure continues to emphasize imparting subject-specific scientific knowledge as well as memorization-based assessment and progression. The modern educational method has been scientifically developed to arouse an interest in creative learning focused on critical thinking (Miller, 2020). They learn to ask probing questions and organize assets to determine realistic answers.

For example, Educators in Loyalist College in Belleville used a virtual environment called 'Second Life' to enhance classroom teaching (Hudson & DeGast-Kennedy, 2009). Their initiative, innovation, and outcomes included the following:

* Initiative: offering a virtual environment for students pursuing custom-related career fields. An example of using the virtual environment: each student assumed the role of an agent (Border Service Officer), with their avatar questioning the travelers wishing to enter Canada. In the virtual environment, interactions are conducted by voice messages, with the people playing the travelers in a separate room from the students. The student interviews three or more passengers, and the entire class watches and examines their exchanges.
* Innovations: Loyalist College used Second Life to construct a fully functional border crossing to educate students on interviewing techniques used by Border Services Officers (BSO) at Canada's key ports of entry. Faculty and instructional programmers, 3D designers, and builders from Loyalist's Virtual World Design Centre were all interested in the creation process. The simulation is used as part of distance training by the Canadian Border Services Agency (BSA) as a pre-training for BSO recruits before they attend training.

- Benefits and outcomes attained: Students get more confidence in their skills and abilities and identify the roles and characteristics of a BSO. They develop their observation skills by watching others and learning through simulations that can replicate dangerous or inaccessible environments.

Enterprise and Entrepreneurship Education

Enterprise education is described as training students to have a more significant potential to process ideas and the skills, qualities, and qualifications to make them a reality. It covers various cognitive, analytical, social, cultural, and functional attitudes, characteristics, and core competencies relevant to every student (Penaluna, 2018). The purpose of enterprise education is to develop graduates who have the knowledge, attitude, and capabilities to generate original ideas in response to defined needs, resources, and shortfalls, as well as the capacity to act on them, even when situations alter and become ambiguous; in other words, brainstorm ideas and making it happen. For example, enterprise education prepares students studying the traditional management information systems MIS course to become entrepreneurs rather than employees.

Entrepreneurship strives to improve students' enterprising competencies, such as their capacity to recognize possibilities and develop projects by being self-employed, creating new companies, or expanding and increasing a portion of an established enterprise. Herring Thorpe Infants School, located in a low-income neighborhood, used enterprise to foster an atmosphere of solid aspirations and difficulty. They had an activity where foundation year students sell the eggs laid by the chickens they take care of, and Grade 1 students design the egg packaging while Grade 2 students measure the cost and earnings. This activity brought various cross-curriculum educational components to life and helped children develop their imagination, initiative, and problem-solving skills.

Entrepreneurship and enterprise education offers programs aimed at improving attitudes, abilities, and competencies expected to substantially affect a particular individual in suitable employment, bringing physical, social, and cultural benefits. They significantly affect placements and events that promote cooperation between academic institutions and external organizations. Thus, they equip the students with the skills to lead a rewarding, self-directed professional career.

One goal of enterprise education is to increase employer interest in schools, colleges, and universities, especially among small and medium-sized businesses (Penaluna, 2018). Employers will be interested in work placements, industry start-up simulations, mock interviews, research and consulting activities, jobs talk, business idea production, enterprise education as pedagogy mentoring, curriculum vitae training, business strategy, presentation, and job application guidance. Many of the activities listed above are examples of how business education can be incorporated into multiple curriculum frameworks.

Technologies for Enterprise Education

Technology in education produces an immersive, experience-based curriculum where students combine theory with computer hardware and software to facilitate and provide an environment that prepares students to understand technology, its evolution, uses, innovations, and social and cultural meanings (Kurt, 2017). There is a variety of technology applications in enterprise education such as:

Virtual and Augmented Reality: Virtual Reality (VR) is an electronic device that provides real-time interactive graphics with 3D environments and objects that enable virtual human interaction with those 3D models. The device comprises thick glasses that go on the eyes and hand controllers to enhance the simulation experience. For Augmented Reality (AR) applications, all that's needed is a smart device's camera to enable the digital object's emergence to the real world.

Virtual Reality objects and environments enable learners to gain more insight and information and use their acquired skills and experience more efficiently as they engage in virtual simulations (Orel, 2020). These environments will be designed to boost the student's active learning while engaging them with virtual objects and avatars that suit their learning curricula, making VR simulators a practical learning tool. Many VR platforms can create a unique, individualized environment that cannot be replicated in the classroom setting and applied in enterprise education in many ways, such as Unity, PG&E, and Labster. (Ahmed Al-Gindy, 2020).

Unity is a development platform used to create 2D and 3D games. Students can create fun simulations and VR/AR tools that improve their skills, knowledge, and performance. For example, CAE Vimedix AR helps students learn ultrasound by allowing them to visualize anatomy and ultrasound cut plane in real time.

In addition, Unity has many virtual solutions for real-world applications such as automotive, transportation and manufacturing, film transportation and cinemas, architecture, engineering, and construction.

PG&E Becker pilot service training is an interactive 3D application developed by Unity. PG&E is one of the largest natural gas and electric energy companies in the US, providing natural gas and electric service to 16 million people throughout a 70,000-square-mile service area in northern and central California. Founded: 1905, Location: HQ San Francisco, CA, Employee #: 23,500, Revenue: $17.6 Billion. Every five years, PG&E gas service technicians must perform a complete tear-down and rebuild a GE Becker VRP-600-CH Pilot as part of preventive maintenance. There are up to 20 pilots in a Field Service Representative's (FSR) territory. Due to the complex nature of parts and components, both the error rate and the time to train the technicians can be high. This results in many support calls related specifically to the rebuild procedure for new and experienced FSRs, causing downtime and damage to equipment.

PG&E deployed a 3D interactive maintenance simulation (built by Heartwood) that allows the FSR to practice each action and step as if they were tearing it down and rebuilding it in the real world. It includes choosing the appropriate tool correctly and showing how it works in the overall system. The simulation was designed to be portable, scalable, and modular on iPads and PCs.

The editor allows users to design scenes, instances of the 3D landscape in Unity and instantly observe the edits' results. Unity also enables users to deploy their games to various platforms, including TV, desktop, and mobile devices. Furthermore, Unity supports VR and augmented reality (AR), making virtual objects appear in the real world and creating games for virtual reality headsets. Most games in Unity include features from the Unity asset store, which also allows users to access artwork, models, and scripts, programs that accomplish tasks in Unity. Finally, Unity will enable users to share their work with others: Unity Team allows for collaboration on projects, while Unity Connect enables users to share their work with potential recruiters.

Labster is yet another platform that gives students access to a realistic lab experience that will let them perform experiments and practice their skills in a fun and risk-free learning environment.

It can be used for a training experience in majors challenging to provide a real-time training experience for the students, such as military training and training in surgical procedures. Moreover, virtual reality offers an excellent service in different majors such as architectural and interior design. The students can do their building designs or interior design using smart devices like laptops or desktops and design software. The role of virtual reality is to enable the students to interact with their designs and gain a 360-degree experience in a 3D virtual world which helps them improve and enhance their creative designing skills of the students. Also, virtual reality and augmented reality allow students to deeply understand their courses, such as visiting historical, natural, and tourism places from all around the world in a 360 degree, that means virtual and augmented reality can enhance the practical experience of the students in different ways and aid in a deep understanding of the surrounding environment and people needs which help in improving imaginative, thinking, and planning skills.

One of the famous virtual and augmented reality applications is the VR park in Dubai mall in the United Arab Emirates. It provides an immersive VR and AR experience for the visitors learning about different environments and objects in 3D, from polar bears in the Antarctic to the dinosaurs in the prehistoric world.

Three-dimension Printing (3D): This is a digital fabrication technology. It enables physical objects from geometrical representation and allows flexible design and customization of 3D objects based on computer-aided design software. Integrating 3D printing in enterprise education is one of the ways that enhance creative design, problem-solving, and thinking out-of-the-box skills as it has many applications in the educational field such as:

1. Biology, science, and medicine: printing different human parts, organs, molecules, and so on. It could be used in the learning process or used for people who have a health problem in their artificial limbs.
2. Math: 3D printing of different geometrical shapes to facilitate solving problem procedure of geometric area, surface, layout, and so on.
3. Physics: different printing objects like planes, cars, balls, to measure physics variables like distance, movements, volume, and evaluate some physics concepts like aerodynamic and gravity.
4. Chemistry: printing 3D molecular models.
5. Geography: printing 3D natural models and topographic maps, which help transform the course learning methods from pure theory to an attractive course.
6. Mechanical, mechatronics, and electrical: printing a 3D prototype of different electrical and mechanical projects like a car, drones, submarines, and robots.

Robotics and Artificial Intelligence (AI): It is a combination of mechanical, electrical, and computer parts that perform a specific task by implementing some programming levels in the computer device of the robot. Artificial Intelligence and intelligent system are always the central part of building a robot where the intelligent system enables the robot to perform the tasks as if it is performed by a human or under his supervision and control. There are many kinds of robotics and Artificial Intelligence, such as humanoid robots that mimic human behavior, autonomous robots that operate independently of human interaction, teleoperated robots used for geometric and weather conditions and controlled by humans, and other types.

Due to its multidisciplinary nature, adding robotics technologies in classrooms and lectures has a beneficial impact in enhancing student's skills and preparing the twenty-first-century graduates. Robotics has a vital role in implementing enterprise education. Some companies produce robots' platforms to integrate entertainment, learning and improving students' skills.

For example, LEGO and VEX robotics companies produce various robotic platforms like VEX IQ, VEX-EDR, VEX-U, VEX-Pro, LEGO-WEDO, and LEGO-Mindstorms. They are suitable for all age groups and educational levels from elementary to higher education. VEX-pro designs products for the industry level, using more advanced microcontrollers and parts. Simply saying, VEX has platforms from elementary to industry which makes it one of the perfect multidisciplinary education platforms suitable for integrating technology in enterprise education.

In 2018 VEX worlds have broken the record for the largest robot competition with 30,000 students of 1075 teams. World Robot Olympiad and FIRST Champion, Robotics Education and Competition (REC), and many other competitions make the learning process easy and funny. Also, engaging robots' activities and competitions in learning stimulate students to build and improve their learning skills that include:

- Control the robot's movements through applying mathematics and programming knowledge.
- Utilize and integrate different sensors, like touch sensor, temperature sensor, distance sensor.
- Troubleshooting strategies and engineering practices.
- Practice teamwork, time, and task management.
- Apply some scientific tracks and terms like motion generation, robot vision, different robot programming languages, and Robot Applications.

Cloud Computing: It is a technology that enables students, teachers, and administrators access to specific required resources. It is a great practical tool that minimizes students' efforts to do their homework as it stores the homework and sometimes exams in the cloud and provides remote educational services via the internet connection. It has a significant impact in emergencies that permit students to physically attend classes like health issues, weather conditions, and distance restrictions.

The Role of Technology in Enterprise Education

Technology and entrepreneurship education adds value to the student's learning journey. Whether they are interested in starting their own business or working for someone else. To bridge the gap between scientific and business students and the skills that employees of the twenty-first century needs. Technical services and methods are introduced to entrepreneurship education and approaches to teaching these technologies are investigated. Thus, students will understand the technology and its capabilities and limitations while focusing on applying an entrepreneurial mindset in acquiring opportunities.

A practical approach to using technology in enterprise and entrepreneurship education has a significant effect on learning to excel and, as a whole, the student's professional growth. It trains them for a fulfilling working life and serves as an essential means of achieving the organizational goal for graduate employment, job prospects, and growth potential. To prosper an employee in the twenty-first century, scientific and technological skills alone are not enough, and there needs to be an entrepreneurial mindset in students. That deficiency can be filled using technical approaches in entrepreneurship education, which will provide a wide variety of programs and procedures, both in and out of the curriculum, and incorporate activities that enhance hands-on skills, enable the student to learn to take initiatives, empower critical thinking skills, and develop communication skills.

The Roles and Tasks of Technology and Entrepreneurial Educators

There are standards to education, and to meet that standard, educators should empower their technology and entrepreneurial skills and know the roles and tasks needed to impact students' education positively. National (2012) and Educators (n.d.) suggest to combine technology with enterprise education to promote students' learning in enterprise education. This can be illustrated in Table 3.1, which summarizes the roles and responsibilities of technology and entrepreneurial educators, where performing these roles in one major will significantly impact the learning process.

Table 3.1 The roles of Technology and Entrepreneurial Educators

Technology Educators	Entrepreneurial Educators
Design, meet, and achieve curricular expectations suited to expand student's opportunities.	Plan and develop a curriculum that provides effective entrepreneurial education.
Engage with communities, community members, and other educators to offer different perspectives on topics.	Contribute through the development of enterprise education and collaborate with students, teachers, and other stakeholders
Motivate and inspire students to become positive, critical thinkers with several paths to achievement.	Inspire students to learn. Promote diversity and inclusion while delivering entrepreneurial education
Educators define, interpret, and assess decisions about learning environments through contemplation. Understand how their behaviors, whether implicit or explicit, impact students' classroom interactions and desire to learn.	Evaluate own practices and understand roles and responsibilities of entrepreneurial educators.

Characteristics of Technology and Entrepreneurial Educator

* **Innovative**—Able to experiment with different pedagogies, activities, exercises, and learning assessments to empower and encourage students. Explore various contexts to enhance their teaching practice.
* **Engaging**—Work with STEM (Science, Technology, Engineering, and Mathematics) educators, entrepreneurs, inventors, innovators, technologists, and other stakeholders in developing and creating a learning experience.
* **Pertinent**—Able to maintain the provision's relevancy by linking trends and needs. Keeping up to date with technology and the market to educate students on the new trends.
* **Empowering**—Enable students to relate their studies with real-world experiences and their aspirations.
* **Deliberate**—Continuously revise and develop their teaching practices to benefit oneself, students, and the institution.

Technology and Entrepreneurship Across Different Educational Levels

It is critical that as students move through the phases, they are presented with sophisticated challenges and increase gradually in the level of complexity. Ultimately, students should gain a comprehensive understanding of Technology and Enterprise, including an understanding of its effect on people, environments, and communities. Learners gain a better experience of learning opportunities that help them meet their goals at each stage of growth. Table 3.2 describes each educational starting from kindergarten level to higher education level.

Kindergarten Level

Students at this level are expected to have the following entrepreneurship skills:

- Engaging in interactive conversations.
- Ability to observe, recognize, and classify surrounding objects.
- Demonstrate the ability of the primary technology tools and smart devices.
- Draw correlation between current experience and skills with new experiences and knowledge.

The suggested technology to be used at this level:

- Creative building blocks like LEGO Kits improve students' understanding of shape, color, buildings, and structures and improve their imagination skills.

Table 3.2 Educational levels descriptions

Educational level	Age	Length
Kindergarten	From 4 to 5 years	2
Primary	From 6 to 12 years	6
Preparatory	From 12 to 15 years	4
Secondary	From 15 to 18 years	3
Higher education (Universities)	+ 18 years	–

* Virtual and augmented reality technology to introduce students to basic designing and programming skills.

Results of using technology at this level:

* Building collaboration, social, and emotional skills.
* Students can represent the surrounding environment objects using some technology tools.

Primary Level

Students at this level are expected to have the following entrepreneurship skills:

* Ability to use technology to solve simple real-life problems.
* Following instructions to perform a task.
* Ability to link basic math, science concepts, and the surrounding world.
* Ability to record accurate data and information.
* Students recognize the various elements of the technology phase through resources to complete concepts step-by-step, such as investigating, devising, producing, and evaluating.
* Demonstrate ability in collaboration and teamwork effectively.

The suggested technology to be used at this level:

* Robotics: Students can build robots, learn how to code adjustment changes robots' behavior and movements, specify what works wrong, and troubleshoot errors.
* Through VR and AR technologies, lectures, books, and activities become more immersive, interactive, riveting, and engaging as, and have become a viable solution for capturing students' concentration and attention.

Results of using technology at this level:

- Students understand the importance of inventions and innovations and how to implement them in the surrounding environment in a beneficial manner.
- Students can test materials for practical and artistic properties and suitability for diverse conditions while considering project requirements.
- Students will have opportunities to adapt ideas and expertise from various disciplines and academic fields and organize systems to realize opportunities, such as fundraising for school trips.

Preparatory Level

Students at this level are expected to have the following entrepreneurship skills:

- Learning programs allow students to create system models to demonstrate how systems or elements operate together to accomplish a specific goal.
- Students identify key design characteristics and functional aspects of technology through opportunities to examine a wide range of past and present technologies. These include visuals, environmental effects, alignment, symmetry, color, line, form, scale, ease of handling, cleaning, and successful operation.

The suggested technology to be used at this level:

- Robotics: Students learn and apply the physical and scientific concepts through robotics like drones, submarines, electronic chips, and sensors. They build prototypes that help to solve real-life problems, apply their learning of cost and estimations in preparing materials and resources.
- Through VR/AR technologies, students will enhance the planning, designing, and coding skills in any desired major, such as, if the student

is interested in history stories, he/she will be able to convert his imagination into a 3D world that helps him/her in presenting and understanding the ideas and lessons correctly.

Results of using technology at this level:

* Students can participate in competitions and challenges that require proposing or performing a technology application.
* This approach gives students opportunities to develop and apply their information skills across their learning areas and develop computer literacy that provides a basis for application in future career environments.

Secondary Level

Students at this level are expected to have the following entrepreneurship skills:

* Ability to work on a project-based idea independently.
* Can initiate and deploy technology in business ideas within groups and teams.
* Students learn that needs are addressed in various ways by researching how inventions are created, adopted, and used by various individuals and societies.

The suggested technology to be used at this level:

* Robotics: Working with robotics enables students to participate in different competitions and challenges. Using robotic kits, students are introduced to the design thinking process, where a problem is presented and how they can work together to provide the solution.
* Through 3D printing technologies, students take a creative approach. They learn how to transform their ideas into real-life solutions through testing and building small-scale prototypes.

Results of using technology at this level:

* Students will develop their design and theories, research and ask about the problem, build and test their prototype, and then present their solution or final product.
* Students will have self-motivation skills to convert an idea from imagination to reality and present the idea confidently.

Higher Education Level

Students at this level are expected to have the following entrepreneurship skills:

* Ability to suggest and evaluate a solution to a complex real-life problem based on some criteria like safety, reliability, cost, constraints, and requirements.
* Students from different majors and backgrounds can utilize technology in a beneficial manner that impacts positively in the deep understanding of the major.
* Understand how to minimize risk, scope out new sources of innovation, use technological tools, and learn from the market.

The suggested technology to be used at this level:

* 3D printing and simulation benefit students from different majors like Medicine students, simulating and imitating patients, and surgical and clinical procedures. This simulation transforms the traditional medicine classes from using the simple images of human body parts to complex human interactions portrayed using modern and advanced simulation technologies.
* The use of intelligent systems helps business students curate data from multiple business scenarios, analyze and predict performance through AI systems and Machine Learning (ML) predictive algorithms that analyze business patterns and determine performance goals.

- AI and ML approaches help train students on the business, manage and analyze data, and improve marketing.
- Cloud computing should be an essential part of the university stage as the students at this stage can use technology independently and efficiently. According to a study implemented in the University of Dammam in Saudi Arabia to evaluate the impact of using technologies and cloud computing in health colleges in a physiology course, the analysis was performed on students in their second year from different health colleges (Medicine, Nursing, Pharmacy, and Dental), where they evaluated suing smart devices and provide the course assessment, resources, and lectures online on the course website which considered as resources center. Thus students can access the course materials whenever they want without time and place restrictions. The result of the study evaluated the relationship between the academic achievement of the student and the use of technology where it concluded that the technology helps the student to significantly increase their academic achievement and progress (Al-Hariri & Al-Hattami, 2017).

Results of using technology at this level:

- Apply knowledge, techniques, skills, and modern tools to solve broadly-defined problems appropriate to the discipline.
- Design systems, components, or processes meeting specified needs for broadly-defined problems appropriate to the discipline.
- Utilize visual communication in technical and non-technical environments.
- Conduct standard tests, measurements, and experiments and analyze and interpret the results to improve processes.
- Develop self-confidence to function effectively as a member and a leader on technical and non-technical teams.

Evaluation Criteria of Students' Progress

Their career ambitions and expectations determine how students desire to progress through the entrepreneurial environment. For some students, it may merely have improved their perspectives which can make them more employable, while for others, it may have given them a goal to become an owner/manager. In enterprise education, the evaluation will mainly focus on innovation outcomes. The outcome cannot be accurately predicted in advance due to the nature of development, which assumes an element of ingenuity and surprise. The learning journey and its mapping offer tools for accurate assessment in this context. The assessment marks the following:

- **Participation**—Learners take action. Learners from any discipline engage with dedicated ideas and concepts.
- **Setback**—Learners focus on limiting risks through awareness of obstacles and embracing setbacks by experimenting and learning from errors to facilitate learner's views/vision.
- **Analyzing**—Learners are aware of their passion and interests. They develop confidence and adapt quickly. Learners take action in a step-by-step progression.
- **Inspiration**—Add value to society and businesses—awareness by realizing their own added value to the community and developing team ideas.

Results and Outcomes of Integrating Technology in Enterprise and Entrepreneurship Education

- Build students' thought, reasoning, and imaginative skills to identify their needs and build and create solutions to these needs.
- Design and focus on curriculum deliverables and map them to student's learning and engagement. The constructed curricula should be based on researching and analyzing student development and contributing to the institution's strategy and content.
- Encourage students and peers to develop their technological and entrepreneurial skills by influencing them and other educators and stakeholders through their experience and knowledge.

- Help educators create strategic plans that include technology and enterprise education topics for institutions and prepare next generations as social leaders.
- Encourage students to 'do' their study in a manner that allows them to recognize and develop strategies, using appropriate technologies that aid in enhancing learner's social and soft skills to build an ultimate objective of establishing and developing a value proposition for others.
- Encourage interdisciplinary frameworks in learning approaches and evaluation using experiential learning methods. The theory comes after experience and gives theory reinforcement and stimulates feedback about the ideas' advantages and disadvantages.
- Enable students to distinguish between 'theoretical learning' and 'practical learning' developed in enterprise education and how to prepare for these components by utilizing technology. For example, Cloud Computing technologies enable students and educators to access learning content through shared data storage. Students will rely less on hardware specifications and access materials remotely, thus enabling learners and educators to teach and learn at their convenience.
- Encourage students to use feedback to evaluate teaching points, objectively examine emotional reactions, and prepare for strategic action. For instance, they use Artificial Intelligence (AI) to develop skills and testing systems and provide a personalized learning experience to students based on their abilities (Rouhiainen, 2019).

Conclusion

When the global economy is experiencing dramatic change, introducing students to technology and enterprise learning will enlighten them in adapting to changes and engaging with individuals and societies. They can develop interest and acquire skills while using equipment and facilities and determine the appropriateness of technological advances. The use of modern technologies: Virtual Reality (VR), Artificial Intelligence (AI), Augmented Reality (AR), and Robotics helps in introducing various pedagogies that allows enterprise education to take place, not only in business schools but also in science and technology student's learning curricula. Technology influences all aspects of people's daily lives and transforms society: information technology and telecommunications influenced where people work, learn, and live. Students develop the experience, skills, understandings, and values required to cope with and contribute to future development. By creating concepts and pushing ideas until they come to fruition, students will experience the significance of technological procedures and systems. Students will also be able to test their theories of integrating or developing technologies by responding to various obstacles and working in environments influenced by technology. They will work both independently and collaboratively, gathering information about topics relating to a problem, focusing on understandings from other disciplines to reinforce conclusions, and objectively examining what others had achieved before them. This approach aims to focus students' awareness on the effective use of information and communication technologies and refining their abilities to react objectively and efficiently to the demands of the rapidly changing world by using and adapting various technologies regularly.

Learning Points and Recommendations

Summary of Key Learning Points

What ways can we use to enhance teaching and learning in business schools? How can technology help both scientific and non-scientific majors? What are the outcomes of integrating technologies across K-12 and University curriculum? This chapter addressed how technology can benefit enterprise and entrepreneurship learning. The educators also introduced the suitable methods of using technology in enterprise and the ways that can be implemented in education, along with the results and outcomes of such an approach.

The Relationship Between Technology, Enterprise, and Entrepreneurship Education:

* Help students develop an entrepreneurial mindset and fulfill graduation and career employment needs.
* Grasp opportunities while exploring technology, its limitation, and capabilities.
* Acquire twenty-first-century skills: observation and communication skills, critical and practical thinking skills, and being more innovative and imaginative in developing solutions.

Results of Implementing Technology with Enterprise and Entrepreneurship Education:

* Promote the learning process through visuals and graphics.
* Improve the quality of education through student development and productivity.
* Understanding the importance of innovation and how to develop it into a project and create a business product.

Recommendations

There are many improvements and recommendation for future work on technology in enterprise education concept, such as proposing an implementation plan that reform the educational curriculum in schools that graduate a student to a modern enterprise education that graduate an entrepreneur. The implementation plan involves working on:

* Determining and evaluating the possibility of implementing technology and enterprise education based on some criteria.
* Identify the requirement to reform the educational curriculum to enterprise education and integrate technology.
* Preparing a practical plan to modify the classrooms for applying technology.
* Preparing a practical plan for developing teachers' and student's technology and enterprise skills and abilities.

References

Ahmed Al-Gindy, C. F. (2020). Virtual reality: Development of an integrated learning. *International Journal of Information and Education Technology, 10*(3), 171–175.

Al-Hariri, T., & Al-Hattami, A. (2017). Impact of students' use on their learning achievements in physiology courses at the University of Dammam. *Journal of Taibah University Medical Science.*

Educators, E. (n.d.). *Underpinning the EEUK fellowship.* Enterprise Educators. http://www.enterprise.ac.uk/wp-content/uploads/2018/09/EEUK-Fellowship-Underpinning-FINAL-FAQ.pdf

Hudson, K., & DeGast-Kennedy, K. (2009). Canadian border simulation at Loyalist College. *Journal For Virtual Worlds Research, 2,* 1–3.

Kurt, S. (2017). Definitions of educational technology. Educational Technology.

Miller, R. (2020). Education system vs. new schools, what is better? *CEOWORLD Magazine.*

National. (2012). *Middle childhood generalist standards.* National Board for Professional Teaching Standards.

Orel, M. (2020). The potentials of virtual reality in entrepreneurship education. In L. Daniela (Ed.), *New perspectives on virtual and augmented reality.* Taylor & Francis Group.

Penaluna, A. (2018). *Enterprise and entrepreneurship education: Guidance for UK higher education providers.* The Quality Assurance Agency for Higher Education (QAA).

Rouhiainen, L. (2019). How AI and data could personalize higher education. *Harvard Business Review.*

Sánchez García, J. C. (2017). Educación emprendedora: Estado del arte. *Propósitos y Representaciones,* 442–443. http://revistas.usil.edu.pe/index.php/pyr/article/view/190

Stephen Perse Foundation. (2017). Teaching methods: Traditional Vs. modern.

4

Measuring the Impact of Simulation-Based Teaching on Entrepreneurial Skills of the MBA/DBA Students

Aidin Salamzadeh, Mehdi Tajpour, and Elahe Hosseini

Introduction

Entrepreneurship is one of the main factors in the development and employability of organizations, as it deals with exploring new entrepreneurial opportunities, which could lead to improved employment rates and income. It could lead to the socio-economic development of societies (Hosseini et al., 2020). Besides, due to the business environments' various volatilities, more attention is being paid to entrepreneurs and entrepreneurial activities, which could help it improve and provide a more

---

A. Salamzadeh (✉) • M. Tajpour
University of Tehran, Tehran, Iran
e-mail: Salamzadeh@ut.ac.ir; tajpour@ut.ac.ir

E. Hosseini
Yazd University, Yazd, Iran
e-mail: elahe.Hosseini@stu.yazd.ac.ir

© The Author(s), under exclusive license to Springer Nature Switzerland AG 2022
D. Hyams-Ssekasi, N. Yasin (eds.), *Technology and Entrepreneurship Education*,
https://doi.org/10.1007/978-3-030-84292-5_4

fertile ground for its development (Acs & Virgill, 2010; Arasti & Salamzadeh, 2018). Also, entrepreneurship is the engine of development in societies, organizations, and even educational sectors (Tajpour et al., 2020). Rapid population growth and increased unemployment rates, especially among the graduates of universities and the higher education institutions' limitations in getting engaged in entrepreneurial activities, have become vital challenges for various societies (Kucel et al., 2016).

Indeed, there are potential entrepreneurs in various organizations, but some entities such as universities and higher education institutions must get proactively engaged with them to find and train the potential entrepreneurs and unleash their power (Toghraee & Monjezi, 2017). These entrepreneurs could become the catalysts of growth and development for their organizations or run their ventures (Salamzadeh, 2018). Then, they could become the change agents of their societies or even the global society (Tajpour et al., 2018). Nevertheless, they need a set of required skills and tools to improve their entrepreneurial journeys, inside or outside their organizations. Such an approach helps them become more creative, innovative, self-confident, take more risks, and hopefully create more value (Barzdins, 2012; Salamzadeh et al., 2017). Therefore, universities and scholars have become more focused on stimulating their students' entrepreneurial minds and motivate them to be more innovative in their current businesses or future ventures (Militaru et al., 2015). Thus, the missions of universities are changing rapidly toward the Third Mission (Guerrero et al., 2014, 2015). Besides, entrepreneurship education, which is already added to various programs' curricula, provides students with most of the required skills needed to live an entrepreneurial life or set up their ventures, primarily through changing their mindsets (Costin et al., 2018).

It is noteworthy that there are various approaches to entrepreneurship education. This chapter focuses on measuring the impact of simulation-based teaching on entrepreneurial skills of the entrepreneurship MBA/DBA students of the University of Tehran. The study scrutinizes whether the simulation-based teaching techniques that were used in their programs have affected their entrepreneurial skills or not. In this study, students were engaged in simulation-based learning techniques. They gained some experiences and faced several challenges, and we examined if those techniques had any significant impact on the entrepreneurial atmosphere of their business and their entrepreneurial skills. Simulation-based teaching included tools to improve the technical, communication, and cognitive skills of the students. Students learned about these three skills through simulation-based teaching techniques during the study and were supposed to improve their entrepreneurial skills.

This study contributes to the existing body of literature in several terms. Firstly, it is a newly introduced approach toward entrepreneurship education, especially in an emerging economy. Secondly, it highlights the importance of using simulation-based teaching techniques in entrepreneurship education, which policymakers and university officials might consider in their policies and strategies. Thirdly, as entrepreneurship education has become a vital concern for various societies, simulation-based teaching's potentials will help them improve their citizens' entrepreneurial skills and, therefore, use their potential as the engines of economic development. Besides, in this study, the impact of simulation-based teaching on improving the entrepreneurial atmosphere in academic settings and universities and its impact on the development of entrepreneurial skills of the entrepreneurship MBA and DBA students have been investigated.

The chapter is structured as follows. First, the literature is reviewed. Then, the research model and the hypotheses are proposed. Then, the research methodology and the results of the analysis are discussed. Finally, the paper concludes with some remarks and learning points.

Literature Review

The simulation includes how real-world experiences are simulated and directed to repeat some aspects of a real-life and stimulate a series of behaviors interactively (Keskitalo & Ruokamo, 2021). Besides, it makes it possible to highlight some specific behaviors, skills, and characteristics in a controlled environment (Ke & Xu, 2020). Such an approach is helpful in various aspects of skill-based learning in which intentional and practical principles of experiential learning are considered (Patel & Dennick, 2017). Simulation enables students to learn through experiential learning techniques, which expose them to real-life venture creation and growth facts (Costello, 2017). Simulation leads to understanding processes, predicting relationships, and developing skills (Torres et al., 2020). Therefore, simulation techniques help students learn about the complexities of small businesses in reaching higher performance outputs (Yasin & Hafeez, 2018). In addition to simulation, such an educational strategy is proposed to maintain students' learning interests to achieve optimal and continuous learning outcomes (Hung et al., 2021). Besides, real-time and interactive decisions are not made exactly according to real-world facts and figures. Nevertheless, generally, decisions are made based on limited information which is not necessarily reliable and accessible. The information might be irrelevant to unknown problems which appear in short periods and might also be competitive (Costin et al., 2018). The simulation-based learning environment enhances participants' performance in interactive and demonstration learning while educating them to observe and care for students' actions/reactions during learning. On the other hand, there is a competition between physical reality and functional intelligence in the simulated environment (Ke et al., 2020). Therefore, simulation activities are a function of the previous and next steps, which instead of emphasizing the processes of doing things in the system, redefines it through its components (Chernikova et al., 2020). Simulation-based teaching is extensively used to develop technical and procedural skills, allowing the students to learn according to a previously defined measurement system that records and evaluates the results. Several scholars suggest that the development of technical skills will improve the students' entrepreneurial skills (Patel & Dennick, 2017).

Today, according to the development of information and communication technology and dramatically increasing use of web-based learning tools and techniques, simulation-based teaching is being used in entrepreneurship and business education and research (Pempek & Calvert, 2009; Akl et al., 2013). In fact, simulation refers to a comprehensive virtual environment that provides opportunities to increase and develop various learners' competencies (Nøhr & Aarts, 2010). Based on the academics' tendency to such methods, simulation has become an essential part of university programs, generally, and specifically in classroom activities (De Freitas, 2006; Moizer & Lean, 2010). Therefore, simulation is a factor affecting businesses' competitive advantage in the international environment and is also an important tool for organizations to better manage information and knowledge (Tajpour & Hosseini, 2020). Improved learners' motivation and entrepreneurial skills and their attempt to get more proactively engaged in challenges are among the simulation outcomes (Wouters et al., 2013). Besides, using simulation-based teaching techniques combined with traditional ones could be very useful. Although simulation-based teaching could not address all the educational needs and challenges, it could be a helpful tool and could offer various techniques for improving learners' engagement in learning processes (Fayolle, 2018).

Since simulation, as an effective teaching tool, significantly helps with active, experiential, and problem-oriented learning, scholars believe that to improve entrepreneurial skills, such an approach could be considered (Ranchhod et al., 2014; Fayolle, 2018). This teaching method's main aim in entrepreneurship education is developing, implementing, and assessing experiential educational programs based on attractive and better learning to stimulate entrepreneurship (Bellotti et al., 2014). Simulation-based assessment is an effective and efficient tool for assessing students' skills in education (Yamazaki et al., 2021). One of the benefits of simulation-based teaching in improving entrepreneurial skills is that these methods are useful tools to create an environment for learners to know what would be the best they can do in their future activities and develop their entrepreneurial skills accordingly (Neto & Mendes, 2012). Besides, simulation provides potential entrepreneurs with more practical experiences in a safe environment to help them set up their ventures in the future.

Simulation-based teaching is a behavioral approach, and it aims to learn complex concepts and skills. Also, this approach is shaped based on social learning theories (Miller et al., 2019). Ease of application, accelerated learning, capacity to motivate and influence the learners, creating an exciting environment and stimulating group discussions, ease of accessibility, and using visual and graphical tools and techniques are among the benefits of these approaches (Thomas & Barker, 2018). Generally speaking, involvement of the five senses in the learning process, increasing self-confidence and critical thinking skills, improved communication and cognitive skills, facing actively with learners, and ability to teach to a wide range of learners are also among the other benefits of such an approach (Makransky et al., 2019). The training results on performance improvement simulation show increased satisfaction and knowledge in the real environment (Strygacz & Sthub, 2018). Some of the research findings are summarized in the Table 4.1 below:

Hypotheses Development

Simulation-based teaching is shaped based on the assumption that education must include three key elements, that is, networks, mentality, and framework (Sidhu et al., 2015). Networks include environmental supports, the framework includes knowledge and realities related to entrepreneurship, and mentality is an overlooked element in the traditional curriculum (Smith et al., 2014). This approach presumes that entrepreneurs' mentality could be defined as a set of behavioral patterns which are efficient tools to strengthen and encourage students' behavioral patterns. Therefore, in such an approach, learners explore their mentalities and compare them with those of the entrepreneurs (Soltanifar et al., 2021). Most of the focus is on the relationship between learners and the subject in question. That is to say, how learners might perceive the information, experiences, and knowledge offered in the educational course (Sidhu et al., 2015). Simulation-based teaching puts the learners in an active role and stimulates their critical thinking skills. They challenge learners, and learners become motivated. These motivations will lead to further developed entrepreneurial skills (Bellotti et al., 2012).

Entrepreneurial skills are shaped as a result of learning and getting information. The more individuals have entrepreneurial skills, the more they might be successful (Soltanifar et al., 2021). Scholars define entrepreneurial skills as the ability to create new and valuable things by dedicating required time and effort, presuming financial collaboration, mental and social risks, and rewards resulted from personal and financial satisfaction, as well as independence (Nieuwenhuizen, 2009). General definitions of entrepreneurial skills suggest that these skills are considered as self-esteem, courage, stubbornness, desire to get an immediate result, and the ability to recognize opportunity (Shabbir et al., 2016). The most

Table 4.1 Summary of the results of previous research

Authors/Year	Title	Conclusion
Hung et al. (2021)	Effects of simulation-based learning on nursing students' perceived competence, self-efficacy, and learning satisfaction: A repeat measurement method	Simulation-based education is effective in improving students' perceived ability, self-efficacy, and satisfaction with learning. Statistically, there has been an improvement in student competence, self-efficacy, and satisfaction with learning by simulation. In addition to simulation, several educational strategies are proposed to maintain students' learning interests to achieve optimal and continuous learning outcomes.
Spadea et al. (2021)	Enhancing the future of simulation-based education in pediatrics	Advanced simulation through technology is a great tool for educating people. It is an effective method of teaching technical and non-technical skills that are used by a large number of people. Also, in this regard, governments and academic institutions should do their utmost to finance education.
Yamazaki et al. (2021)	Assessment of blood pressure measurement skills in second-year medical students after ongoing simulation-based education and practice	Measuring students' different skills are due to repeated practice based on simulation and improve the knowledge and experience of mastering the curriculum. Simulation-based assessment is an effective and efficient tool for assessing students' skills in education.
Chernikova et al. (2020)	Simulation-Based Learning in Higher Education: A Meta-Analysis	The use of technology has positive effects on learning. Students who already had a high level of knowledge benefited more. Students who already have little knowledge learn better when guided by examples. Findings were high in various fields of higher education, including management. The result shows that simulation is one of the most effective tools to facilitate the learning of complex skills in different domains.

(continued)

Table 4.1 (continued)

Authors/Year	Title	Conclusion
Ke et al. (2020)	Investigating educational affordances of virtual reality for simulation-based teaching training with graduate teaching assistants	Virtual reality-based learning environment enhances participants' performance through appropriate actions and reactions of students while working, which leads to a competition between physical reality and functional intelligence in the simulated environment.
Campos et al. (2020)	Simulation-based education involving online and on-campus models in different European universities	Due to the globalization of simulation-based learning experience, it can be made available to students from different geographical areas and universities, which leads to the development of interdisciplinary skills, the ability to work in teams and multicultural learning processes, the development of international cooperation, and interdisciplinary in education.
Jamil and Isiaq (2019)	Teaching technology with technology: approaches to bridging learning and teaching gaps in simulation-based programming education	In simulation-based teaching, the adaptation of students' learning and interaction procedures emerges as empowerment factors. On the other hand, the negative consequences of participatory tasks, distractions of students between learning and physical environment are changed and corrected.
Dodds et al. (2018)	Using simulation-based education to help social work students prepare for practice	Simulation is a combination of professional knowledge and practical skills. Modern technologies provide interactive and comprehensive learning experiences, enabling students to develop practical skills safely. It facilitates the gap between knowledge and skills through interactive and comprehensive simulations by modern technology.

(continued)

Table 4.1 (continued)

Authors/Year	Title	Conclusion
Strygacz and Sthub (2018)	Combining Simulation-Based Training and Flipped Classroom in Project Management Learning	Simulation-based learning through management experiences is a simulated real-life preparation project that helps solve problems. The training results on performance improvement simulation show increased satisfaction and knowledge in the real environment.
Blackmore et al. (2018)	Simulation-based education to improve communication skills: a systematic review and identification of current best practice	Advances in communication skills taught through simulation can translate into measurable benefits beyond the simulation center, but this evidence is limited by the way most studies are designed. Good communication skills lead to high-quality services.

Source: Authors' elaboration

critical entrepreneurial skills include personal skills such as innovativeness, creativity, risk-taking, the ability to face unknown subjects, accepting challenges, responsibility, and exploring entrepreneurial opportunities in volatile environments. Interpersonal skills include effective interaction with others, effective communication, negotiation, impressing others, and leadership skills. Finally, process skills include designing and organizing, analyzing, synthesizing, evaluating, and acting skills (Rudmann, 2008). In sum, according to the extant literature, in this research, simulation-based teaching is composed of three main skills, that is, technical, communication, and cognitive skills.

Technical skills or expertise is the building block of creative and entrepreneurial action (Nikraftar & Hosseini, 2017). These skills include written skills, evaluation or assessment skills, business management skills, technological skills, organizational skills, networking skills, mentorship and coaching skills, role-playing skills, and teamwork (Salamzadeh et al., 2016; Hatch, 2018). Besides, these include operational skills required to produce products or render services, skills required to supply raw material, procurement, and exploring skills (Bellotti et al., 2012). The second category includes *communication skills*. Previous research revealed that improved communication skills in students could significantly affect their activities and social behavior. Hence, by using communication skills, people can become aware of their behavior and performance. In this way, they strengthen their managerial ability to be a suitable basis for correcting and improving behaviors and personality development (Tajpour et al., 2018). Good communication skills lead to high-quality services (Blackmore et al., 2018). Also, it makes them more self-confident, and therefore, it impacts their entrepreneurial skills (Katz et al., 2020). Learners should be able to use their abilities and skills to creatively and entrepreneurially design their business plans. These skills include active listening skills, straight-talking skills, non-verbal communication skills, stress management skills, and emotion control skills (Bellotti et al., 2012). Finally, *cognitive skills* make knowing possible for us (Alisinanoğlu et al., 2012). These skills include problem-solving skills, and they aim to adjust and balance the processes that lead to behavioral disorder (Kim et al., 2011; Khahande Karnama et al., 2017). Cognitive skills lead to decreased anxiety in critical conditions and would expedite collaborative and supportive behaviors, improving our knowledge regarding the environment. Based on these skills filtering and recognizing the correct information from the wrong ones becomes possible (Reed, 2020; Yasin et al., 2020). Learning skills such as self-confidence, rational caution, purposefulness, and courage to make decisions and decision-making are some of the issues that can improve people's cognitive skills (Sabokro et al., 2018).

These skills are assumed to improve entrepreneurial skills in an innovative atmosphere (Tajpour et al., 2020). Therefore, in organizational science literature, it is generally defined based on individuals' perception of their work environment (García-Buades et al., 2015). Despite the intense technical and organizational competition, managers try to recognize and create an appropriate atmosphere in which innovation is appreciated and improved continuously and could increase productivity. All organizations need new and innovative thoughts to survive in today's intense competition. Ideation and new processes could be a basis for organizations to adapt to the dynamic external environment and create a competitive advantage (Wilkinson et al., 2020). An innovative atmosphere is about common understanding among the organization's members

4 Measuring the Impact of Simulation-Based Teaching...

regarding procedures, methods, and behaviors that promote a new generation of knowledge and methods (Moolenaar et al., 2010). It reveals the feedback that individuals might receive regarding the organization's support from innovative and creative behaviors. These include organizational support mechanisms that motivate creative employees to use their capabilities and talents creatively to act entrepreneurially and stimulate employees' motivation to use their best capabilities and become more productive in terms of entrepreneurial activities (Williams et al., 2013; Gegenhuber, 2020). Providing such an atmosphere is a common asset for employees and organizations, and it is a function of organizational structure, employee's citizenship behavior, and their attempt to understand organizational support (Machado & Davim, 2020). Thus, the following hypotheses are proposed and studied in this research (Fig. 4.1).

H_{1a}: Technical skills significantly affect the development of entrepreneurial skills of MBA and DBA students.

H_{2a}: An innovative atmosphere affects the relationship between technical skills and the development of entrepreneurial skills of MBA and DBA students.

H_{1b}: Communication skills significantly affect the development of entrepreneurial skills of MBA and DBA students.

H_{2b}: An innovative atmosphere affects the relationship between communication skills and the development of entrepreneurial skills of MBA and DBA students.

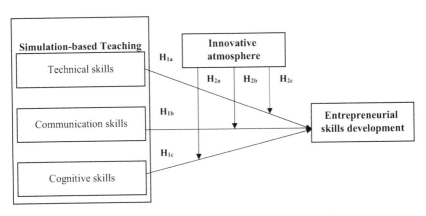

Fig. 4.1 Theoretical framework. (Source: Authors' elaboration)

H_{1c}: Cognitive skills significantly affect the development of entrepreneurial skills of MBA and DBA students.

H_{2c}: An innovative atmosphere affects the relationship between cognitive skills and the development of entrepreneurial skills of MBA and DBA students.

Research Methods

As discussed earlier, this research investigates the impact of simulation-based teaching on the development of entrepreneurial skills. Besides, it scrutinizes whether an innovative atmosphere would impact this relationship. This study's statistical population includes 557 students of entrepreneurship MBA and DBA programs at the University of Tehran. The students were studying entrepreneurship programs in various faculties, including the faculty of entrepreneurship, faculty of management, and faculty of engineering during 2020. The sample size was derived from Cochran's formula and was equal to 231. These students had studied for at least one year and were executives with more than three years of experience. A researcher-made questionnaire with 30 questions was designed and verified by experts (expert validity) (Henseler et al., 2015). A 5-point Likert-type scale was used (1—completely disagree, to 5—completely agree) (Table 4.2). A Likert scale is a tool for measuring people's attitudes and is used to prepare attitude questionnaires in management and humanities. In general, three standard scales have been introduced by

Table 4.2 Variables, components, questions, and Cronbach's alpha

Variables	Components	Questions	Cronbach's alpha
Simulation-based teaching	Technical skills	1–6	0.845
	Communication skills	7–12	0.746
	Cognitive skills	13–18	0.867
Innovative atmosphere	–	19–24	0.805
Entrepreneurial skills development	–	25–30	0.824

Rennes Likert, known as the five-degree, seven-degree, and nine-degree scales. These scales can be used to express agreement or determine the importance of items. The most common form of the Likert spectrum is 5 degrees. This scale can also be used to express agreement or assess importance or status. In this study, a 5-point Likert scale has been used. This scale measures only the subject and issue under study and not another irrelevant issue. It also expresses a more or less positive or negative tendency and not an indifferent tendency. The questions regarding entrepreneurial, technical, communication, and cognitive skills were drawn from Azim and Al-Kahtani (2014) and Garcia-Esteban and Jahnke (2020), and the innovative atmosphere was measured based on Dubey and Ghai (2011) and Chen et al. (2020). The questionnaire was distributed online, and 227 sound questionnaires were gathered and analyzed. Smart PLS3 was used to analyze the data (Kline, 2015).

The validity and reliability of the questionnaire were ensured through various methods. For ensuring the validity of the questionnaire, construct and content validity were checked. Therefore, before distributing the questionnaire, the authors asked seven experts and faculty members to ensure the content validity. Their comments and points were considered in the early draft, and they checked the final questionnaire for approval. Cronbach's alpha and composite reliability were used to ensure reliability (Fornell & Larcker, 1981). Table 4.2 shows the values for Cronbach's alphas for all the variables, which are higher than 0.7, and therefore, it shows the reliability of the measurement tool.

Besides, to ensure the reliability of the questionnaire, partial least square measures are considered. In this method, reliability is checked by factor loadings and composite reliability. The closer the values of factor loadings to one would be, the more reliable they will be. Factor loadings must also be higher than 0.4 (Hulland, 1999). Cronbach's alpha and composite reliability values are higher than 0.7 and, therefore, are acceptable. Average variance extracted (AVE) values are also more than 0.5. Therefore, the variables' reliability is ensured (Table 4.3).

To ensure the questionnaire's convergent and divergent reliability, AVE and the square root of AVE are calculated, respectively (Table 4.4). The results ensure the questionnaire's convergent reliability, as the AVE values

Table 4.3 Validity and reliability measures

Variables	Components	Composite reliability	AVG	rho	R^2	R^2-adjusted	Q^2
Simulation-based teaching	Technical skills	0.876	0.554	0.856	0.821	0.802	0.703
	Communication skills	0.883	0.559	0.874	–	–	–
	Cognitive skills	0.826	0.546	0.764	–	–	–
Innovative atmosphere	–	0.899	0.598	0.877	–	–	–
Entrepreneurial skills development	–	0.863	0.518	0.821	0.432	0.802	0.703

Table 4.4 Divergent validity

Components	1	2	3	4	5
Cognitive skills	0.773				
Communication skills	0.592	0.668			
Entrepreneurial skills development	0.640	0.648	0.744		
Innovative atmosphere	0.580	0.590	0.720	0.870	
Technical skills	0.354	0.512	0.514	0.362	0.748

were higher than 0.5 (Ebrahimi et al., 2019). Also, as the square root of AVE values are greater than the correlation values, its divergent reliability is ensured (Fornell & Larcker, 1981).

Results

Based on student responses, 27% were from the Faculty of Entrepreneurship, 39% from the Faculty of Management, and 34% from the Faculty of Engineering, University of Tehran. The model's fitness was measured by investigating the measurement, structural, and general models (Hair et al., 2017). To ensure the model fitness in partial least squares, several measures are used. T-values were calculated using the software accordingly (Fig. 4.2). As the t-values were higher than 1.96 at the confidence level of 95%, its fitness was approved (Thomas, 2003).

4 Measuring the Impact of Simulation-Based Teaching...

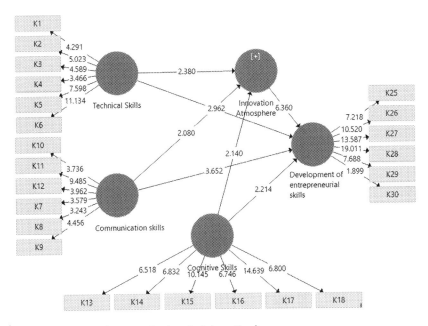

Fig. 4.2 T-values. (Source: Authors' elaboration)

The second measure to ensure the fitness of the structural model is R^2, which is also calculated. The values might be below 0.19, 0.33, and 0.67, showing weak, moderate, and strong values (Hosseini et al., 2020). According to the outputs, the values for variables of entrepreneurship skills development and innovative atmosphere were 0.821 and 0.432, respectively (Fig. 4.3).

Predictive Relevance (Q^2 Values)

Q^2 values are calculated for dependent variables and show the predictive validity of a model. The values might be 0.35 (strong effect), 0.15 (moderate effect), and 0.02 (weak effect) (Kline, 2015). These values were 0.707 and 0.355, respectively, for entrepreneurship skills development and innovative atmosphere. It ensures the predictive relevance of the variables.

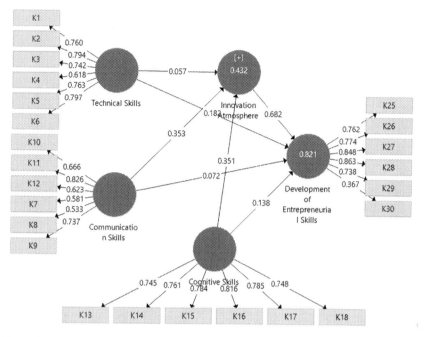

Fig. 4.3 Factor loadings, and R^2. (Source: Authors' elaboration)

The Goodness of Fit (GoF)

The general model includes both measurement and structural models. GoF values could be 0.1 (weak effect), 0.25 (moderate effect), and 0.36 (strong effect). The calculated value for the general model was 0.385, which reveals strong goodness of fit.

$$GOF = \sqrt{average(Commonality) \times average(R2)}$$

Standardized Root Mean Square Residual (SRMR) values are also calculated. There are various views among the scholars. For instance, a series of scholars believe that the values must be lower than 0.05, while others consider values below 0.08 acceptable. Generally, values less than 0.1 reveal an acceptable fitness (Kline, 2015). Bentler-Bonett index or

4 Measuring the Impact of Simulation-Based Teaching... 93

normed fit index (NFI) is also measured. The results show that the fitness is acceptable (Table 4.5).

Moreover, to analyze the mediating role of innovation atmosphere, the variance accounted for (VAF) value was calculated, which was 0.569, which

$$\text{VAF} = (a \times b) / (a \times b) + c$$

a: The amount of the mediator and independent variable pathway coefficient: 0.254
b: The amount of the mediator and dependent variable pathway coefficient: 0.682
c: The amount of the dependent and independent variable pathway coefficient: 0.131

Finally, to test the hypotheses, t-values were calculated. The findings revealed that all the hypotheses were supported (Table 4.6). It reveals that

Table 4.5 SRMR and NFI

	SRMR	NFI
Acceptable values	≥0.10	≤0.9
Calculated values	0.039	0.913

Table 4.6 Hypothesis test results

Path	t-test	Influence coefficient	Result
Technical skills—Entrepreneurship skills development	2.962	0.182	Supported
Technical skills—Innovation atmosphere-Entrepreneurship skills development	2.380	0.057	Supported
Communication skills—Entrepreneurship skills development	3.652	0.072	Supported
Communication skills—Innovation atmosphere-Entrepreneurship skills development	2.080	0.353	Supported
Cognitive skills—Entrepreneurship skills development	2.214	0.138	Supported
Cognitive skills—Innovation atmosphere-Entrepreneurship skills development	2.140	0.351	Supported

skills targeted at simulation-based teaching significantly affected the development of entrepreneurship skills of the entrepreneurship MBA and DBA students of the University of Tehran. Besides, the mediating role of the innovation atmosphere was supported.

Conclusion

Today, simulation-based teaching techniques are not used widely in business and entrepreneurship programs. Nevertheless, as their importance has been highlighted in the literature, proponents of such teaching methods try to investigate them. In the present chapter, the authors have investigated the impact of the skills targeted at simulation-based teaching (including technical, communication, and cognitive skills) on the development of entrepreneurial skills of the entrepreneurship MBA and DBA students of the University of Tehran. Besides, it was studied whether an innovative atmosphere might impact those relationships. Findings revealed that the innovative atmosphere significantly impacts the relationship between simulation-based teaching and entrepreneurial skills development. According to the literature, one of the required tools for developing the students' entrepreneurial skills is to use simulation-based teaching techniques in line with the organizational atmosphere. An inappropriate atmosphere might impact the relationship between the teachers and students and become a barrier to creativity. Simulation-based teaching might lead to developing entrepreneurship skills and be considered successful if it increases the students' imagination, creativity, flexibility, and absorption capacity in real-life situations.

Based on the results of H_{1a} and H_{2a}, technical skills targeted in simulation-based teaching could significantly affect the development of entrepreneurship skills, both directly and through the mediating role of the innovative atmosphere. It reveals the importance of paying attention to technical skills, which are essential in the labor markets. These skills make students qualified for the market opportunities and also equip them with the necessary skills to become entrepreneurs or find appropriate jobs. It will directly lead to the improvement of total entrepreneurial activities and also the employment rates. These skills include the ones needed for industrial settings and general markets, which face profound technological changes and allow them to update and enhance skills. Besides, due to the organizational environment's dynamism and innovativeness of competitors, improving these skills has become a mandate for any organization. Thus, organizations tend to create a supportive and innovative atmosphere to recognize the changes and address such dynamisms adequately. Such an atmosphere could motivate individuals to act more entrepreneurially. It is suggested that team workshops be formed in these simulations and that members be asked to present ideas in groups because interpersonal relationships that are based on innovation prevent stress and tension in doing activities. Given that people tend to solve problems linearly, try to expand brainstorming sessions with people who think nonlinearly. To increase the skills of students, a survey should be conducted with their educational needs, and educational programs should be developed by the needs. These findings are in line with those of Patel and Dennick (2017) and Thomas and Barker (2018).

Based on the results of H_{1b} and H_{2b}, communication skills in simulation-based teaching could positively impact entrepreneurship skill development, which could be improved further in an innovation atmosphere. Communication skills are among the most important life skills that could facilitate our social lives, help us improve our networks, and succeed in our personal and business lives. To communicate appropriately, one must be aware of a message's aim and content to provide relevant feedback. People can solve their problems, but they have to adapt to the circumstances and the time. Turn emotional and stressful situations into safe and calm environments through communication skills. Thus, communication skills lead to changes in behavior and changes in some situations that are out of control. Entrepreneurship deals with exploring and creating opportunities based on the socio-economic needs of a target group. Therefore, any entrepreneur must communicate with people. Besides, simulation-based teaching techniques could provide students with the required skills to participate in market situations and create value. Students should learn how to decode other's messages and address their needs accordingly. The students' communication skills could significantly improve their activities, behaviors, and self-confidence. It will increase their entrepreneurial skills, especially in a supportive and innovative environment. Individuals will present their ideas without fear and stress, which could lead to sharing ideas and information more efficiently. Therefore, it is suggested that simulation-based teaching techniques must be used more frequently to let the students learn how to communicate, and it might be facilitated by making the atmosphere more innovative. It is suggested that by teaching communication skills, one can strengthen emotional intelligence as well as form a problem-oriented coping style. Also, in reviewing communication skills, increasing the skill of saying no and eliminating extra sentences when negotiating can lead to personal growth and increase the entrepreneurial spirit. That one learns how to apply knowledge, guidance, and practice at the same time. It is suggested that concise communication skills training be considered. Because short circuits always win, even the tech industry supports this rule. As one reaches the final steps of negotiation, more should be said in fewer words. So find ways to get rid of clutter you do not need. By teaching communication skills, one can express one's values and differences with any other person in the market or organization. Through communication skills, one must constantly ask oneself why this action should be taken, asking why these put you on the path to achieving goals. Holding meetings with investors in line with communication skills is recommended because short presentations in this field cause people to be flexible in different situations. These findings are in line with the findings of Rudmann (2008), Costin et al. (2018), Makransky et al. (2019), and Wilkinson et al. (2020).

Finally, according to H_{1c} and H_{2c}, cognitive skills considered in simulation-based teaching techniques could positively affect students' entrepreneurial skills. It could be facilitated in an innovative atmosphere. Cognitive skills, such as problem-solving, deal with complex issues and problems like setting up a new venture or expanding it. Therefore, these skills must be considered in simulation-based teaching and could significantly impact entrepreneurial skills development. Previous studies have also supported these findings (e.g., Ranchhod et al., 2014; Miller et al., 2019; Makransky et al., 2019). Thus, effective problem-solving, which is a cognitive issue, could become a foundation for developing ideas and choosing the best choices to succeed in an entrepreneurial journey. Such skills could help individuals face occupational and professional tensions more effectively. That is why scholars consider these skills required for anyone, especially entrepreneurs. Entrepreneurs have to make decisions repeatedly, and their cognitive maps and skills could help them make crucial decisions. They use these skills to frame and understand the problem and apply them to explore, evaluate, and exploit entrepreneurial opportunities.

Learning Points

- Enterprise and entrepreneurship educators should consider technical skills (such as written skills, evaluation or assessment skills, business management skills, technological skills, organizational skills, networking skills, mentorship and coaching skills, role-playing skills, and teamwork) in their simulation-based teaching techniques to develop the MBA and DBA students' entrepreneurship skills.
- Enterprise and entrepreneurship educators should develop communication skills (such as active listening skills, straight-talking skills, nonverbal communication skills, stress management skills, and emotion control skills) in their simulation-based teaching techniques to develop the MBA and DBA students' entrepreneurship skills.
- Enterprise and entrepreneurship educators should consider cognitive skills (such as sustained and multiple simultaneous attention skills, response inhibition skills, fast information processing skills, cognitive flexibility and control skills, and pattern recognition skills) in their simulation-based teaching techniques to develop the MBA and DBA students' entrepreneurship skills.
- Providing an innovative atmosphere could improve the impact of simulation-based teaching on developing the MBA and DBA students' entrepreneurship skills.

References

Acs, Z. J., & Virgill, N. (2010). Entrepreneurship in developing countries. In *Handbook of entrepreneurship research* (pp. 485–515). Springer.

Akl, E. A., Kairouz, V. F., Sackett, K. M., Erdley, W. S., Mustafa, R. A., Fiander, M., … Schünemann, H. (2013). Educational games for health professionals. *Cochrane Database of Systematic Reviews, 3*. https://doi.org/10.1002/14651858. CD006411.pub4

Alisinanoğlu, F., Özbey, S., & Kesicioğlu, O. S. (2012). Impact of social skill and problem behavior training program on children attending preschool: A survey. *Academic Research International.*

Arasti, Z., & Salamzadeh, A. (2018). A review of the status of social entrepreneurship research and education in Iran. In *Entrepreneurship education and research in the Middle East and North Africa (MENA)* (pp. 325–346). Springer.

Azim, M. T., & Al-Kahtani, A. H. M. (2014). Entrepreneurship education and training: A survey of the literature. *Life Science Journal, 11*(1), 127–135.

Barzdins, J. (2012). Developing health care management skills in times of crisis: A review from the Baltic region. *International Journal of Healthcare Management, 5*(3), 129–140. https://doi.org/10.1179/2047971912Y.0000000015

Bellotti, F., Berta, R., De Gloria, A., Lavagnino, E., Antonaci, A., Dagnino, F., ... Mayer, I. S. (2014). Serious games and the development of an entrepreneurial mindset in higher education engineering students. *Entertainment Computing, 5*(4), 357–366. https://doi.org/10.1016/j.entcom.2014.07.003

Bellotti, F., Berta, R., De Gloria, A., Lavagnino, E., Dagnino, F., Ott, M., ... Mayer, I. S. (2012). Designing a course for stimulating entrepreneurship in higher education through serious games. *Procedia Computer Science, 15,* 174–186. https://doi.org/10.1016/j.procs.2012.10.069

Blackmore, A., Kasfiki, E. V., & Purva, M. (2018). Simulation-based education to improve communication skills: A systematic review and identification of current best practice. *BMJ Simulation and Technology-Enhanced Learning, 4*(4), 159–164. https://doi.org/10.1136/bmjstel-2017-000220

Campos, N., Nogal, M., Caliz, C., & Juan, A. A. (2020). Simulation-based education involving online and on-campus models in different European universities. *International Journal of Educational Technology in Higher Education, 17*(1), 1–15. https://doi.org/10.1186/s41239-020-0181-y

Chen, L., Luo, F., Zhu, X., Huang, X., & Liu, Y. (2020). Inclusive leadership promotes challenge-oriented organizational citizenship behavior through the mediation of work engagement and moderation of organizational innovative atmosphere. *Frontiers in Psychology, 11,* 560594.

Chernikova, O., Heitzmann, N., Stadler, M., Holzberger, D., Seidel, T., & Fischer, F. (2020). Simulation-based learning in higher education: A meta-analysis. *Review of Educational Research, 90*(4), 499–541.

Costello, G. J. (2017). More than just a game: The role of simulation in the teaching of product design and entrepreneurship to mechanical engineering students. *European Journal of Engineering Education, 42*(6), 644–652. https://doi.org/10.1080/03043797.2016.1211992

Costin, Y., O'Brien, M. P., & Slattery, D. M. (2018). Using simulation to develop entrepreneurial skills and mindset: An exploratory case study. *International Journal of Teaching and Learning in Higher Education, 30*(1), 136–145.
De Freitas, S. (2006). *Learning in immersive worlds* (pp. 3–71). Joint Information Systems Committee.
Dodds, C., Heslop, P., & Meredith, C. (2018). Using simulation-based education to help social work students prepare for practice. *Social Work Education, 37*(5), 597–602. https://doi.org/10.1080/02615479.2018.1433158
Dubey, R., & Ghai, S. (2011). Innovative atmosphere relating to success factors of entrepreneurial managers in the organization agility: An empirical study. *International Journal of Innovation Science, 2*(3), 97–102. https://doi.org/10.1260/1757-2223.2.3.97
Ebrahimi, P., Ahmadi, M., Gholampour, A., & Alipour, H. (2019). CRM performance and development of media entrepreneurship in digital, social media, and mobile commerce. *International Journal of Emerging Markets, 16*(1), 25–50. https://doi.org/10.1108/IJOEM-11-2018-0588
Fayolle, A. (2018). Personal views on the future of entrepreneurship education. In *A research agenda for entrepreneurship education*. Edward Elgar Publishing.
Fornell, C., & Larcker, D. F. (1981). Evaluating structural equation models with unobservable variables and measurement error. *Journal of Marketing Research, 18*(1), 39–50.
García-Buades, M. E., Ramis-Palmer, C., & Manassero-Mas, M. A. (2015). Climate for innovation, performance, and job satisfaction of local police in Spain. *Policing: An International Journal of Police Strategies & Management, 38*(4), 722–737. https://doi.org/10.1108/PIJPSM-02-2015-0019
Garcia-Esteban, S., & Jahnke, S. (2020). Skills in European higher education mobility programmes: Outlining a conceptual framework. *Higher Education, Skills and Work-Based Learning, 10*(3), 519–539. https://doi.org/10.1108/HESWBL-09-2019-0111
Gegenhuber, T. (2020). Book review: Cultural entrepreneurship: A new agenda for the study of entrepreneurial processes and possibilities.
Guerrero, M., Urbano, D., & Salamzadeh, A. (2014). Evolving entrepreneurial universities: Experiences and challenges in the Middle Eastern context. In *Handbook on the entrepreneurial university*. Edward Elgar Publishing.
Guerrero, M., Urbano, D., & Salamzadeh, A. (2015). Entrepreneurial transformation in the Middle East: Experiences from Tehran Universities. *Technics Technologies Education Management, 10*(4), 533–537.

Hair, J. F., Jr., Ringle, C., Sarstedt, M., & Gudergan, S. P. (2017). *Advanced issues in partial least square structural equation modeling.* SAGE.

Hatch, M. J. (2018). *Organisation theory: Modern, symbolic, and postmodern perspectives.* Oxford University Press.

Henseler, J., Ringle, C. M., & Sarstedt, M. (2015). A new criterion for assessing discriminant validity in variance-based structural equation modeling. *Journal of the Academy of Marketing Science, 43*(1), 115–135. https://doi.org/10.1007/s11747-014-0403-8

Hosseini, E., Tajpour, M., & Lashkarbooluki, M. (2020). The impact of entrepreneurial skills on manager's job performance. *International Journal of Human Capital in Urban Management, 5*(4), 361–372. https://doi.org/10.22034/IJHCUM.2020.04.08

Hulland, J. (1999). Use of partial least squares (PLS) in strategic management research: A review of four recent studies. *Strategic Management Journal, 20*(2), 195–204.

Hung, C. C., Kao, H. F. S., Liu, H. C., Liang, H. F., Chu, T. P., & Lee, B. O. (2021). Effects of simulation-based learning on nursing students' perceived competence, self-efficacy, and learning satisfaction: A repeat measurement method. *Nurse Education Today, 97*, 104725. https://doi.org/10.1016/j.nedt.2020.104725

Jamil, M. G., & Isiaq, S. O. (2019). Teaching technology with technology: Approaches to bridging learning and teaching gaps in simulation-based programming education. *International Journal of Educational Technology in Higher Education, 16*, 25. https://doi.org/10.1186/s41239-019-0159-9

Katz, N. H., Lawyer, J. W., Sweedler, M., Tokar, P., & Sossa, K. J. (2020). *Communication and conflict resolution skills.* Kendall Hunt Publishing.

Ke, F., Pachman, M., & Dai, Z. (2020). Investigating educational affordances of virtual reality for simulation-based teaching training with graduate teaching assistants. *Journal of Computing in Higher Education.* https://doi.org/10.1007/s12528-020-09249-9

Ke, F., & Xu, X. (2020). Virtual reality simulation-based learning of teaching with alternative perspectives taking. *British Journal of Educational Technology, 51*(6), 2544–2557. https://doi.org/10.1111/bjet.12936

Keskitalo, T., & Ruokamo, H. (2021). Exploring learners' emotions and emotional profiles in simulation-based medical education. *Australasian Journal of Educational Technology, 3*, 15–26.

Khahande Karnama, A., Dehghan Najm Abadi, A., & Tajpour, M. (2017). The relationship between entrepreneurial orientations and occupational performance at TUMS student health center. *Journal of Payavard Salamat, 11*(2), 124–133.

Kim, M. J., Doh, H. S., Hong, J. S., & Choi, M. K. (2011). Social skills training and parent education programs for aggressive preschoolers and their parents in South Korea. *Children and Youth Services Review, 33*(6), 838–845. https://doi.org/10.1016/j.childyouth.2010.12.001

Kline, R. B. (2015). *Principles and practice of structural equation modeling*. Guilford Publications.

Kucel, A., Róbert, P., Buil, M., & Masferrer, N. (2016). Entrepreneurial skills and education-job matching of higher education graduates. *European Journal of Education, 51*(1), 73–89. https://doi.org/10.1111/ejed.12161

Machado, C., & Davim, J. P. (Eds.). (2020). *Entrepreneurship and organizational innovation*. Springer.

Makransky, G., Mayer, R. E., Veitch, N., Hood, M., Christensen, K. B., & Gadegaard, H. (2019). Equivalence of using a desktop virtual reality science simulation at home and in class. *PLoS One, 14*(4), e0214944.

Militaru, G., Pollifroni, M., & Niculescu, C. (2015). The role of technology entrepreneurship education in encouraging to launch new ventures. In *Balkan Region conference on Engineering and Business Education* (Vol. 1, pp. 274–281). Sciendo.

Miller, Z. A., Amin, A., Tu, J., Echenique, A., & Winokur, R. S. (2019). Simulation-based training for interventional radiology and opportunities for improving the educational paradigm. *Techniques in Vascular and Interventional Radiology, 22*(1), 35–40. https://doi.org/10.1053/j.tvir.2018.10.008

Moizer, J., & Lean, J. (2010). Toward endemic deployment of educational simulation games: A review of progress and future recommendations. *Simulation & Gaming, 41*(1), 116–131.

Moolenaar, N. M., Daly, A. J., & Sleegers, P. J. (2010). Occupying the principal position: Examining relationships between transformational leadership, social network position, and schools' innovative climate. *Educational Administration Quarterly, 46*(5), 623–670.

Neto, J., & Mendes, P. (2012). Game4Manager: More than virtual managers. In *Handbook of research on serious games as educational, business and research tools* (pp. 108–134). IGI Global.

Nieuwenhuizen, C. (Ed.). (2009). *Entrepreneurial skills*. Juta and Company Ltd.

Nikraftar, T., & Hosseini, E. (2017). The effect of prior knowledge on entrepreneurial opportunity recognition (the case study of tourism agencies participating in tourism fairs in Shiraz). *Journal of Entrepreneurship Development, 9*(4), 731–748. https://doi.org/10.22059/jed.2017.61551

Nøhr, C., & Aarts, J. (2010). Use of "serious health games" in health care: A review. *Information Technology in Health Care: Socio-Technical Approaches, 160.*

Patel, R., & Dennick, R. (2017). Simulation-based teaching in interventional radiology training: Is it effective? *Clinical Radiology, 72*(3), 266–2e7. https://doi.org/10.1016/j.crad.2016.10.014

Pempek, T. A., & Calvert, S. L. (2009). Tipping the balance: Use of advergames to promote the consumption of nutritious foods and beverages by low-income African American children. *Archives of Pediatrics & Adolescent Medicine, 163*(7), 633–637. https://doi.org/10.1001/archpediatrics.2009.71

Ranchhod, A., Gurău,.C., Loukis, E., & Trivedi, R. (2014). Evaluating the educational effectiveness of simulation games: A value generation model. *Information Sciences, 264*, 75–90. https://doi.org/10.1016/j.ins.2013.09.008

Reed, S. K. (2020). *Cognitive skills you need for the 21st century.* Oxford University Press.

Rudmann, C. (2008). *Entrepreneurial skills and their role in enhancing the relative independence of farmers.* Forschungsinstitut für biologischen Landbau (FiBL).

Sabokro, M., Tajpour, M., & Hosseini, E. (2018). Investigating the knowledge management effect on managers' skills improvement. *International Journal of Human Capital in Urban Management, 3*(2), 125–132. https://doi.org/10.22034/IJHCUM.2018.02.05

Salamzadeh, A. (2018). Start-up boom in an emerging market: A niche market approach. In *Competitiveness in emerging markets* (pp. 233–243). Springer.

Salamzadeh, A., Arasti, Z., & Elyasi, G. M. (2017). Creation of ICT-based social start-ups in Iran: A multiple case study. *Journal of Enterprising Culture, 25*(1), 97–122. https://doi.org/10.1142/S0218495817500042

Salamzadeh, Y., YousefNia, M., Radovic Markovic, M., & Salamzadeh, A. (2016). Strategic management development: The role of learning school on the promotion of managers' competence. *Economía y Sociedad, 21*(50), 1–25.

Shabbir, M. S., Shariff, M. N. M., & Shahzad, A. (2016). Mediating role of perceived behavioral control and stakeholders' support system on the relationship between entrepreneurial personal skills and entrepreneurial intentions of its employees in Pakistan. *International Business Management, 10*(9), 1745–1755.

Sidhu, I., Johnsson, C., Singer, K., & Suoranta, M. (2015). A game-based method for teaching entrepreneurship. *Applied Innovation Review, 1*(1), 51–65.

Smith, K., Williams, D., Yasin, N., & Pitchford, I. (2014). Enterprise skills and training needs of postgraduate research students. *Education and Training, 56*(8/9), 745–763. https://doi.org/10.1108/ET-05-2014-0052

Soltanifar, M., Hughes, M., & Göcke, L. (2021). *Digital entrepreneurship: Impact on business and society.* Springer Nature.

Spadea, M., Ciantelli, M., Fossati, N., & Cuttano, A. (2021). Enhancing the future of simulation-based education in pediatrics. *Italian Journal of Pediatrics, 47*(1), 1–3. https://doi.org/10.1186/s13052-021-00989-7

Strygacz, I., & Sthub, A. (2018). Combining simulation-based training and flipped classroom in project management learning. *Higher Education Studies, 8*(3), 85–93.

Tajpour, M., & Hosseini, E. (2020). The effect of intelligence and organizational culture on corporate entrepreneurship in Shiraz Gas Compa. *Human Resource Management in the Oil Industry, 12*(45), 335–354.

Tajpour, M., Hosseini, E., & Moghaddm, A. (2018). The effect of managers strategic thinking on opportunity exploitation. *Scholedge International Journal of Multidisciplinary Allied Studies, 5*(2), 68–81.

Tajpour, M., Hosseini, E., & Salamzadeh, A. (2020). The effect of innovation components on organizational performance: The case of the governorate of Golestan Province. *International Journal of Public Sector Performance Management, 6*(6), 817–830. https://doi.org/10.1504/IJPSPM.2020.110987

Thomas, C. M., & Barker, N. (2018). Simulation elective: A novel approach to using simulation for learning. *Clinical Simulation in Nursing, 23,* 21–29. https://doi.org/10.1016/j.ecns.2018.08.003

Thomas, R. M. (2003). *Blending qualitative and quantitative research methods in theses and dissertations.* Corwin Press.

Toghraee, M. T., & Monjezi, M. (2017). Introduction to cultural entrepreneurship: Cultural entrepreneurship in developing countries. *International Review of Management and Marketing, 7*(4), 67–73.

Torres, A., Domańska-Glonek, E., Dzikowski, W., Korulczyk, J., & Torres, K. (2020). Transition to online is possible: Solution for simulation-based teaching during the COVID-19 pandemic. *Medical Education, 54*(9), 858–859. https://doi.org/10.1111/medu.14245

Wilkinson, A., Donaghey, J., Dundon, T., & Freeman, R. B. (Eds.). (2020). *Handbook of research on employee voice.* Edward Elgar Publishing.

Williams, D., Smith, K., Yasin, N., & Pitchford, I. (2013). Evaluating the state of enterprise training for postgraduate researchers in the UK. *Education and Training, 55*(8/9), 849–867. https://doi.org/10.1108/ET-06-2013-0083

Wouters, P., Van Nimwegen, C., Van Oostendorp, H., & Van Der Spek, E. D. (2013). A meta-analysis of the cognitive and motivational effects of serious games. *Journal of Educational Psychology, 105*(2), 249.

Yamazaki, Y., Hiyamizu, I., Joyner, K., Otaki, J., & Abe, Y. (2021). Assessment of blood pressure measurement skills in second-year medical students after ongoing simulation-based education and practice. *Medical Education Online, 26*(1), 1841982. https://doi.org/10.1080/10872981.2020.1841982

Yasin, N., & Hafeez, K. (2018). Enterprise simulation gaming: Effective practices for assessing student learning with SimVenture Classic and VentureBlocks. In *Experiential learning for entrepreneurship* (pp. 51–69). Palgrave Macmillan.

Yasin, N., Khansari, Z., & Sharif, T. (2020). Assessing the enterprising tendencies of Arab female undergraduate engineering students in the Sultanate of Oman. *Industry and Higher Education, 34*(6), 429–439.

5

Teaching Digital Marketing: A Malaysian University Perspective

Amiruddin Ahamat and Jing Ai Pang

Introduction

The recent hike in digital trends has changed the global economy where most consumers are now driven to shop and do businesses online as it is cost-effective and time-saving (Kemp, 2019). It allows companies to reach out to their targeted customers via content marketing, chat bots, and programmatic advertising. However, digital trends also prompt companies to generate, distribute, modify, and extend content efficiently and effectively toward their audience (Semeradova & Weinlich, 2014). Consumers are also given the opportunities to communicate, navigate, and gain more information through digital technologies.

A. Ahamat (✉)
Faculty of Technology Management & Technopreneurship, Universiti Teknikal Malaysia Melaka (UTeM), Melaka, Malaysia
e-mail: amiruddin@utem.edu.my

J. A. Pang
PPS Global Network Sdn Bhd, Petaling Jaya, Malaysia

Slijepčević and Radojevic (2018) stated that digital technologies have pushed global companies to embrace it as a vital component for their business and marketing strategies. E-commerce via platforms such as Lazada, Shopify, and Amazon has become a new trend for companies to adapt for the benefit of their business. This is because customers are always using digital technologies in their daily routine and these online tools have become essential for them. Research on digital trends shows that artificial intelligence (AI) has been utilized as a data analytic tool for companies to be data-driven and subsequently deliver first-class and customized customer experience technology (Watton, 2019).

Digital trends also enable companies to utilize customers' data to optimize customer experience without violating their privacy. Hence, the e-commerce trend emerges as an opportunity for businesses to market their products to the targeted audience. A study by Bu et al. (2019) found that global digital consumers are more interested to shop online rather than in physical shops. Furthermore, Xu et al. (2018) posit that the rise in artificial intelligence (AI), robotics, technologies innovation, virtual reality (VR), augmented reality (AR), Big Data, and the internet of things (IoT) are the new trends in Industrial Revolution 4.0 (IR 4.0). These latest technologies offer advanced communication and autonomous bots to improve the quality of life including in work, education, and communities. This is supported by Leurent and Shook (2019) who found that IR 4.0 drives manufacturers to use advanced manufacturing systems and new technologies to efficiently and effectively produce quality products.

The discussion above hence shows that these digital trends provide each category of the industry with an opportunity to enhance their productivity, the quality of their goods and services, as well as implementing innovation on technologies. As a result, users will be able to digitalize their lifestyle with technologies. Following the continuous improvement of digital technologies, the future of job market demand will change and people need to be ready for it. This is supported by Evans (2019) who reported that the future job market will face new nature of work, self-employment, gig economy, and a rise in demand for qualified skills needed in jobs.

According to Green et al. (2018), the gig economy will be the future career in the market particularly for young people who are employed to work at flexible working hours for a specific period. This also applies to freelancers with short-term contracts with independent organizations. Manyika (2017) suggests that the future job market shall comprise digital-related jobs for digital talents that allow workers to work at flexible hours. This gives a high possibility of self-employment in the future job market. As the future job market changes, universities and colleges will have to respond and implement changes on the teaching modules or curriculum for students to gain skills, knowledge, and abilities that are relevant to the market needs.

Evans (2019) posits that the education sector should respond to the new market trends by building a foundation of skills, adaptability, and flexibility; retaining their expectation and high commitment to learning; and providing students with sufficient support. Moreover, an improvement on the existing teaching methods is also necessary to ensure effective learning and achieve the intended learning outcomes. Such changes in the teaching modules and methods will help students to avoid unemployment in the future. As the current global trend is moving toward digitalization, graduates need to equip themselves with the latest set of skills to meet the future job market requirement. According to Spiller and Tuten (2019), many industries demand marketing graduates be equipped with digital marketing skills as the market trend is moving toward the digital world.

In addition, Beitelspacher et al. (2018) stated that the majority of employers demand marketing graduates who are equipped with both digital and practical skills as part of their recruitment requirements. The global digital trends show that there is a huge number of users who are online and most likely engaged with the digital world. This facilitates companies to target their audience with the use of digital technologies, hence necessitating future graduates to equip themselves with relevant skills to be ready for the future working environment. Following the emergence of the digital trends and the current demand for IT literate candidates by the job market, education institutions like universities and colleges need to adapt their curriculum and teaching modules to prepare students for the real working environment. These institutions are responsible to produce students with the skills, knowledge, and ability that meet the business and market needs.

According to Frederiksen (2015), several marketing courses offered by universities or colleges are deemed obsolete due to the failure of modifying and adapting the academic content with the current advancement in technology and digital trends. Furthermore, there is a perception that the prominent issue of unemployment among Malaysian graduates is caused by their lack of employability skills (Shukri et al., 2014). This traces back to the absence of teaching modules or curriculum innovations that fit the current educational context. It subsequently causes students to be left behind the new digital trends and affects their future careers. Concerning the theme of this chapter, the notion on digital entrepreneurship is theoretically significant with regard to the entrepreneur in new business creation where "the mechanisms by which entrepreneurs shape ventures are often contingent on factors such as the industry sector, talent, institutional characteristics of the national economy, and experiences of the entrepreneurs themselves" (Beckman et al., 2012, p. 203; Ghobakhloo & Tang, 2013).

This demonstrates the importance to investigate the competencies required to be a successful digital entrepreneur beyond entrepreneurial competencies (e.g., Manolova et al., 2007; Revell-Love & Revell-Love, 2016). Thus, signifies the need to pursue Welter (2011) in studying the context-specific influences in resource-scare environments and where digital technology is becoming both a trigger and an enabler (Lusch & Nambisan, 2015) of entrepreneurial behaviors in the university practices. Welter (2011) calls for more empirical research to grasp how context can be an asset (where it facilitates entrepreneurship in the higher education context) or a liability (challenges that constrain entrepreneurship) in the process of digital marketing teaching delivery effectiveness. Therefore, this study aims to examine the effectiveness of teaching delivery of the Digital Marketing subject. The main purpose is to identify the factors that would affect the teaching delivery effectiveness in digital marketing education from the Malaysian perspective.

Background of the Case

The Teaching of Digital Marketing Course

Among the common method used in teaching the Digital Marketing subject is a pedagogical approach. Such a method is particularly common among digital marketing educators from countries like the United States, Brazil, Turkey, and United Kingdom (Habib, 2015; Liu & Levin, 2018; Tugrul, 2017; Duffy & Ney, 2015). Noordink (2010) stated that the pedagogical approach involves lecturers giving lectures with different types of teaching methods for different subjects. According to Weston (2013), it involves several principles of pedagogy such as motivation and direction of activity that would affect students' learning progress and it relates to the lecturers-students interactions.

The motivation pedagogy requires educators to motivate students that creates a good relationship for them to understand each other well during lectures (Weston, 2013). Meanwhile, the direction of activity pedagogy involves students participating in activities that could facilitate them on learning by doing which involves experience on the course. It helps students to be active in learning which would improve the teaching quality. In the pedagogical approach, most education institutions use approaches like teacher-centered approach and student-centered approach (Duffy & Ney, 2015; Tugrul, 2017; Liu & Levin, 2018). These approaches aim to provide institutions with the best teaching method and ensure that students can gain knowledge from lecturers.

Thus, part of this research aims to determine the method that best suits lecturers to teach the Digital Marketing subject. Further explanation on the approaches will be given in the latter part of this study. Moreover, most universities in the United States and the United Kingdom use digital media such as Twitter, YouTube, and Facebook as pedagogical tools to teach digital marketing (Spiller & Tuten, 2019; Duffy & Ney, 2015; Liu & Levin, 2018; McCorkle & Payan, 2017). This indicates that the pedagogical tools have been modernized with the inclusion of digital media.

The modernized pedagogical approach has made classroom interaction easier for educators and students during lessons (Jackson & Ahuja, 2016).

Buzzard et al. (2011) believe that digital media has changed the interactions between educators and students from the authentic model to a new model of the Web 2.0 interactive world. It helps students to learn and explore the latest advancement in digital marketing. However, Cole (2009) argues that integrating digital media with traditional pedagogical methods requires education institutions to modify the existing educational contents that support students' interaction.

Student-Centered Approach Through Problem-Based Learning (PBL)

The student-centered approach involves activities like problem-based learning (PBL), active learning, self-directed learning, and self-regulated learning (Mascolo, 2009). It drives students to be independent in learning while educators giving them guidance that helps to clarify their understanding of the topic. Several methods are often employed in the student-centered approach, which are integrative approach, active learning approach, and corporative learning approach. In this research, the Digital Marketing subject only focuses on the integrative approach, active learning approach, and flipped classroom approach. The flipped classroom is also part of the student-centered approach, but it requires educators to guide students during in-class activities (Nguyen et al., 2015).

Generally, PBL has gained prominence in the Malaysian education environment. According to Sadrina et al. (2018), PBL has been employed to change the ineffective traditional teaching method into the student-led approach (p.144). The traditional teaching method is more teacher-centered where lecturers are the one who conducts the lessons with fewer students' anticipation in the classroom. According to Bose (2019), the PBL teaching method is suitable for marketing students especially when there is a new subject for students to learn and adapt to. This is because such an approach facilitates lecturers to approach their students while promoting easier and better understanding among students at the same time.

PBL is often used to expose students to problem-solving theories through students' engagement (Allen et al., 2011). This allows students to have active learning and focus on real-world problems and assignments. The assessments of the Digital Marketing subject will be mainly based on problem-solving. Shih and Tsai (2017) propose that PBL through digital media can affect students' learning and it is also part of the student-centered approach. Therefore, PBL might be one of the best ways for lecturers to conduct effective teaching of digital marketing.

Active Learning Using Digital Media Tools

According to Chan and Leung (2016), the use of digital media tools like Facebook and Twitter encourages students to be active in learning. The active learning approach refers to a learning environment where students have high engagement or involvement during lessons. Unlike traditional teaching method that makes students passive, the utilization of problem-based learning requires students to brainstorm and suggest solutions to assigned problems. Such active learning helps students to build their understanding of the real-world implications (Mascolo, 2009). Through this approach, students get to be independent and responsible in their learning. A study by Ueda and Ban (2018) reported that students in a Japanese university gained strong motivation as they completed the active learning projects given by the university. This suggests that active learning provides students the chance to undergo new learning by exploring the topic further with guidance from the lecturers.

Flipped Classroom: Teaching Method for Marketing

According to Li (2019), the teaching of marketing via flipped classroom enables lecturers and students to collaborate and together strive to achieve the learning objective. Such collaboration encourages interaction between them and the lesson will be more interesting for students to follow. Green (2015) stated that flipped classroom has become popular in education where it not only promotes face-to-face interaction but also focuses on task-based activities and hands-on activities among students. The flipped classroom has replaced the traditional instruction teaching method to allow students to learn through self-learning before the lecture.

The implementation process for flipped classrooms requires students to do prior preparation before entering the class (Shih & Tsai, 2017). The lecturers act as the guide by assigning activities to enhance students' knowledge and understanding of the Digital Marketing subject. Such guidance is often delivered through pre-recorded media to enhance the teaching effectiveness of digital marketing. Moreover, Green (2015) suggests that the implementation of the flipped classroom serves as an innovative strategy that helps lecturers to provide effective teaching delivery for students in digital marketing. The flipped classroom is suitable to be used to teach the Digital Marketing subject as it involves media closely related to the subject and facilitates students to adapt the subject at a faster pace. Shih and Tsai (2017) also stated that flipped classroom provides students and lecturers with the flexibility on teaching and learning the Digital Marketing subject. Therefore, lecturers have the option to use a flipped classroom for teaching to improve their teaching effectiveness and encourage active learning as well.

Effective Teaching Delivery in Digital Marketing

According to Kini and Podolsky (2016), lecturers' teaching effectiveness is never dependent solely on their experience. This is because some lecturers may have the knowledge but not necessarily the skills to deliver effective teaching to students. It shows that there is a relationship between teaching effectiveness and students' achievement (Kini & Podolsky, 2016). In the academic context, the quality of teaching is closely related to teaching effectiveness. Educators have to devise the right teaching approach that facilitates students' learning. McCorkle and Payan (2017) suggest that educators should provide students with beneficial real-time experience, facilitate skill development, and enhance their future career during the teaching of the Digital Marketing subject. As a result, students will be able to gain experience and skills that can be gained through relevant project cases given by the educators, which will add to their employability and translate into a high possibility for them to be employed in the future.

Furthermore, students can adapt to the market needs by equipping themselves with effective and ethical skills and tools for marketing jobs (Cowley, 2017). In this regard, effective teaching delivery allows students to be directly involved with the target audience via available products or services. They will have the opportunity to understand the market needs and propose an appropriate marketing strategy for the case. Allowing students to be involved in projects case also enables them to directly engage with the market situation. Several universities from Japan and the United States have utilized the method in allowing students to apply their knowledge practically through the cases (Cowley, 2017; Ueda & Ban, 2018; McCorkle & Payan, 2017). This enables students to improve their skills to market a product through the usage of digital media tools.

Teaching delivery effectiveness plays an important role in students' future careers. Educational institutions need to ensure that their lecturers are capable of delivering knowledge to students in an effective way. There are many factors to consider when it comes to teaching delivery effectiveness in class such as lecturers' teaching style, students' characteristics, teaching model, and classroom climate. According to Rohm et al. (2018), educational institutions should take into consideration these factors so that the teaching will be on par with the employment requirement for undergraduates.

Barwani et al. (2012) posit that teaching strategies are one of the factors that determine teaching delivery effectiveness in class. This is because lecturers often have different kinds of teaching strategies to be utilized in their classes. These teaching strategies can be based on their professionalism, expectation, and leadership (Antony et al., 2019). In this regard, lecturers' level of professionalism can affect the effectiveness of their teaching as they might have less experience in conducting lectures and vice versa. Meanwhile, lecturers' teaching style depends on the clarity of teaching and their methods of teaching during class. According to Van de Grift (2014), teaching strategies cover teaching practices that may comprise the conventional or constructivist paradigm of teaching and learning. The teaching method depends on which teaching approach that a lecturer wishes to use.

In response to the issue, Caro et al. (2016) suggest that the role of a lecturer is to provide necessary processes that guide students on their studies. This implies that lecturers must have the content knowledge and enthusiasm in teaching with the right teaching method. Therefore, it is the lecturers' responsibility to adapt the teaching strategies (i.e., teacher-centered or student-centered approach) either from the conventional or constructivist paradigm that are appropriate and best suit their classroom needs. Furthermore, student's level of ability and family background seems to be varied on the effectiveness of teaching delivery (Caro et al., 2016). Students' knowledge and understanding of the context can affect their learning of the Digital Marketing subject. This is because they often possess an insufficient level of motivation, self-discipline, and higher-order thinking skills (Gao, 2014). Subsequently, it implies that students have different traits that give different reactions to the teaching. For example, active students are more common to corporate with the lecturers during the teaching and learning process which then translates into effective teaching as opposed to inactive students. Gao (2014) also stated that each student will respond differently to the teaching strategies as most learners are digital natives who grew up with technology while most lecturers are digital immigrants.

A study by Benson et al. (2014) found that most students do not apply the knowledge of marketing to digital media but rather opt to use it for social purposes. Educators need to influence and teach students about utilizing digital media for business purposes. However, most learners prefer the student-centered approach in class as it promotes self-learning. Kyriakides et al. (2013) suggest that students' characteristics such as their traits, characteristics during class, and learning abilities can affect teaching effectiveness. Students' different response toward different teaching methods is probably due to their individual preference toward various learning styles. This means that there are several types of learning dimensions which are active-reflective, sensing-intuitive, visual-verbal, and sequential-global that are used to measure students' learning style preference (Kim et al., 2019).

Students with different characteristics often have the learning style that gives them comfort in learning. The learning style measurement is based on Felder's Index of Learning Style (ILS) that was developed following an experiment to find out students' learning style preferences (Felder & Spurlin, 2005). Each learning dimension has its preference among students where active-reflective is the preference to process information, sensing-intuitive is the preference to receive information, visual-verbal is the preference to the presentation (videos or pictures), and sequential-global is the preference to understand the information in sequence. In the context of effective teaching, students' characteristics portray insignificant influence as the factor lies in the lecturers' teaching method (Bose, 2019; Alvi & Gillies, 2020).

Teaching Model for Digital Marketing

The model for digital marketing should be consistent with the emerging students and business needs of the twenty-first century (Wymbs, 2011). This is because the teaching model is one of the factors that can affect teaching effectiveness and students' learning outcome. Teaching model that is not updated based on the market needs will result in students' knowledge that is left behind the curve. Such a teaching model is deemed ineffective for teaching and causes students to gain irrelevant skills and knowledge for the market. The teaching and learning model works as a fundamental use for education by marketing educators (Crittenden & Crittenden, 2015). Its context and content must be on par with the latest education requirement so that educational institutions can produce students with the right digital and marketing skills in the digital world.

Furthermore, the teaching model can help lecturers and students with experiential learning comprising a combination of theory and practices with digital as the core content of the subject (Rohm et al., 2018). The teaching model serves as a guide for lecturers to do their teaching plans. Li (2019) proposes that the teaching model should be a three-in-one model that involves case study teaching, real project, and practical learning. This will allow lecturers to improve students' applied ability and training for the benefit of their future careers. Moreover, Li (2019) also suggests that the teaching model context should be task-driven and combine both marketing theory with advanced technology. Through this way, students will be more motivated in learning and subsequently promote effective teaching in digital marketing.

Meanwhile, Rohm et al. (2018) propose that the teaching model should have contents that provide students with deeper learning on the subject. It shows that teaching content should demonstrate effective teaching toward students. Therefore, lecturers should reform the teaching model from time to time for it to meet the market requirement. According to Kim (2019), the teaching model for a digital marketing course should provide students with effective teaching. This is because the digital world is constantly evolving and the market trends can change as well. Thus, the teaching model should be developed or reformed with a work-ready purpose for students. The latest teaching content will help lecturers to deliver effective teaching as well.

Classroom Climate Affecting Teaching Delivery Effectiveness

Classroom climate is another factor that can affect the teaching delivery effectiveness in class. Antony et al. (2019) suggest that the internal and external classroom interaction between lecturers and students can affect teaching effectiveness. In this regard, the interaction between lecturers and students should be flexible whereby students should feel comfortable during lectures. According to Jani et al. (2015), the internal and external of a classroom will affect the class commencement and understanding between the lecturers and students. The use of traditional methods by lecturers might create unnecessary difficulty for students to interact with them.

Therefore, lecturers must try to understand students' behavior and thinking so that they can adapt to the learning process faster. Noesgaard and Ørngreen (2015) posit that the learning environment must be supportive and resourceful so that both students and lecturers can interact with each other well during lectures. Following the significant importance of interaction that happens between lecturers and students during lessons, the researcher believes that it is suitable for students to have a student-centered approach. Such an approach will encourage students to be active in learning and increase their confidence in learning. Jani et al. (2015) found that lecturer-group interaction and lecturer-individual student interaction can affect the teaching effectiveness in class. This suggests that there should be a good interaction between lecturers and students to achieve effective teaching.

Several types of research have demonstrated that active engagement from lecturers often poses a significant impact on the effectiveness of teaching. This is because it encourages students to engage more actively in class and motivates them to learn the subject (Kardes, 2020). Lecturers need to pay attention to students to keep the interaction going in class and subsequently lead toward effective teaching and learning for that particular subject. According to Powers et al. (2020), students prefer to have active engagement through the use of technology in class as it facilitates and encourages them to have better interaction with their lecturer. This will benefit students with effective teaching of the Digital Marketing subject. However, several situations can cause the classroom climate to change into online learning especially when students and lecturers interact in video conference meetings (Graul, 2020).

Conceptual Framework

This study proposes a conceptual framework driven by the context of digital marketing teaching delivery as a dependent variable while the instructor's teaching style, students' characteristics, teaching model, and classroom climate are the independent variables. The framework is designed in Fig. 5.1 below.

Based on the literature review context, Fig. 5.1 presents a conceptual framework demonstrating the relationship between factors of teaching effectiveness and the outcome of teaching delivery in digital marketing. The framework suggests that the influence of teaching effectiveness in digital marketing is shaped by various factors including teaching style, student's characteristics, teaching model, and classroom climate. This is the conceptual basis on which the relationship between context and digital marketing in a resource-scarce environment is examined in this chapter. The hypotheses tested are presented as follows:

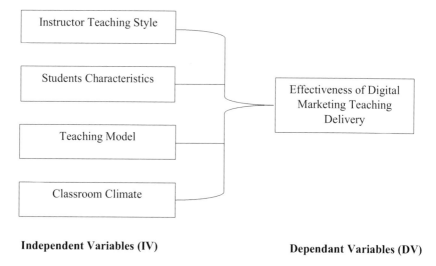

Fig. 5.1 Conceptual framework of effectiveness of digital marketing teaching delivery

H10 Lecturer teaching style would not affect the effectiveness of teaching delivery in digital marketing.

H11 Lecturer teaching style would affect the effectiveness of teaching delivery in digital marketing.

H20 Students' characteristics would not affect the effectiveness of teaching delivery in digital marketing.

H21 Students' characteristics would affect the effectiveness of teaching delivery in digital marketing.

H30 The teaching model would not affect the effectiveness of teaching delivery in digital marketing.

H31 Teaching model would affect the effectiveness of teaching delivery in digital marketing.

H40 Classroom climate would not affect the effectiveness of teaching delivery in digital marketing.

H41 Classroom climate would affect the effectiveness of teaching delivery in digital marketing.

Methodology

This study has employed descriptive research to identify the factors that affect teaching delivery effectiveness in the Digital Marketing subject. Descriptive research allows researchers to conduct testing and comparison to obtain clarity on phenomena of the topic of interest, characteristics of the phenomena, or situation (Ivey, 2016). It is used in this study to describe and interpret the numerical data to support the objective of the study. Saunders et al. (2016) believe that descriptive analysis helps to describe and make a comparison on the numerical data which focuses on the central tendency that includes mean, median, and mode as the data measurement and also dispersion involving the dispersion of data value around the central tendency.

Descriptive Analysis

The descriptive analysis in this study was based on the data obtained from a total of 143 respondents. The demographic profile consists of gender, course, race, year of study, and the students took Digital Marketing subject. The data indicate that male respondents consist of 23.8% ($n = 34$) of the total frequency while female respondents consist of 76.2% ($n = 109$) of the total frequency. The respondents are undergraduate students from a technical public university in Malaysia. These students comprise 1 student from the first year with 0.7%, 87 students from the second year with 60.8%, 1 student from the third year with 0.7%, and 54 students from the fourth year with 37.8%. All respondents have already taken the Digital Marketing subject during the undergraduate level.

Pearson Correlation Coefficient Analysis

According to Gogtay and Thatte (2017), Pearson correlation coefficient analysis is often used to determine the relationship between two or more variables. This research used the analysis to determine the relationship between the independent and dependent variables. It also measures the strength between the variables of the research. Saunders et al. (2016) state that the result of the coefficient analysis will show a value ranging from −1 to +1. This study investigates whether the proposed factors have a positive or negative relationship in influencing the effectiveness of teaching delivery of the Digital Marketing subject.

Table 5.1 contains the results of Pearson correlation coefficient analysis for all variables under investigation in this research. The results show that all independent variables have a positive relationship with the dependent variables. Among the correlation coefficients, the strongest linear relation is between lecturers' teaching style and effectiveness of teaching delivery in the Digital Marketing subject with a Pearson correlation coefficient of 0.666 and the significant level is 0.000, where $p < 0.05$. This indicates that the two variables are significant and that there is a strong positive relationship between these variables.

The second strongest linear relationship is observed between teaching model and effectiveness of teaching delivery in Digital Marketing subject which recorded a Pearson correlation of 0.658 and significant level of 0.000, where $p < 0.05$. This indicates that these two variables are significant. The relationship between the teaching model and the effectiveness of teaching delivery in digital marketing shows a strong positive relationship.

Meanwhile, the correlation value between classroom climate and effectiveness of teaching delivery in the Digital Marketing subject is 0.496 and the significant level is 0.000, where $p < 0.05$. This suggests that there is a strong positive relationship between the two variables, hence indicating that they are significant. Finally, investigation on the relationship between students' characteristics and effectiveness of teaching delivery in the Digital Marketing subject reveals a correlation value of 0.336 with a significant level of 0.000, where $p < 0.05$. This points out the strong

5 Teaching Digital Marketing: A Malaysian University Perspective

Table 5.1 Pearson correlation coefficient analysis

		ETDM	LTS	SC	TM	CC
Effective Teaching Delivery Method (ETDM)	Pearson correlation Sig. (2-tailed) N	1 143	0.666[a] 0.000 143	0.336[a] 0.000 143	0.658[a] 0.000 143	0.496[a] 0.000 143
Lecturer Teaching Style (LTS)	Pearson correlation Sig. (2-tailed) N	0.666[a] 0.000 143	1 143	0.391[a] 0.000 143	0.652[a] 0.000 143	0.439[a] 0.000 143
Students' Characteristics (SC)	Pearson correlation Sig. (2-tailed) N	0.336[a] 0.000 143	0.391[a] 0.000 143	1 143	0.453[a] 0.000 143	0.452[a] 0.000 143
Teaching Model (TM)	Pearson correlation Sig. (2-tailed) N	0.658[a] 0.000 143	0.652[a] 0.000 143	0.453[a] 0.000 143	1 143	0.559[a] 0.000 143
Classroom Climate (CC)	Pearson correlation Sig. (2-tailed) N	0.496[a] 0.000 143	0.439[a] 0.000 143	0.452[a] 0.000 143	0.559[a] 0.000 143	1 143

[a] Correlation is significant at the 0.01 level (2-tailed)

positive relationship between the two variables. Therefore, these variables are significant.

The results in Table 5.2 show that the factor of students' characteristics has the lowest correlation value as compared to other independent variables with the coefficient correlation of 0.336. It indicates that such a factor does not affect the effectiveness of teaching delivery in digital marketing. The reason behind this might be because students have different personality reactions toward the lesson. According to Kim et al. (2019), marketing students tend to have more interest in learning by watching video clips and taking online exams. This suggests their inclined preference over visual learning rather than verbal learning.

Besides, students with different personalities often portray different interests in the teaching method. This might be because the teaching method being utilized on the course does not tally with students' learning style preferences (Nja et al., 2019). Students' characteristics will unlikely affect the effectiveness of teaching as the lecturers and their teaching style are responsible to motivate students to learn despite their cultural background. This means that students' characteristics do not affect teaching

Table 5.2 Summary of Pearson correlation coefficient result

Independent variables	Correlation	Interpretation
Lecturer teaching style	0.666	Strong positive relationship
Students' characteristic	0.336	Strong positive relationship
Teaching model	0.658	Strong positive relationship
Classroom climate	0.496	Strong positive relationship

effectiveness as lecturers' teaching style is the main factor for teaching effectiveness (Bose, 2019).

In support of the above discussion, lecturers' teaching style has recorded the highest coefficient correlation with 0.666. This indicates its significant effect on the effectiveness of teaching delivery in digital marketing. Lecturers' teaching style varies in different approaches where it can be either teacher-centered or student-centered. According to Antony et al. (2019), the teaching method affects the effectiveness of teaching based on the procedure, method, and process. This shows that lecturers' teaching style is relevant and suitable for students in the Digital Marketing subject. Furthermore, teaching strategies are important for effective teaching as most marketing lecturers prefer to employ problem-based learning as their teaching method, which is suitable to introduce a completely new subject to students (Bose, 2019).

Finally, the teaching model and classroom climate also affect the effectiveness of teaching in Digital Marketing subjects with coefficient correlation values of 0.658 and 0.496, respectively. The teaching model affects the effectiveness of teaching if the model is not at par with the latest market requirement. Laverie et al. (2020) support this notion by pointing out that the teaching model and teaching material for the Digital Marketing subject must have the capability to deliver the most recent knowledge and application for students. This shows that the teaching model for the Digital Marketing subject does have a prominent impact on effective teaching. Meanwhile, classroom climate is also a critical factor for teaching effectiveness where lecturers must practice active engagement to motivate students in the class (Kardes, 2020). This indicates that the interaction between students and lecturers during a lecture is important for effective teaching to happen, as supported by the respondents' agreement on this notion.

Findings from the analysis show that all independent variables in this study (i.e., lecturers' teaching style, students' characteristics, teaching model, and classroom climate) have been identified to have a positive relationship with the effectiveness of teaching delivery in digital marketing. Lecturers' teaching styles with different approaches can affect teaching effectiveness where it must be relevant and suitable for students to learn effectively (Kardes, 2020). Meanwhile, students' characteristics and different learning preferences are also found to affect teaching effectiveness (Bose, 2019). Both lecturers' teaching styles and students' characteristics are related to one another as well as the classroom climate factor.

Furthermore, the teaching model of the subject affects the effectiveness of teaching in terms of delivering the latest learning content (Cheng, 2019). Whereas, classroom climate is a prominent factor in terms of the learning environment and readiness (Powers et al., 2020). With these factors being identified, lecturers and universities may consider it as they implement their education strategy. This can help lecturers to enhance their teaching effectiveness and ensure that students can improve their learning efficacy in digital marketing.

The results also found that studying digital marketing allows students to grasp a better understanding and knowledge as well as more awareness of digital marketing in the marketplace (Hossain et al., 2019). It enables students to know more about digital marketing and digital skills to be equipped for their future careers. Digital Marketing subject also serves as an opportunity for students to use their creative ideas in proposing better campaigns together with different technological devices for digital marketing (Kim et al., 2018; Mourey, 2019). All these impacts shall help students to have a higher chance of getting employed in the future.

Finally, findings reported in this study suggest that factors such as lecturers' teaching style, teaching model, and classroom climate have a significant relationship with the effectiveness of teaching delivery. This is because lecturers' teaching plays a vital role in teaching effectiveness (Antony et al., 2019) and the teaching model guides both lecturers and students in achieving effective teaching and learning of the latest information and trends (Kim, 2019). Meanwhile, classroom climate shows that the students-lecturers interaction in class affects the effectiveness of teaching (Kardes, 2020). However, students' characteristics do not have a significant relationship with the effectiveness of teaching delivery. This is because students are mostly ready to learn while lecturers' teaching plays an important role to motivate students on learning (Karagiannopoulou & Entwistle, 2019).

Conclusion

The present study has found several factors that are proven to affect the effectiveness of teaching delivery concerning the Digital Marketing subject. Thus, it is advised for both lecturers and educational institutions to consider these factors. Based on this discussion, it is concluded that students' characteristics do not influence the effectiveness of teaching delivery in the Digital Marketing subject in the context of the Malaysian perspective. Furthermore, the majority of students agree that other factors like teaching style, teaching model, and classroom climate do affect the effectiveness of teaching delivery in digital marketing. As lecturers' style in teaching digital marketing can be based on students' suggestions, this can result in better interaction between students and lecturers and encourage more students to learn the Digital Marketing subject.

References

Allen, D. E., Donham, R. S., & Bernhardt, S. A. (2011). *New directions for teaching and learning*. Wiley Periodicals, Inc.

Alvi, E., & Gillies, R. M. (2020). Teachers and the teaching of self-regulated learning (SRL): The emergence of an integrative, ecological model of SRL-in-context. *Education Sciences, 10*(98), 1–19.

Antony, J., Karamperidis, S., Antony, F., & Cudney, E. A. (2019). Understanding and evaluating teaching effectiveness in the UK higher education sector using experimental design: A case study. *International Journal of Quality & Reliability Management, 36*(2), 202–216.

Barwani, T. A., Al-Ani, W. T., & Amzat, I. H. (2012). An effective teaching model for public school teachers in the Sultanate of Oman: Students' stance. *Education, Business and Society: Contemporary Middle Eastern Issues, 5*, 23–46.

Beckman, C. M., Eisenhardt, K., Kotha, S., Meyer, A., & Rajagopalan, N. (2012). The role of the entrepreneur in technology entrepreneurship. *Strategic Entrepreneurship Journal, 6*(3), 203–206.

Beitelspacher, L. S., Crittenden, V., & Sosnowski, D. (2018). Solving for X: Creating a culture of readiness. Retrieved from BizEd, https://bized.aacsb.edu/articles/2018/06/solving-for-x-creating-a-culture-of-career-readiness

Benson, V., Morgan, S., & Filippaios, F. (2014). Social career management: Social media and employability skills gap. *Computers in Human Behaviour, 30*, 519–525.

Bose, I. (2019). Enhancing student learning through action research experiment with the selected group of business students. *The Online Journal of Quality in Higher Education, 6*(2), 50.

Bu, L., Wang, J., Wang, K. W., & Zipser, D. (2019). *China digital consumer trends 2019* (pp. 1–20). McKinsey Digital.

Buzzard, C., Crittenden, V. L., Crittenden, W. F., & McCarty, P. (2011). The use of digital technologies in the classroom: A teaching and learning perspective. *Journal of Marketing Education, 33*(2), 131–139.

Caro, D. H., Lenkeit, J., & Kyriakides, L. (2016). Teaching strategies and differential effectiveness across learning contexts: Evidence from PISA 2012. *Studies in Educational Evaluation, 49*, 30–41.

Chan, W. T., & Leung, C. H. (2016). The use of social media for blended learning in tertiary education. *Journal of Educational Research, 4*(4), 771–778.

Cheng, Y. C. (2019). *Paradigm shift in education: Towards the third wave of effectiveness.* Routledge.

Cole, M. (2009). Using wiki technology to support student engagement: Lessons from the trenches. *Computers & Education, 52*(1), 141–146.

Cowley, S. W. (2017). The Buzz Feed marketing challenge: An integrative social media experience. *Marketing Education Review, 27*(2), 109–114.

Crittenden, V., & Crittenden, W. (2015). Digital and social media marketing in business education: Implications for the marketing curriculum. *Journal of Marketing Education, 37*(2), 71–75.

Duffy, K., & Ney, J. (2015). Exploring the divides among students, educators, and practitioners in the use of digital media as a pedagogical tool. *Journal of Marketing Education, 37*, 1–10.

Evans, S. (2019). Tomorrow's world: Future of the labour market. *Youth Commission Report, 3*, 1–25.

Felder, R. M., & Spurlin, J. (2005). Applications, reliability, and validity of the index of learning styles. *International Journal of Engineering Education, 21*(1), 103–112.

Frederiksen, L. W. (2015). 3 Key digital marketing skills students don't learn in college. Retrieved from Fast Company, http://www.fastcompany.com/3041253/3-key-digital-marketing-skills-students-dont-learn-in-college

Gao, S. (2014). Relationship between science teaching practices and students' achievement in Singapore, Chinese Taipei, and the US: An analysis using TIMSS 2011 data. *Frontiers of Education in China, 9*, 519–551.

Ghobakhloo, M., & Tang, S. H. (2013). The role of owner/manager in adoption of electronic commerce in small businesses: The case of developing countries. *Journal of Small Business and Enterprise Development, 20*(4), 754–787.

Gogtay, N., & Thatte, U. (2017). Principles of correlation analysis. *Journal of the Association of Physicians of India, 65*, 78–81.

Graul, A. R. (2020). Successful strategies for content creation and design of online class. *Journal on Empowering Teaching Excellence, 4*, 13–21.

Green, D. D., McCann, J., Lopez, N., Vu, T., & Ouattara, S. (2018). Gig economy and the future of work: A Fiverr.com case study. *Management and Economics Research Journal, 4*, 281–288.

Green, T. (2015). Flipped classroom: An agenda for innovative marketing education in the digital era. *Marketing Education Review, 25*(3), 179–191.

Habib, S. (2015). Teaching approaches in advertising: Creativity and technology. *Journal of Advertising Education, 19*, 17–25.

Hossain, M. A., Jahan, N., Fang, Y., Hoque, S., & Hossain, M. S. (2019). Nexus of electronic word-of-mouth to social networking sites: A sustainable chatter of new digital social media. *Sustainability, 11*, 759.

Ivey, J. (2016). Is descriptive research worth doing? *Pediatric Nursing, 42*(4), 189.

Jackson, G., & Ahuja, V. (2016). Dawn of the digital age and the evolution of the marketing mix. *Journal of Direct, Data and Digital Marketing Practice, 17*, 170–186.

Jani, S. H., Shahid, S. A., Thomas, M., & Francis, P. (2015). The predictors of lecturers' teaching effectiveness for public and private universities in Malaysia. *International Journal of Social Science and Humanity, 5*(4), 384–388.

Karagiannopoulou, E., & Entwistle, N. (2019). Students' learning characteristics, perceptions of small-group university teaching, and understanding through a "meeting of minds". *Frontiers in Psychology, 10*, 1–12.

Kardes, I. (2020). Increasing classroom engagement in international business courses via digital technology. *Journal of Teaching in International Business, 31*(1), 51–74.

Kemp, S. (2019). Digital 2019: Global internet use accelerates. Retrieved from Wearesocial, https://wearesocial.com/blog/2019/01/digital-2019-global-internet-use-accelerates

Kim, D.-H., Hettche, M., & Spiller, L. (2019). Incorporating third-party online certifications into a marketing course: The effect of learning style on student responses. *Marketing Education Review, 29*, 1–14.

Kim, T., Karatepe, O., Lee, G., & Demiral, H. (2018). Do gender and prior experience moderate the factors influencing attitude toward using social media for festival attendance? *Sustainability, 10*, 3509.

Kim, Y. (2019). Developing a work-ready social media marketing analytic course: A model to cultivate data-driven and multi-perspective strategy development skills. *Journal of Innovative Education, 17*, 163–188.

Kini, T., & Podolsky, A. (2016). *Does teaching experience increase teacher effectiveness? A review of the research* (p. 15). Learning Policy Institute.

Kyriakides, L., Christoforou, C., & Charalambous, C. Y. (2013). What matters for student learning outcomes: A self-analysis studies exploring factors of effective teaching. *Teaching and Teacher Education, 36*, 143–152.

Laverie, D., Humphrey, W., Manis, K. T., & Freberg, K. (2020). The digital era has changed marketing: A guide to using industry certifications and exploration of student perception of effectiveness. *Marketing Education Review, 30*, 1–24.

Leurent, H., & Shook, E. (2019). *Leading through the fourth industrial revolution: Putting people at the centre* (pp. 1–23). World Economic Forum.

Li, Y. (2019). Research on teaching reform of application-oriented curriculum of marketing course in the internet plus education era. *1st international symposium on Education, Culture and Social Sciences (ECSS 2019)*, pp. 478–481.

Liu, Y., & Levin, M. A. (2018). A progressive approach to teaching analytic in the marketing curriculum. *Marketing Education Review, 28*, 14–27. https://doi.org/10.1080/10528008.2017.1421048

Lusch, R., & Nambisan, S. (2015). Service innovation: A service-dominant logic perspective. *MIS Quarterly, 39*(1), 155–175.

Manolova, T. S., Carter, N. M., Manev, I. M., & Gyoshev, B. S. (2007). The differential effect of men and women entrepreneurs' human capital and networking on growth expectancies in Bulgaria. *Entrepreneurship Theory and Practice, 31*(3), 407–426.

Manyika, J. (2017). *Technology, jobs, and the future of work* (pp. 1–6). Mckinsey Global Institute.

Mascolo, M. F. (2009). Beyond student-centered and teacher-centered pedagogy: Teaching and learning as guided participation. *Pedagogy and the Human Sciences, 1*, 3–27.

McCorkle, D., & Payan, J. (2017). Using twitter in the marketing and advertising classroom to develop skills for social media marketing and personal branding. *Journal of Advertising Education, 21*, 33–43.

Mourey, J. A. (2019). Improve comedy and modern marketing education: Exploring consequences for divergent thinking, self-efficacy, and collaboration. *Journal of Marketing Education, 42*, 1–15.

Nguyen, B., Yu, X., Japutra, A., & Chen, C.-H. S. (2015). Reverse teaching: Exploring student perceptions of "flip teaching". *Active Learning in Higher Education, 17*, 1–11.

Nja, C. O., Umali, C.-U. B., Asuquo, E. E., & Orim, R. E. (2019). The influence of learning styles on academic performance among science education undergraduates at the University of Calabar. *Educational Research and Reviews, 14*, 618–624.

Noesgaard, S. S., & Ørngreen, R. (2015). The effectiveness of e-learning: An explorative and integrative review of the definitions, methodologies, and factors that promote e-learning effectiveness. *Electronic Journal of e-Learning, 13*(4), 278–290.

Noordink, M. (2010). *Different ways of teaching, different pedagogical approaches.* Retrieved from Marlijne Noordink, http://marlijnenoordink.blogspot.com/2010/10/different-ways-of-teaching-different.html

Powers, S. L., Barcelona, R. J., Trauntvein, N. E., & McLaughlin, S. (2020). The role of classroom design in facilitating student engagement in recreation and leisure education. *A Journal of Leisure Studies and Recreation Education, 35*, 1–15.

Revell-Love, C., & Revell-Love, T. (2016). Competencies of women entrepreneurs utilizing information marketing businesses. *Journal of Small Business and Enterprise Development, 23*(3), 831–853.

Rohm, A. J., Stefl, M., & Clair, J. S. (2018). Time for a marketing curriculum overhaul: Developing a digital-first approach. *Journal of Marketing Education, 41*, 1–13.

Sadrina, S., Mustapha, R., & Ichsan, M. (2018). The evaluation of project-based learning in Malaysia: propose a new framework for polytechnics system. *Jurnal Pendidikan Vokasi, 8*(2), 143–150.

Saunders, M., Lewis, P., & Thornhill, A. (2016). *Research methods for business students* (7th ed.). Pearson Education Limited.

Semeradova, T., & Weinlich, P. (2014). New trends in digital marketing and the possibilities of their application in business marketing strategies. *24th International Business Information Management Association Conference*, pp. 1–5.

Shih, W. L., & Tsai, C. Y. (2017). Students' perception of a flipped-classroom approach to facilitating online project-based learning in marketing research courses. *Australasian Journal of Educational Technology, 33*(5), 32–49.

Shukri, M., Manaf, N. H., & Islam, R. (2014). Malaysian graduates' employability skills enhancement: An application of the importance-performance analysis. *Journal for Global Business Advancement, 7*(3), 181–197.

Slijepčević, M., & Radojevic, I. (2018). *Current trends in digital marketing communication*. Faculty of Management, Belgrade Metropolitan University.

Spiller, L., & Tuten, T. (2019). Assessing the pedagogical value of branded digital marketing certification programs. *Journal of Marketing Education, 41*, 1–14.

Tugrul, T. O. (2017). Perceived learning effectiveness of a course Facebook page: Teacher-led versus student-led approach. *World Journal on Educational Technology: Current Issues, 9*(1), 35–39.

Ueda, T., & Ban, H. (2018). Active learning on digital marketing for advertising a University Museum Exhibition. *Procedia Computer Science, 126*, 2097–2106.

Van de Grift, W. J. (2014). Measuring teaching quality in several European countries. *School Effectiveness and School Improvement, 25*, 295–311.

Watton, J. (2019). *Experience index 2019 digital trends* (pp. 1–48). Econsultancy Adobe.

Welter, F. (2011). Contextualizing entrepreneurship—conceptual challenges and ways forward. *Entrepreneurship Theory and Practice, 35*(1), 165–184.

Weston, C. (2013). *Five principles of pedagogy*. Retrieved from Ed Tech Now, https://edtechnow.net/2013/05/12/pedagogy/

Wymbs, C. (2011). Digital marketing: The time for a new "academic major" has arrived. *Journal of Marketing Education, 33*(1), 93–106.

Xu, M., David, J. M., & Kim, S. H. (2018). The fourth industrial revolution: Opportunities and challenges. *International Journal of Financial Research, 9*, 90–94.

Part II

Technology and Entrepreneurship Education

6

Simulation-based Teaching Pedagogy and Entrepreneurship Education: A Bibliometric Analysis

Pritpal Singh Bhullar and Monika Aggarwal

Introduction

The higher education institutions, across the globe, have been making sincere attempts to penetrate entrepreneur education among the students since the last decade (Hornsby et al., 2018). As a result, rapid growth has been witnessed in entrepreneurial education across various disciplines (Fayolle et al., 2016). The aim of stimulating entrepreneurship training in academics does not remain confined to only provide entrepreneurship knowledge but also to make them graduated in this specific discipline (Nabi et al., 2017). It has become the need of an hour to bring the students from diversified backgrounds under one umbrella and deliver a cross-cultural orientation of entrepreneurship (Stefanic et al., 2020).

P. S. Bhullar (✉)
Maharaja Ranjit Singh Punjab Technical University, Bathinda, India
e-mail: mgtpritpal@mrsptu.ac.in

M. Aggarwal
UIAMS, Panjab University, Chandigarh, India
e-mail: monikaa@pu.ac.in

© The Author(s), under exclusive license to Springer Nature Switzerland AG 2022
D. Hyams-Ssekasi, N. Yasin (eds.), *Technology and Entrepreneurship Education*,
https://doi.org/10.1007/978-3-030-84292-5_6

Since a couple of years ago, the entrepreneurship education mode was caged within the stories of success and failures of male-dominated entrepreneurial businesses. The conventional pedagogy was highly criticized by the academic evaluators and business practitioners as it was not able to equip the students with the requisite temperament to face the heat of a real business environment (Poisson-de Harro & Turgut, 2012). The tough challenge ahead of institutions is to create a synergy between the current entrepreneurial process and associated skills and competencies required for a real-life business environment (Fox & Pittaway, 2018). Innovative pedagogies are being embraced by the institutions to boost the effectiveness of entrepreneurship education for potential entrepreneurs by connecting the theory into practices (Nabi et al., 2017). To engage the budding entrepreneurs as co-learners, the role of creative relational type of learning has been gaining weightage in academics (Hjorth, 2011). Simulation pedagogies are being used to facilitate the in-depth understanding of entrepreneurial concepts, problem-solving, and decision-making among students (Wu & Anderson, 2015).

Heitzmann et al. (2019) termed simulation as a tool to tackle the real problem or events on a virtual or small scale and to convert this interaction with the decision-making of potential entrepreneurs. Cook et al. (2013) described simulation as an "educational tool or device with which the students physically interact with an impersonator of real life." Beaubien and Baker (2004) observed the role of simulation in education as a tool that reproduces the real-life characteristics of an event or situation and gives more clarity to students. Numerous research studies have been conducted on the application of simulation-based teaching and learning in the field of engineering, medical, business management, faculty education, prospective nurses to develop motor skills, technical skills, and diagnostic competencies (Hegland et al., 2017; Brubacher et al., 2015; Cook, 2014; Cook et al., 2013; Alfred & Chung, 2011). Simulation pedagogy helps in bridging the gap between theoretical and real-life decision-making with the help of experiential learnings (Tabak & Kyza, 2018). The more precisely the reality of the business scenario is imitated in the simulation games, the more the phenomena and a higher level of relations complexity between them are encompassed by its scenario (Wawer et al., 2010). The significance of simulations as a diversified facet of a technology-enhanced alternative has immense scope for entrepreneurship education (Smith, 2007). Simulation-based pedagogy assists the students in understanding the complexity of "real" business strategies and gives significantly higher benefits in the success of students (Tompson & Dass, 2000).

Still, confined research has been performed to know the effectiveness of simulation-based pedagogies with different learning conditions in the entrepreneurship stream. The existing review papers in the literature have a prime focus on simulation-based education in various streams of educations except for entrepreneurship (Chernikova et al., 2019; Tiwari et al., 2014; Ciucan-Rusu, 2012). The focus of the existing research studies remained narrow within entrepreneurial education. Thus, the existing research papers are extensive in the discussion of the scope of simulation in various disciplines of academics but not comprehensive in their coverage of entrepreneurial key areas.

Against the above backdrop, this chapter aims to bridge all the gaps between the scope for simulation in entrepreneurial education. It provides an ample review of both perspectives, namely simulations and entrepreneurship training while reviewing literature from the past to the present, connecting dots, discussing the development and advancement and their relevance in the present context of innovative pedagogies. This chapter reviews both the past and current research in this emerging field of simulation, touching upon all the critical areas like simulation games in entrepreneurial education and for understanding the sudden shift in pedagogical techniques.

Literature Review

Entrepreneurship can be defined from various aspects like a venture of small business (Shane & Venkataraman, 2000), creation of new opportunity (Blenker et al., 2011), and innovation (Drucker, 2002). From this context, simulation becomes part of entrepreneurial educations from multidimensional aspects like role play, computer games, action learning, serious games, experiential learnings, and video role play (Fayolle et al., 2016; Pittaway & Cope, 2007; Ulijn et al., 2004; Stewart & Knowles,

2003; Hindle, 2002; Leitch & Harrison, 1999). Davidsson and Verhagen (2017) observed the pivotal role of simulation in enabling the students to face real-life complexities by offering various learning opportunities.

Deb and Bhatt (2020) stress the advantages of integrated digital learning to boost the skill-based entrepreneurial training. The study further documented that employing stream-specific gamification in education could potentially contribute to the learning of target students. Kriz and Auchter (2016) examined the adequacy of serious games and simulation for entrepreneurial education in the context of validation and fidelity. Huebscher and Lendner (2010) stated in their research about the significant role of simulations through extending their knowledge about entrepreneurial decision-making variables. Goldstein and Gafni (2019) recommended virtual learning teaching to teach entrepreneurial skills. This strategy further helps in boosting the motivation among students to decode the business world uncertainties. Niebuhr and Tegtmeier (2019) also advocated the applications of advanced technologies like virtual reality to infuse entrepreneurial factors into the learning process. Sarmila et al. (2019) and Torres-Toukoumidis et al. (2019) observed the positive effect of gamification on the entrepreneurial impact on the students and in developing the entrepreneurial competencies. Prensky (2001) documented the applications of simulation techniques to increase knowledge, improve skills, and enable positive learning outcomes. Many studies advocate the existence of the right extent of fidelity in simulation games to increase their effectiveness (Pellegrino & Scott, 2004; Billhardt, 2004; Hindle, 2002). Grossman et al. (2009) reported simulation as a tool to engage inexperience and potential entrepreneurs into more proximal practices of real-life businesses. The duration of the simulation exercise plays a significant role in becoming familiar with the learning environment. Davidsson and Verhagen (2017) explored that role play, communication with target customers, and simulated discussions can also be considered as part of simulation other than a computer or software-based games. Numerous previous studies proposed that the streamlining of pedagogies in delivering entrepreneurship education helps in enhancing the performance of students as well as nurturing their entrepreneurial competence by maintaining the balance with other teaching modules (Zhang & Price, 2020; Aries et al., 2020; Kariv et al., 2019).

The pragmatic significance of simulation in nurturing entrepreneurship among students along with developing academic interest has led to the rapid rise in the scope of simulation games in recent times. This rapid growth associated with emerging research areas calls for a dire need for a systematic review of extended literature. The recent literature regarding the scope of simulation in entrepreneurship set the conceptual framework and boundaries for diving deeper in exploring the research in this field. The research based on the combination of simulation and entrepreneurship has carved a space for differentiation from other research domains in academics. Thus, it has become imperative to recognize the main contributors that mold the research to establish the legitimacy of the rising importance of simulation in the entrepreneurial domain among researchers, academicians, and practitioners.

As a researcher note, it has been observed that minor attempts have been made to perform a comprehensive bibliometric analysis based on the earlier attainments and future scope of simulation in developing entrepreneurship. Despite these endeavors to consolidate the previous researchers on simulation, a wide gap has been found in the literature that makes it a tough nut to crack to obtain a complete clarity of this topic. The current knowledge about simulation seems to be fragmented and needs a clearer picture because of the existing vacuum. Moreover, an in-depth bibliometric analysis of existing literature can add value to the future development of simulation-based entrepreneurial education research by identifying the leading influential researchers in this field. Hence, the present study aims to review the simulation-based entrepreneurial education literature published in renowned scholarly journals of entrepreneurship, business management, and other allied academic areas to explore and discuss the present themes and purposive areas for future areas.

Research Questions

In particular, the present study focuses on addressing the research questions:

RQ1: Who are the leading influential contributors to the literature on simulation-based entrepreneurship education?
RQ2: Which corner of the globe put more emphasis on promoting entrepreneurial education by applying simulation games and other simulation-based modes.
RQ3: How can the literature on simulation-based entrepreneurship education be advanced?

The present study endeavors to address these research questions by analyzing the literature on entrepreneurship education pedagogy using bibliometric analysis techniques (Caviggioli & Ughetto, 2019; Xu et al., 2018). These bibliometric techniques have been well explored to contribute to regulating the existing research literature from a multidimensional perspective by reviewing a major chunk of relevant scholarly work (Caviggioli & Ughetto, 2019). Furthermore, it has been observed that these bibliometric techniques remained focus on the statistical framework by leaving no stone unturned for the biases that may have an impact on the literature review (Xu et al., 2018). Research question one was addressed by applying bibliographic coupling and co-occurrence analysis based on the existing research literature. The second research question was solved by performing citation analysis, whereas for achieving the third research objective, the widening scope of pedagogy was identified from the previous studies. The finding of the present study gives a clear view of the existing condition and stretch the existing literature by presenting the future scope of simulation to overcome the existing barriers. Thus, it provides gainful insights for practitioners and scholars for future academic research.

Research Design

Bibliographic coupling, citation analysis, and co-authorship analysis were applied by using VOSviewer. VOSviewer has been considered a reliable bibliometric analysis tool to examine and visualize bibliometric data utilizing various options (Van Eck & Waltman, 2014). In specific, VOSviewer was used to examine the co-occurrences of keywords from bibliometric datasets like Scopus, Web of Sciences, and so on (Fahimnia et al., 2015). Therefore, the co-word analysis was done by applying VOSviewer, whereas the co-citation and dynamic co-citation analyses have been performed using Gephi (Khanra et al., 2020).

In the bibliometric coupling technique, two journal articles citing a publication were coupled as high instances of mutual reference suggest an intellectual capital common to both (Khanra et al., 2020). This technique was built on backward citation chaining. However, it has attracted critiques because of its limitations in assessing the older articles (Khanra et al., 2020). The study acknowledges the influential authors who have produced most citations to their study. The study identified Neck H. M. (2011), most cited author for his work, followed by Fiet J. O. (2001) and Piperopoulos & Dimov (2015) in terms of several citations.

Citation Analysis

This technique determines the intensity of appreciation for a publication based on its citation count (Khanra et al., 2020; Xu et al., 2018). The study acknowledges the top ten authors, organizations, and countries, respectively, from the citation analysis.

Co-authorship Analysis

Co-authorship analysis highlight that the tendency of co-authors to cite comparable publications within a network can have a substantial impact on the literature of a research topic (Khanra et al., 2020). Hence, it is imperative to recognize impactful associations of authors to comprehend the structure of literature related to the given research issue (Khanra et al., 2021).

Data Analysis

The keywords used to extract the documents from Scopus include "Entrepreneurship Education" and "Pedagogy" or "Simulation Teaching".

Totally 202 documents published during the period 1999 till April 24, 2021 were found, and out of these 182 papers were analyzed.

Table 6.1 shows the acceptance and rejection criteria for the inclusion of the documents in this research study.

Here the scope of this chapter is confined to documents published only in the English language. Three documents published in Croatian, Portuguese, and Spanish languages were found in Scopus which were ignored for analysis. Final papers published were included and three papers in the press were excluded. Further total documents include 144 articles, 19 book chapters, and 19 conference papers.

The statistics depicted in Table 6.2 show the year-wise publication of the documents downloaded for this study. From the year 1988 till 2007 only six documents were published. Further from the year 2011 till 2021, 91% of the documents were published out of the total publication in SCOPUS in the domain under study. It shows that academic interest in entrepreneurial education hovered only after the year 2011. Maximum documents, that is, 25 (13.74%) were published in the year 2016 followed by 23 (12.63%) publications in the year 2018, and 20 (11%) in the year 2017. From the year 1997 to 2000 and then from the year 2002 to 2005, 1995, and from 1989 to 1993, there was no publication. The year 1988, 1994, 1995, 1996, 2001, 2006, and 2007 had only one document published each year.

Table 6.3 shows the source-wise publications. Journal titled *Education and Training* has published a maximum (22 documents) during the period under study. *Journal of Entrepreneurship Education* is at number 2 with 11 documents published followed by *Industry and Higher Education* (9 documents). *International Journal of Entrepreneurial Behaviour and Research, International Journal of Entrepreneurship and Small Business*, and *Journal of Small Business and Enterprise Development* had published seven documents each.

Table 6.1 Acceptance criteria

Acceptance	Rejection
All English text	Croatian (1), Portuguese (1), and Spanish (1)
Papers published as article (144), book chapters (19), and conference papers (19)	Review papers (7), book (6), and editorial (1)
Final papers	Articles in press (3)

6 Simulation-based Teaching Pedagogy and Entrepreneurship... 141

Table 6.2 Year-wise documents published

Year	Number	Year	Number	Year	Number	Year	Number
2021	7	2015	19	2009	3	1997–2000	0
2020	17	2014	16	2008	4	1996	1
2019	18	2013	4	2007	1	1995	0
2018	23	2012	6	2006	1	1994	1
2017	20	2011	11	2002–2005	0	1989–1993	0
2016	25	2010	3	2001	1	1988	1

Table 6.3 Source-wise publication

Name of journal	Documents published
Education and Training	22
Journal of Entrepreneurship Education	11
Industry and Higher Education	9
International Journal of Entrepreneurial Behaviour and Research	7
International Journal of Entrepreneurship and Small Business	7
Journal of Small Business and Enterprise Development	7
International Journal of Management	5
Journal of Small Business Management	5
International Journal of Engineering Education	4
Entrepreneurship and Regional Development	3
Proceedings Frontiers in Education Conference Fie	3
Academy of Entrepreneurship Journal	2 documents each
Advances in the Study of Entrepreneurship Innovation and Economic Growth	
Contributions to Management Science	
International Entrepreneurship and Management Journal	
Journal of Business and Entrepreneurship	
Journal of Business Venturing	
Journal of Development Economics	
Journal of Education for Business	
Journal of Enterprising Communities	
Journal of Small Business and Entrepreneurship	
Journal of Technology Transfer	
Journal of Vocational Education and Training	
Studies in Higher Education	
Technological Forecasting and Social Change	

Table 6.4 Country-wise publications

Country	Number of documents published
United States	59
United Kingdom	39
Sweden	14
Australia	11
Denmark, Finland	10
Nigeria	9
India, Malaysia	8
China, Italy	7
Canada	6
France	5
Netherlands	4
Germany, Greece, Indonesia, Ireland, Poland	3
Ghana, New Zealand, Norway, Portugal, Russian Federation, South Africa, Spain, Switzerland, Uganda	2
Austria, Croatia, Egypt, Estonia, Israel, Kuwait, Mauritius, Morocco, Peru, Slovakia, South Korea, Taiwan, UAE	1
Undefined	2

The statistics reported in Table 6.4 indicate that the United States has published a maximum of 59 papers followed by the UK publishing 39 papers, Sweden 14 papers, Australia 11, and Denmark and Finland publishing 10 papers each. It was also found that European Commission is the leading funding authority funding studies related to entrepreneurship (six documents funded) followed by Covenant University, Directorate-General for Employment, Social Affairs, Inclusion, European Social Fund, Innovation Growth Lab, National Science Foundation each funded two documents. Similarly, Aarhus Universitet has published seven documents, followed by Babson College with five documents. The Chalmers University of Technology, Queensland University of Technology, Coventry University, Covenant University published four documents each. Universities like the University of Worcester, Purdue University, University of South Wales, University of Michigan, Michigan State University, Aalto University, Jonkoping International Business School, EMLYON Business School have published three documents each.

Bibliometric Analysis

Bibliometric analysis has been studied as co-authorship, co-occurrence keywords wise, document-wise citation analysis, bibliographic coupling, and co-citations.

Figure 6.1 presents co-authorship analysis. Out of 397 authors, 67 meet the threshold of publishing a minimum of 2 documents. There are 28 clusters of 67 authors in the co-authorship network author-wise. Cluster 1 of 8 authors comprises Blenker, Frederiksen, Jones, Korsgaard, Neergaard, Robinson, Tanggaard, and Thrane. Seven authors are grouped in cluster 2 including Bellotti, Berta, De Gloria, Lavagnine, Ott, Romero,

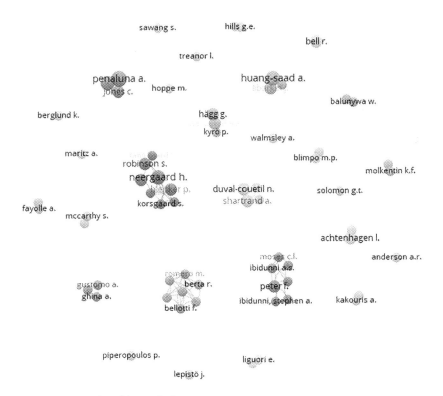

Fig. 6.1 Co-authorship analysis

and Usart. Ibidunni, Maxwell, Moses, Motilewa, Olokundun, and Peter are in cluster 3.

Figure 6.2 shows keywords-wise co-occurrence analysis. Out of 593 keywords, 45 meet the threshold of a minimum of three occurrences. These 45 items are divided into seven clusters of keywords. The most prominent keywords occurring together include education, education computing, engineering education, engineering entrepreneurship, engineers, innovation, innovation education, learning outcome, personal training, students, teaching, and undergraduate students. The focus is basically on undergraduate engineering and entrepreneurship. Cluster 2 includes ten keywords including curriculum, design thinking, educational development, entrepreneur, entrepreneurial education, entrepreneurial learning, entrepreneurship pedagogy, learning, secondary education, and student. This cluster focuses on entrepreneurship education. Cluster 3 talks about outcomes including creativity, curricula, design, engineering, engineering students, professional aspects, self-efficacy, societies, and

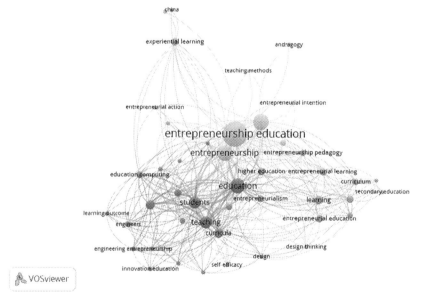

Fig. 6.2 Co-occurrences keyword-wise

6 Simulation-based Teaching Pedagogy and Entrepreneurship...

institutions. Figure 6.2 shows that teaching methods are the area that is still gray and needs attention for future research.

Document-wise citation analysis as presented in Table 6.5 shows that out of 182 documents 99 meet the threshold of having a minimum of five citations. Top cited documents are of Neck & Greene (2011) with maximum citations followed by Fiet (2001), Piperopoulos & Dimov (2015), Hills (1998), Jones (2010), Edelman et al. (2008), and Kassean et al. (2015). All these authors have more than 100 citations as shown in Table 6.5 and are connected as shown in Fig. 6.3. This table shows a list of documents having more than 40 citations.

Figure 6.4 shows the results of bibliographic coupling. Out of 182 documents, 115 met the threshold of a minimum of three citations. Bibliographic coupling is just similar to co-citations which are explained in the next part of this chapter. This coupling happens when two documents refer to a common third document in their bibliographies meaning thereby that the coupled work relates to the same type of subject matter.

Figure 6.5 shows a network of co-citation analysis. Out of 9420 cited references, 50 meet the threshold of having a minimum of 5 references. Further 50 cited documents are divided into five clusters.

Cluster 1 comprises Blenker, Fayolle, Gibb, Hannon, Jones, Kassean, Katz, Mwasalwiba, Neck, and Shane.

Table 6.5 Document-wise citation analysis

Document	Citations	Links	Document	Citations	Links
Neck H.M. (2011)	497	44	Blenker P. (2011)	69	10
Fiet J.O. (2001)	269	10	Solomon G.T. (1994)	63	3
Piperopoulos P. & Dimov (2015)	212	9	Robinson S. (2016)	61	11
Hills G.E. (1998)	182	11	Fayolle A. (2016)	59	7
Jones B. (2010)	168	12	Middleton K.W. (2014)	58	3
Edelman L.F. (2008)	142	9	Duval-Couetil N. (2016)	56	0
Kassean H. (2015)	107	11	Täks M. (2014)	54	0
Gibb A. (2011)	86	8	Blenker P. (2008)	47	6
Mueller S. (2011)	77	0	Blenker P. (2012)	45	8
Anderson A.R. (2008)	77	9	Kirby D.A. (2011)	42	2

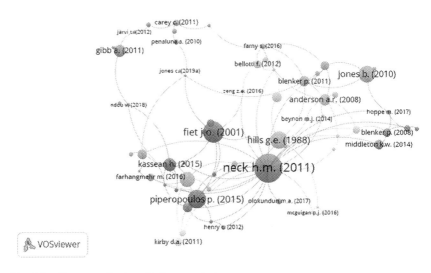

Fig. 6.3 Document-wise citation analysis

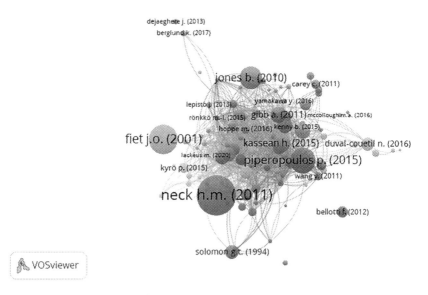

Fig. 6.4 Bibliographic coupling

Cluster 2 comprises Ajzen, Davidsson, Fiet, Gorman, Hong, Katz, Kuratko, Lobler, Pittaway, Shane, Shepherd, and Solomon.

6 Simulation-based Teaching Pedagogy and Entrepreneurship...

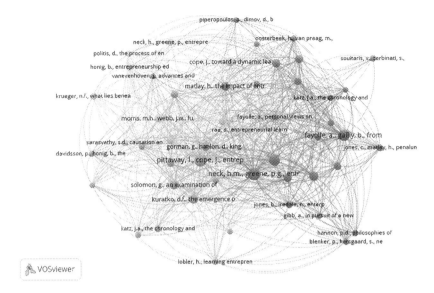

Fig. 6.5 Co-citation analysis

Cluster 3 includes Fayolle, Martin, Matlay, Nabi, Oosterbeek, Piperopolous, Pittaway, Rideout, Souitaris, and Vanevenhoven.

Cluster 4 includes Bae, Cope, Honig, Kruger, Morris, Neck, Politis, Rae, Rasmussen, and Sarasvathy.

Cluster 5 comprises Fayolle only.

Neck H.M. (2011) being the most coupled author, all these items are clubbed in seven clusters. *Cluster 1* carries 22 documents including Antonaci (2015), Armstrong (2014), Bellotti (2012), Berglund (2006), Beynon (2014), Blenker (2008), Dakung (2017), Do Paco (2011), Farhangmehr (2016), Fatoki (2014), Hermeling (2011), Hills (2018), Manimala (2017), Neck (2011), Olokundun (2017), Piperopoulos & Dimov (2015), Pistrui (2012), Reuel (2016), Robinson (2014), Solomon (2014), and Wang (2011). These documents talk about a framework for designing an entrepreneurial course to stimulate and motivate participants to take entrepreneurship with contents like business plans, serious games, and simulations. Few of these papers also analyze the impact of courses on the intentions of students from engineering and business backgrounds.

Cluster 2 is with authors like Achtenhagen (2013), Bandera (2018), Bell (2019), Dzisi (2017), Fayolle et al. (2016), Holzmann (2018), Hoppe (2016), Huq (2017), Jones (2017), Kakouris (2015), Kassean et al. (2015), Lynch (2021), Marliyah (2018), Mueller (2011), Mukesh (2020), Ndou (2018), Nyadu (2018), Pathak (2019), Schmidt (2015), Shankar (2016), and Yamakawa (2016).

This cluster focuses on teaching pedagogy including games, design thinking, research, experimentation, use of technology, real-world experience for entrepreneurship education that crafts mindsets and enhances learning. It also concludes that there is a need to revisit the entrepreneurship education framework in light of changes in the current scenario.

Co-citations

The more deep-dive into the documents suggests that entrepreneurship teaching pedagogy should foster the ability of the student to practice entrepreneurship (Neck & Greece, 2011), self-efficacy, a combination of theory and practice (Anderson & Jack, 2008). Literature also suggests that there are three approaches to entrepreneurial teaching (Ertmer & Newby, 1993). Behaviorism approach advocates stimulus-response psychology wherein students are given lesson content, reinforcers and then they respond. The cognitive approach talks about designing a proper structure, sequence, and outline of information so that students absorb and use the information when needed. The constructive approach assumes that students constantly construct understanding and represent. Further courses should have a minimum engagement of adjunct faculty (Blenker et al., 2011).

The teaching pedagogy should include serious games and simulations, design-based thinking, reflective learning, practice-based pedagogy or learning through practice (Neck & Greece, 2011; Gibb, 2011), case study and lectures by entrepreneurs (Hills, 1998; Blenker et al., 2011), starting start-up activities (Edelman et al., 2008), real-world experience (Mueller, 2011), action and reflective process (Kassean et al., 2015; Blenker et al., 2011). Course work should be student-oriented (Fiet, 2001; Mueller, 2011), experimental-oriented (Hills, 1998; Blenker et al.,

2011), and curiosity-based (Robinson et al., 2016). The components should not only be related to business; rather, they should be richer, deeper, and wider (Jones & Iredale, 2010). It should include starting a business (Neck & Greece, 2011) and development of a business plan (Hills, 1998; Mueller, 2011). It should not only focus on the theory which is usually boring but should also have a component of the theory-based practice of specific skills (Fiet, 2001).

As far as the simulation is concerned, it is found that simulation facilitates decision-making, problem-solving, enhancing skill sets and curiosity, and motivation (Morote & Price, 2018). There are a couple of software like Marketplace (King & Newman, 2009), Sim Venture (Costin et al., 2018), Sharkworld, GoVenture software, and Lemonde Stand (Morote & Price, 2018) on which case studies have been written, and it was concluded that such simulations are effective. A couple of other simulation games that have been tested and developed at MIT Sloan School include INNOV8 (IBM), Platform Wars, Clean Smart, Salt Seller, Informatist, Moblab, and so on. Few examples from India include Moneybhai developed by moneycontrol and ICICI direct. Goi (2018) also emphasized the effectiveness of the use of simulators in business education and learning. These serious games replicate the problems and challenges of entrepreneurs (Costin et al., 2018), enhance visibility, challenge students' creativity (Blazic & Novak, 2015), and finally enhance the level of entrepreneurial skills and competencies.

Conclusion and Directions for Future Work

From the foregoing analysis, it can be concluded that the academic interest arose in the entrepreneurial teaching pedagogy only in this decade. It was found that 91% of the documents were published only after the year 2011. This decade has seen growing interest in the domain of entrepreneurship education and teaching pedagogy. Source-wise publications show that journals titled *Education and Training*, *Journal of Entrepreneurship Education*, and *Industry and Higher Education* are the leading journals publishing documents related to the theme under study. The United States has been exploring entrepreneurial education maximum followed by the United Kingdom, Sweden, Australia, Denmark, and Finland. Even the funding authorities like European Commission, Covenant University, Directorate-General for Employment, Social Affairs, Inclusion, European Social Fund, Innovation Growth Lab, National Science Foundation have been funding entrepreneurship-related research studies. Among Universities, Aarhus Universitet, Babson College, Chalmers University of Technology, Queensland University of Technology, Coventry University, and Covenant University are leading academic institutions working in the domain. Neck (2011), Fiet (2001), Piperopoulos & Dimov (2015), Hills (1998), Jones (2010), Edelman et al. (2008), and Kassean et al. (2015) are the leading influential contributors to the literature on entrepreneurship education.

The contributors have been emphasizing how the entrepreneurship course framework should be and how it can foster entrepreneurship attitudes and intentions. Literature also suggests that there should be a combination of both theory and practicals to enhance the impact of entrepreneurship courses. The course should have a minimum engagement of adjunct faculty. Course work should be student-oriented, experimental-oriented, and curiosity-based. Teaching pedagogy should largely have techniques like serious games and simulations, design-based thinking, reflective learning, practice-based case study and lectures by entrepreneurs, starting start-up activities, real-world experience, action, and reflective processes. It should encourage participants to start their ventures, learn out of the experience of others. Teaching methodology has been found as the gray area which needs more serious research.

Ultimately following model can be drawn as the conclusion of existing literature on entrepreneurial education and pedagogy (Fig. 6.6):

The entrepreneurship education framework has been quite established as of now. The teaching pedagogies have been suggested, and their impact on entrepreneurial intentions has also been tested in the past and is being tested. There is a dearth of literature on the collection and development of simulation games and measurement of the impact of specific simulation games on entrepreneurship, though the literature suggests that such games influence and encourage entrepreneurship. Thus, it is suggested that the future research direction for entrepreneurship education should

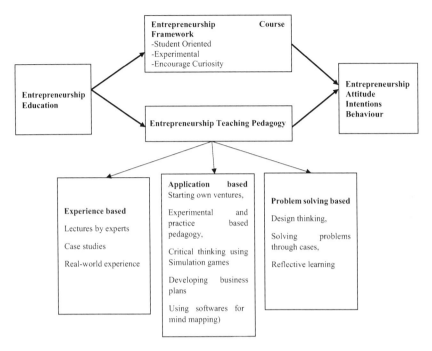

Fig. 6.6 Entrepreneurship teaching pedagogy model

be toward developing games and analyzing the impact of simulation games—game-wise.

References

Alfred, M., & Chung, C. (2011). Design, development, and evaluation of a second generation interactive Simulator for Engineering Ethics Education (SEEE2). *Science and Engineering Ethics, 18*(4), 689–697. https://doi.org/10.1007/s11948-011-9284-0

Anderson, A. R., & Jack, S. L. (2008). Role typologies for enterprising education: The professional artisan? *Journal of Small Business and Enterprise Development, 15*(2), 259–273.

Aries, A., Vional, V., Saraswati, L., Wijaya, L., & Ikhsan, R. (2020). Gamification in the learning process and its impact on entrepreneurial intention. *Management Science Letters, 10*(4), 763–768.

Beaubien, J. M., & Baker, D. P. (2004). The use of simulation for training teamwork skills in health care: How low can you go? *BMJ Quality and Safety,* *13*(Suppl 1), 51–56. https://doi.org/10.1136/qshc.2004.009845

Billhardt, B. (2004). The promise of online simulations. *Chief Learning Officer, 3,* 38–41.

Blazic, A. J., & Novak, F. (2015). Challenges of business simulation games: A new approach of teaching business. Retrieved June 10 from https://www.intechopen.com/books/e-learning-instructional-design-organizational-strategy-and-management/challenges-of-business-simulation-games-a-new-approach-of-teaching-business

Blenker, P., Korsgaard, S., Neergaard, H., & Thrane, C. (2011). The questions we care about: Paradigms and progression in entrepreneurship education. *Industry and Higher Education, 25*(6), 417–427.

Brubacher, S. P., Powell, M., Skouteris, H., & Guadagno, B. (2015). The effects of e-simulation interview training on teachers' use of open-ended questions. *Child Abuse & Neglect, 43*(1), 95–103. https://doi.org/10.1016/j.chiabu.2015.02.004

Caviggioli, F., & Ughetto, E. (2019). A bibliometric analysis of the research dealing with the impact of additive manufacturing on industry, business and society. *International Journal of Production Economics, 208,* 254–268.

Chernikova, O., Heitzmann, N., Fink, M. C., Timothy, V., Seidel, T., & Fischer, F. (2019). Facilitating diagnostic competences in higher education: A meta-analysis in medical and teacher education. *Educational Psychology Review, 32*(1), 157–196. https://doi.org/10.1007/s10648-019-09492-2

Ciucan-Rusu, L. (2012). Action and reaction–case study from a business simulation. *Procedia Economics and Finance, 3,* 1243–1249. https://doi.org/10.1016/s2212-5671(12)00303-6

Cook, D. A. (2014). How much evidence does it take? A cumulative meta-analysis of outcomes of simulation-based education. *Medical Education, 48*(8), 750–760. https://doi.org/10.1111/medu.12473

Cook, D. A., Brydges, R., Zendejas, B., Hamstra, S. J., & Hatala, R. (2013). Technology enhanced simulation to assess health professionals: A systematic review of validity evidence, research methods, and reporting quality. *Academic Medicine, 88*(6), 872–883. https://doi.org/10.1097/ACM.0b013e31828ffdcf

Costin, Y., O'Brien, M. P., & Slattery, D. M. (2018). Using simulation to develop entrepreneurial skills and mind-set: An exploratory case study. *International Journal of Teaching and Learning in Higher Education, 30*(1), 136–145.

Davidsson, P., & Verhagen, H. (2017). Types of simulation. In B. Edmonds & R. Meyer (Eds.), *Simulating social complexity. Understanding complex systems* (pp. 23–37). Springer. https://doi.org/10.1007/978-3-319-66948-9_3

Deb, R., & Bhatt, D. K. (2020). Technology integration through digital learning hub in skill-oriented entrepreneurial education. *Journal of Engineering Education Transformations, 33*, 503–509.

Drucker, P. (2002). The discipline of innovation. *Harvard Business Review, 80*, 95–100, 102, 148.

Edelman, L. F., Manolova, T. S., & Brush, C. G. (2008). Entrepreneurship education: Correspondence between practices of nascent entrepreneurs and textbook prescriptions for success. *The Academy of Management Learning and Education, 7*(1), 56–70.

Ertmer, P. A., & Newby, T. J. (1993). Behaviorism, cognitivism, constructivism: Comparing critical features from an instructional design perspective. *Performance Improvement Quarterly, 26*(2), 43–71.

Fahimnia, B., Sarkis, J., & Davarzani, H. (2015). Green supply chain management: A review and bibliometric analysis. *International Journal of Production Economics, 162*, 101–114.

Fayolle, A., Verzat, C., & Wapshott, R. (2016). In quest of legitimacy: The theoretical and methodological foundations of entrepreneurship education research. *International Small Business Journal, 34*(7), 895–904.

Fiet, J. O. (2001). The pedagogical side of entrepreneurship theory. *Journal of Business Venturing, 16*(2), 101–117.

Fox, J., & Pittaway, L. (2018). Simulations in entrepreneurship educations: Serious games and learning through play. *Entrepreneurship Education and Pedagogy, 1*(1), 61–89.

Gibb, A. (2011). Concepts into practice: Meeting the challenge of development of entrepreneurship educators around an innovative paradigm: The case of the International Entrepreneurship Educators Programme (IEEP). *International Journal of Entrepreneurial Behaviour and Research, 12*(2), 146–165.

Goi, C. L. (2018). The use of business simulation games in teaching and learning. *Journal of Education for Business, 94*(5), 342–349.

Goldstein, A., & Gafni, R. (2019). Learning entrepreneurship through virtual multicultural teamwork. *Issues in Informing Science & Information Technology, 16*, 276–305.

Grossman, P., Compton, C., Igra, D., Ronfeldt, M., Shahan, E., & Williamson, P. (2009). Teaching practice: A cross-professional perspective. *Teachers College Record, 111*(9), 2055–2100.

Hegland, P. A., Aarlie, H., Strømme, H., & Jamtvedt, G. (2017). Simulation-based training for nurses: Systematic review and meta-analysis. *Nurse Education Today, 54*(1), 6–20. https://doi.org/10.1016/j.nedt.2017.04.004

Heitzmann, N., Seidel, T., Opitz, A., Hetmanek, A., Wecker, C., Fischer, M., Ufer, S., Schmidmaier, R., Neuhaus, B., Siebeck, M., Stürmer, K., Obersteiner, A., Reiss, K., Girwidz, R., & Fischer, F. (2019). Facilitating diagnostic competencies in simulations: A conceptual framework and a research agenda for medical and teacher education. *Frontline Learning Research, 7*(4), 1–24. https://doi.org/10.14786/flr.v7i4.384

Hills, G. E. (1998). Variations in University entrepreneurship education: An empirical study of an evolving field. *Journal of Business Venturing, 3*(2), 109–122.

Hindle, K. (2002). A grounded theory for teaching entrepreneurship using simulation games. *Simulation and Gaming, 33*(2), 236–241.

Hjorth, D. (2011). On provocation, education, and entrepreneurship. *Entrepreneurship and Regional Development, 23*(1–2), 49–63.

Hornsby, J., Messersmith, J., Rutherford, M., & Simmons, S. (2018). Entrepreneurship everywhere: Across campus, across communities, and across borders. *Journal of Small Business Management, 56*(1), 4–10.

Jones, C. (2010). Entrepreneurship education: Revisiting our role and its purpose. *Journal of Small Business and Enterprise Development, 17*(4), 500–513. https://doi.org/10.1108/14626001011088697

Jones, B., & Iredale, N. (2010). Viewpoint: Enterprise education as pedagogy. *Education and Training, 52*, 7–18. https://doi.org/10.1108/00400911011017654

Kariv, D., Matlay, H., & Fayolle, A. (2019). Introduction: Entrepreneurial trends meet entrepreneurial education. In *The role and impact of entrepreneurship education*. Edward Elgar Publishing.

Kassean, H., Vanevenhoven, J., Liguori, E., & Winkel, D. E. (2015). Entrepreneurship education: A need for reflection, real-world experience and action. *International Journal of Entrepreneurial Behaviour and Research, 21*(5), 690–708.

Khanra, S., Dhir, A., Islam, A. N., & Mäntymäki, M. (2020). Big data analytics in healthcare: A systematic literature review. *Enterprise Information Systems, 14*(7), 878–912.

Khanra, S., Kaur, P., Joseph, R. P., Malik, A., & Dhir, A. (2021). A resource-based view of green innovation as a strategic firm resource: Present status and future directions. *Business Strategy and the Environment,* 1–19. https://doi.org/10.1002/bse.2961KHANRAETAL.19

King, M., & Newman, R. (2009). Evaluating business simulation software: Approach, tools and pedagogy. *On the Horizon, 17*(4), 368–377.

Kriz, W., & Auchter, E. (2016). 10 years of evaluation research into gaming simulation for German entrepreneurship and a new study on its long-term effects. *Simulation and Gaming, 47*(2), 179–205.

Leitch, C., & Harrison, R. (1999). A process model for entrepreneurship education and development. *International Journal of Entrepreneurial Behaviour and Research, 5*(3), 83–109.

Morote, E. S., & Price, C. (2018). *Learning through play: A new model to teach entrepreneurship.* In a National Symposium on 'Transforming Teaching Through Active Learning held on November 16–17 at Stetson University, Miami, Florida.

Mueller, S. (2011). Increasing entrepreneurial intention: Effective entrepreneurship course characteristics. *International Journal of Entrepreneurship and Small Business, 13*(1), 55–74.

Nabi, G., Linan, F., Fayolle, A., Krueger, N., & Walmsley, A. (2017). The impact of entrepreneurship education in higher education: A systematic review and research agenda. *Academy of Management Learning & Education, 16*(2), 277–299.

Neck, H. M., & Greece, P. G. (2011). Entrepreneurship Education: Known Worlds and New Frontiers. *Journal of Small Business Management, 49*(1), 55–70. https://doi.org/10.1111/j.1540-627X.2010.00314.x

Neck, H. M., & Greene, P. G. (2011). Entrepreneurship education: Known Worlds and New Frontiers. *Journal of Small Business Management, 49,* 55–70. https://doi.org/10.1111/j.1540-627X.2010.00314.x

Niebuhr, O., & Tegtmeier, S. (2019). Virtual reality as a digital learning tool in entrepreneurship: How virtual environments help entrepreneurs give more charismatic investor pitches. In L. Daniela (Ed.), *Digital entrepreneurship* (pp. 123–158). Springer.

Pellegrino, J., & Scott, A. (2004). *The transition from simulation to game-based learning.* In Proceedings of the interservice/industry training, simulation and education conference Entrepreneurship Education and Pedagogy 1(1) (I/ITSEC), Orlando, FL, 6–9 December, 2004. National Training and Simulation Association.

Piperopoulos, P., & Dimov, D. (2015). Burst bubbles or build steam? Entrepreneurship education, entrepreneurial self-efficacy, and entrepreneurial intentions. *Journal of Small Business Management, 53*(4), 970–985. https://doi.org/10.1111/jsbm.12116

Pittaway, L., & Cope, J. (2007). Entrepreneurship education: A systematic review of the evidence. *International Small Business Journal, 25*(5), 477–506.

Poisson-de Harro, S., & Turgut, G. (2012). Expanded strategy simulations: Developing better managers. *Journal of Management Development, 31*(3), 209–220.

Prensky, M. (2001). Fun play and games: What makes games engaging. *Digital Game Based Learning, 5*, 1–5.

Robinson, S., Neergaard, H., Tanggaard, L., & Krueger, N. (2016). New horizons in entrepreneurship: From teacher-led to student-centered learning. *Education and Training, 58*, 661–683.

Sarmila, M. S., Ramlee, S., Sabarudin, A., Arsad, N., Nor, M. M., Batcha, Z. K., et al. (2019). *Student's perception on entrepreneurial education programs for graduate startups in selected ASEAN universities*. In International Visual Informatics Conference (550–559).

Shane, S., & Venkataraman, S. (2000). The promise of entrepreneurship as a field of research. *Academy of Management Review, 25*(1), 217-226.

Smith, K. (2007). Supporting e-learning in enterprise: The TE3 project. *Education and Training, 49*(8/9), 656–670.

Stefanic, I., Campbell, R. K., Russ, J. S., & Stefanic, E. (2020). Evaluation of a blended learning approach for cross-cultural entrepreneurial education. *Innovations in Education and Teaching International, 57*(2), 242–254.

Stewart, J., & Knowles, V. (2003). Mentoring in undergraduate business management programmes. *Journal of European Industrial Training, 27*(2–4), 147–159.

Tabak, I., & Kyza, E. (2018). Research on scaffolding in the learning sciences: A methodological perspective. In F. Fischer, C. Hmelo-Silver, S. Goldman, & P. Reimann (Eds.), *International handbook of the learning sciences* (pp. 191–200). Routledge.

Tiwari, S. R., Nafees, L., & Krishnan, O. (2014). Simulation as a pedagogical tool: Measurement of impact on perceived effective learning. *The International Journal of Management Education, 12*(3), 260–270. https://doi.org/10.1016/j.ijme.2014.06.006

Tompson, G., & Dass, P. (2000). Improving students' self-efficacy in strategic management: The relative impact of cases and simulations. *Simulation and Gaming, 31*(1), 22–41.

Torres-Toukoumidis, A., Robles-Bykbaev, V., Cajamarca, M., Romero-Rodríguez, L. M., Chaljub, J., & Salgado, J. P. (2019). Gamified platform framing for entrepreneur competencies. *Journal of Entrepreneurship Education, 22*(4), 1–9. Retrieved June 16, 2020, from https://www.abacademies.org/articles/gamified-platform-framing-for-entrepreneur-competencies-8360.html

Ulijn, J., Duill, M., & Robertson, S. (2004). Teaching business plan negotiation: Fostering entrepreneurship among business and engineering students. *Business Communication Quarterly, 67*(1), 41–57.

Van Eck, N. J., & Waltman, L. (2014). Visualizing bibliometric networks. In *Measuring scholarly impact* (pp. 285–320). Springer.

Wawer, M., Milosz, M., Muryjas, P., & Rzemieniak, M. (2010). Business simulation games in forming of students' entrepreneurship. *International Journal of Euro-Mediterranean Studies, 3*, 49–71.

Wu, Y., & Anderson, O. R. (2015). Technology-enhanced STEM (science, technology, engineering, and mathematics) education. *Journal of Computers in Education, 2*(3), 245–249. https://doi.org/10.1007/s40692-015-0041-2

Xu, X., Chen, X., Jia, F., Brown, S., Gong, Y., & Xu, Y. (2018). Supply chain finance: A systematic literature review and bibliometric analysis. *International Journal of Production Economics, 204*, 160–173.

Zhang, J., & Price, A. (2020). Developing the enterprise educators' mindset to change the teaching methodology: The case of Creating Entrepreneurial Outcomes (CEO) Programme. *Entrepreneurship Education, 3*(3), 1–23.

7

Understanding the Possibilities and Conditions for Instructor-AI Collaboration in Entrepreneurship Education

Mamun Ala, Mulyadi Robin, Tareq Rasul, and Danilo Wegner

Introduction

The principal aim of entrepreneurial education (EE) is to promote students' insights into commercial opportunities and develop their ability to act on them. As suggested by Jones and English (2004), EE should include instruction related to opportunity identification, commercialization of new ideas, creating new business ventures, organizing resources, and risk management. Traditionally business schools focus on disciplines such as management, marketing, accounting, finance, and information

---

M. Ala (✉) • M. Robin • T. Rasul
Australian Institute of Business, Adelaide, SA, Australia
e-mail: Mamun.Ala@aib.edu.au; Mulyadi.robin@aib.edu.au; tareq.rasul@aib.edu.au

D. Wegner
The University of Sydney, Camperdown, NSW, Australia
e-mail: danilo.lopomobeteto@sydney.edu.au

© The Author(s), under exclusive license to Springer Nature Switzerland AG 2022
D. Hyams-Ssekasi, N. Yasin (eds.), *Technology and Entrepreneurship Education*,
https://doi.org/10.1007/978-3-030-84292-5_7

systems. Generally, the intended learning outcomes (i.e. skills and competencies) of EE include creativity, innovation, industry-specific knowledge, decision-making, risk-taking, problem-solving, leadership qualities, ethics, and social responsibility. The graduates are expected to demonstrate the ability to improve the competitiveness of their firms through innovation and improving dynamic capabilities (Alvarez & Barney, 2000; Ibrahim & Vyakarnam, 2003; Pittaway & Cope, 2007). Essentially, EE is not in contradiction with the notion that the goal of education is also to inspire students to value ethics, integrity, and emotions and act in the best interest of the community.

Given that entrepreneurs need to work in an environment that is characterized by major economic changes, uncertainties, rapid technological advancements, and continuous changes in governing institutions, regulations, and rules, the importance of visionary entrepreneur has become important more than ever (Kuratko, 2005; Von Graevenitz et al., 2010; Fayolle, 2018). According to McMullen and Shepherd (2006), various elements of entrepreneurial action such as knowledge, motivation, and stimulus largely depend on the degree of perception of uncertainty and the readiness to bear uncertainty. Joseph Schumpeter (1883–1950), a pioneering scholar in the theory of competition and innovation, has argued that entrepreneurs should possess some distinct characteristics: they should be visionary and guided by intuition, and they should always seek out new technology, novel production processes, new consumer goods, new forms of organization, and new markets (Ibrahim & Vyakarnam, 2003; Schumpeter, 1934). This also indicates the importance of a dynamic approach in entrepreneurship education. Accordingly, this chapter presents an in-depth discussion on how to combine traditional pedagogy with novel technology such as artificial intelligence (AI) in helping students to develop their entrepreneurial vision, entrepreneurial intentions, and new-venture initiation.

In this chapter, we argue that an instructor-AI collaboration in EE, where possible, can be an optimal approach as it would allow students with different abilities to learn from instructors (e.g. through asking questions and clarifying misunderstanding) and at the same time apply sophisticated computer technology in supporting their creativity and exploration. AI is often viewed as an extended capability of a computer system to perform tasks in the intelligent domain. The concept of AI was coined in 1956 by John McCarthy in an academic conference in the United States (Buchanan, 2005). The evolution of this subject is phenomenal and fundamentally based on six other subject areas, namely natural language processing, knowledge representation, automated reasoning, machine learning, computer vision, and robotics (Russell, 1997).

The outline of the chapter is as follows. The next section examines whether the conventional entrepreneurial curriculum successfully contributes to the academic and social goals and meets the needs and expectations of students and society at large. It also presents a discussion on why the recent socio-cultural, technological, and pandemic-related changes, including mass digitalization, working remotely or working from home, asynchronicity, and global communities of practice, demand new approaches to enhance learners' experience and maximize the achievement of learning outcomes in entrepreneurship education. While computer systems with 'intelligence' are already performing many tasks that were commonly associated with humans, there are growing interests, concerns, and uncertainty regarding the wider application of AI in education. Accordingly, the chapter includes a discussion on the trends in AI adoption in entrepreneurship education and how AI is likely to reshape curriculums, teaching, and assessment, as well as its positive and negative impacts on teaching and learning. Further, this chapter explores the enormous potential of AI specifically in entrepreneurship education. A rich discussion is presented on the possibilities and conditions for an effective instructor-AI collaboration that can make an important contribution to all the key areas of teaching and learning in entrepreneurship education, such as the curriculum, instruction, assessment, and feedback. An instructor-AI collaboration has the potential to improve curriculums, pedagogical practices, learner motivation, and engagement, which are critical to achieving learning outcomes. The chapter concludes with the argument that while integrating AI in entrepreneurship education is capital intensive, it is worth investing in instructor-AI collaboration as it facilitates the progress of learners by providing them with customized learning support without unduly limiting individual choice.

Current Entrepreneurial Curriculum and the Need for New Approaches

Given the recognition of the importance and contribution of entrepreneurship to the broader society, it is not surprising that there is increasing interest in entrepreneurship education (Harmeling & Sarasvathy, 2013; Mwasalwiba, 2010; Piperopoulos & Dimov, 2015). Further, central to this is the perceived effectiveness of the practical impact that entrepreneurship education has in enhancing entrepreneurial competencies among students (Ahmed et al., 2020; Oftedal et al., 2018; Wu et al., 2019).

Over the last three decades, empirical research has demonstrated some support of the efficacy of entrepreneurship education programs in driving innovation, effectiveness, and competitive advantage across different contexts—nations, companies, and individuals (Byrne et al., 2014; Chaturvedi, 2021; Rauch & Hulsink, 2015; Santos et al., 2019). For example, there is a growing consensus that entrepreneurship is considered an important way to influence the competitiveness of any country or industry (Ratten & Jones, 2021a) and that it is an important skill set that can potentially make a positive difference in society (Ratten & Jones, 2021b). Further, prior research also indicates that entrepreneurship can be learned (Ahmed et al., 2020; Byrne et al., 2014; Neck & Corbett, 2018) and that it is globally recognized across cultures (Adekiya & Ibrahim, 2016; Delanoë-Gueguen & Fayolle, 2019; Fiore et al., 2019; Nabi et al., 2017; Wu et al., 2019).

The majority of the entrepreneurial curriculum has been designed around Jamieson's (1984) framework that aims to equip students with knowledge about entrepreneurship (raising awareness and providing an understanding of the basics of starting and running a new venture), developing students' practical skills required for entrepreneurship (e.g. identifying new business opportunities), and developing managerial skills in entrepreneurship (e.g. managing growth and new product development) (Fayolle & Gailly, 2015; Fiore et al., 2019; Foster & Lin, 2003). Recently, educators have also realized the value of teaching students through entrepreneurship—where educators utilize entrepreneurship education to develop broader skill sets for students like networking, adopting an entrepreneurial mindset, and value creation (Fiore et al., 2019; Hoppe et al., 2017; Matlay et al., 2010).

As such, the two modalities of the conventional entrepreneurship education curriculum are to foster an understanding of entrepreneurship as a construct at a philosophical level and to develop and train the skills required for successful entrepreneurship or entrepreneurial activities (Neck & Corbett, 2018; Newbery et al., 2018; Wu et al., 2019). This requires educators to address the ontological dimension of entrepreneurship—defining entrepreneurship, why it exists, and the roles of educators and participants when developing the entrepreneurial curriculum, as well as addressing the didactical dimension of "making the most appropriate choices with regard to a specific audience and the knowledge educators have about the participants in terms of objectives, contents, methods, and expected results" (Fayolle, 2018, p. 694).

Further, there are two approaches toward entrepreneurship education: a narrower view that focuses on the start-up context of entrepreneurship—the 'hard' skills associated with entrepreneurship such as identifying business opportunities, raising finances, and creating new ventures, among others (Jones & English, 2004; Neck & Corbett, 2018)—and the other, a broader perspective on developing enterprising behavior (Higgins et al., 2018; Newbery et al., 2018). While the two schools vary, they are complementary to a certain extent. As argued by Ratten (2020b, p. 757), the "primary goal of entrepreneurship education programs is to equip students with practical knowledge to act in an entrepreneurial manner" and thus necessitating to go beyond "what is entrepreneurship" toward developing both the hard and the soft skills associated with entrepreneurship (Foster & Lin, 2003; Jones et al., 2017).

Theoretically, these approaches provide a holistic educative approach that not only allows students to meet both academic and practical outcomes but also encourages educators to augment their curriculum based on the development stages of their target audience (Chaturvedi, 2021; Lewis & Henry, 2018). However, recent empirical evidence indicates that a conventional classroom-based approach to teaching has limited impact on enhancing entrepreneurial knowledge (Fayolle & Gailly, 2015; Oftedal et al., 2018; Rideout & Gray, 2013). Consequently, scholars have argued that "it is now accepted that traditional classroom teaching methods are not appropriate for entrepreneurship" (Lewis & Henry, 2018, p. 266).

Pedagogical Approaches

As the field of entrepreneurship education matures, we have seen an evolutionary shift in its pedagogical approach—from a teacher-centered and didactic approach in the 1980s, action-oriented teaching methods in the 1990s, and experiential learning and action research in the 2000s to a learner-centered period in the 2010s (Hägg & Gabrielsson, 2019; Lewis & Henry, 2018). These evolutionary shifts were arguably triggered by the growth of empirical research on entrepreneurship, as well as a response to the changing environment. In particular, scholars have raised the need to bridge the gap between the pedagogical approaches with the academic goals and practical outcomes, and addressing the needs of students and society at large (Ahmed et al., 2020; Fayolle, 2018; Oftedal et al., 2018). This necessitated a gradual shift from an approach that emphasizes acquiring knowledge to one that emphasizes the co-creation of knowledge (Hägg & Gabrielsson, 2019; Kirby, 2004). Further, recent theorizing argues for the need to develop a unified approach in entrepreneurship education to create value (Jones et al., 2020).

Hägg and Gabrielsson (2019) also found that the main educational perspective has shifted from mainly focusing on the instructor-centered approach in the 1980s to the learner, learning process, and the learning environment in the 1990s and 2000s and, finally, toward the interaction between the learner and broader society (see Table 7.1). The teaching methods have also evolved, from the use of the more traditional lectures and case studies in the 1980s, adopting action-oriented teaching methods in the 1990s, to experiential learning (action and reflection) in the 2000s, and adopting an experiential and constructivist perspective on learning in the 2010s (Hägg & Gabrielsson, 2019). These are consistent with the evolution in general business education, and the pedagogical approach shifted from how to teach about entrepreneurship to how entrepreneurship can be used to teach valuable life lessons beyond starting a new venture or being an entrepreneur (Harmeling & Sarasvathy,

Table 7.1 Evolution of pedagogy in research on entrepreneurship education

Time period	1980s: teacher-centered period	1990s: process-centered period	2000s: context-centered period	2000s: learner-centered period
Pedagogical development	Traditional (didactic) approach to learning	Centered on the process of learning	Added emphasis on real-world learning opportunities	Constructivist (progressive) approach to learning
Main educational perspective	Instructor and the content to be delivered	Learner and the learning process	Learning environment	Interaction between learner and (broader) society (responsibility)
Educational challenge	Deciding what should be included in entrepreneurship education	Understanding the target of entrepreneurship education	Incorporating hands-on experience in entrepreneurship education	Making assessments and measuring impact of entrepreneurship education

Source: Hägg and Gabrielsson (2019)

2013; Kyrö, 2018; Lewis & Henry, 2018). Essentially, a hallmark of the learner-centered period is the adoption of practical hands-on experiential learning.

However, the shift in pedagogical approach has also led to an increasingly complex entrepreneurial curriculum that necessitates a multidisciplinary approach (Nabi et al., 2017; Oosterbeek et al., 2010). Further, as Fayolle (2018) argues, "the 'client' of entrepreneurship education is the society in which it is embedded. It means that entrepreneurship learning and entrepreneurship outcomes should adequately meet the social and economic needs of all the stakeholders involved (pupils, students, families, organizations, and countries)". As such, the volatility brought about by the recent socio-cultural, technological, pandemic-related changes, including mass digitalization, working remotely or working from home, asynchronicity, and global communities of practice, demand new approaches to enhance learners' experience and maximize the achievement of learning outcomes in post-secondary entrepreneurship education.

COVID-19 and Entrepreneurship Education

Arguably one of the watershed moments in modern history, the unprecedented global impact of the COVID-19 pandemic not only has affected the economy and education in general but also makes the case for the relevance of entrepreneurship and entrepreneurship education across different contexts (Bacq & Lumpkin, 2020; Castro & Zermeño, 2020; Ratten, 2020a).

In line with previous researchers who theorize the importance of teaching for, in, and through entrepreneurship, both the hard and soft skills associated with entrepreneurship have been argued to be relevant in the aftermath of the COVID-19 pandemic. For example, Maritz et al. (2020) highlight the importance of individuals with entrepreneurial and growth mindsets in enabling businesses to pivot during the initial stages of the crisis through "creative recombination of competence and resources" (p. 2). Further, they argue that as the changes brought about by the COVID-19 pandemic are likely to act as external enablement for new venture creation, entrepreneurship will play a key role in kick-starting the economy.

This is true even for educators, who had to innovate under pressure and "repurpose their existing teaching methods to incorporate more digital technology" (Ratten, 2020b) as lockdowns necessitated a move toward online teaching (Liguori & Winkler, 2020). Further, as evidenced by social distancing requirements and extensive lockdowns around the world, students and educators alike were also required to work remotely and have been thrusted to a process of mass digitalization. This brings with it a different set of challenges for entrepreneurship educators in planning their curriculum.

Scholars also highlight the need for entrepreneurship educators to adapt to the new pedagogical approaches such as blended and asynchronous learning, which enables a mixture of both online and face-to-face modes, as well as fully online education (Maritz et al., 2020; Ratten & Jones, 2021a; Secundo et al., 2021). While these approaches have been around prior to the pandemic, Ratten (2020b, p.757) argues that there will be "a lasting legacy of online learning…requiring technology to play a pivotal role in entrepreneurship education".

Further, yet another challenge for entrepreneurship educators is replicating the rich campus experience that often is a feature among high-quality entrepreneurial curriculum, especially as experiential learning has become a key part of teaching entrepreneurship over the last decade or so (Hägg & Gabrielsson, 2019). Further, prior research on distance learning in entrepreneurship education posits that effective learning is contingent on open and frequent communication, as well as high-quality online collaboration and engagement among students (Ratten, 2020b; Secundo et al., 2021). As such, this has necessitated a re-design of courses designed for the physical classroom to satisfy online learning requirements. However, as COVID-19 brought about an accelerated shift to online teaching, many educators still cannot update their curriculum to incorporate technological advances that enable students to engage with authentic learning environments (Ratten, 2020b; Ratten & Jones, 2021b).

Scholars have argued that given the increasing number and growing influence of digital natives, the next evolution in entrepreneurship education would be the need to increase interaction with technology by introducing simulation games, augmented reality, and artificial intelligence to complement existing pedagogical approaches (Tkachenko et al., 2019). Krishnamurthy (2020) predicts that AI-enabled algorithms may replace the direct human interaction (of educators) in the learning process in the near future, citing an example of Jill Watson, an AI-based teaching assistant at Georgia Tech University who has been running since 2016.

Current Application of AI in Entrepreneurship Education

Whether AI will replace human creativity and imagination is still a matter of debate (Dreyfus, 2007); however, AI has somewhat exceeded human capabilities in terms of speed and accuracy in many areas (Jarrahi, 2018; Lemaignan et al., 2017). In a variety of industries, AI has been used to improve efficiency (Makridakis, 2017), which has also positively influenced the relevant economy to grow. The power of AI to analyze complex problems in a relatively short period has enabled this technology to create opportunities and address challenges of the education sector as well (Fox et al., 2018).

AI's impact on education and the knowledge base has been viewed from three perspectives (Wang et al., 2018):

- AI will take learners' social, cultural, and psychological conditions and their aspirations into account to design customized or individualized programs; therefore, learners' thinking and personality will be well aligned to better understand the concepts.
- AI will allow researchers and professionals to get a job done by using intelligent tools or systems; therefore, the researchers and professionals will have more time for imagination, exploration, and innovation.
- The progress of AI will enrich the existing knowledge base to encourage and motivate people to meet new targets for the betterment of society and mankind.

It is believed that in the future, with the help of AI, new, engaging, and effective educational modes will be explored and developed. This will also enable researchers and practitioners to increase the capacity of AI to be adapted to the requirements of other advanced technologies (Wang et al., 2018). In this sense, it is worth noting that AI has already been playing a critical role in entrepreneurship education. This is a relatively new stream of education that has a complicated pedagogic history (Pittaway & Cope, 2007) but has gained notable attention among researchers and practitioners because of its contribution to developing learners' entrepreneurial skills, competencies, and mindsets (Anggadwita et al., 2017). AI has been found to play a role in revitalizing learners' entrepreneurial awareness and discouraging constraints associated with entrepreneurial activities. According to Nuseir et al. (2020), for learners, AI can establish entrepreneurial cultures, infuse entrepreneurial behavior and mindsets, and educate them to become an independent enterprise. In the next section, it will be discussed in more detail how AI-based simulation technologies, namely serious games, have been used in entrepreneurship education.

It is not surprising that AI-based simulations increase learners' knowledge and skills and assist them, to a great extent, to meet the learning outcomes (Prensky, 2001). Serious games, which are AI-based simulations, focus on experiential learning that allows learners to run simulated ventures in mediated environments (Hindle, 2002; Low et al., 1994). How to deal with entrepreneurship in the simulated environment always makes academics and practitioners a little concerned. Based on three characteristics, namely fidelity, verification, and validity, serious games address these concerns (Feinstein & Cannon, 2002).

In a simulation, fidelity refers to the portion that looks real (Pegden et al., 1995). Fidelity at a moderate level has been found useful in serious games (Billhardt, 2004). It has been found in the literature that too much fidelity was not very useful to get the best of a simulated environment (Billhardt, 2004; Pegden et al., 1995). For entrepreneurship education in a simulated environment, learners need to get an adequate amount of challenge without irrelevant, detailed information within a specific time period (Hindle, 2002). Without too much fidelity, entrepreneurship learners feel more engaged and learn more in a mediated environment (Vogel et al., 2006). Low et al. (1994, p. 384) stated that "the ideal game will be rich enough to capture critical aspects of the entrepreneurial process, but sufficiently simple to minimize the danger of confounding factors".

In previous research, it has been found that technical reliability is critical for entrepreneurship education (Hindle, 2002). Verification is the second characteristic that ensures technical reliability in the serious games space to increase learners' engagement (Fox et al., 2018). In addition, the effective verification ability of simulated serious games increases learners' intuitiveness in the entrepreneurship education space (Low et al., 1994). The third characteristic is validation in assessing the simulated serious games in the entrepreneurship education space. It ensures that the simulated entrepreneurship environment correctly represents a situation that exists (Pegden et al., 1995). Uncertainty in the simulated reality should be balanced for the learners to measure their skills and effectiveness meaningfully (Fayolle, 2013).

As suggested by Low et al. (1994), simulated AI-based serious games increase learners' engagement in experiential learning and increase learners' skills through the learning-by-doing approach. An AI-based simulated environment makes virtual environments immersive to learners. The ability of serious games to solve complicated problems through feedback loops encourages learners' reflective learning process (Fox et al., 2018). In addition to complete simulated entrepreneurship education, mixed serious games, in which both simulations and real activities are combined, have gained popularity (Hindle, 2002). To make entrepreneurship education more effective, the importance of disruptive events and the ability to behave in disruptive ways in the AI-based simulated environment is crucial (Fox et al., 2018). To make the simulated serious games environment more meaningful, catastrophic failure needs to be included as well, which will teach the learners to deal with bankruptcy and insolvency. To sum up this section, with the advancement of technologies, entrepreneurship education has been particularly benefitted by virtual reality and AI-based simulated environments, and this discipline will continue to grow.

The Possibilities and Conditions for an Effective Instructor-AI Collaboration

It is beyond the scope of this chapter to present a detailed discussion of the technical side of AI. The existing AI technologies to support instructors and students include the following:

- *Virtual Classroom*—it can be accessed from anywhere in the world and enables teachers to easily manage a large class.
- *Interactive smart board*—it responds to user input and can play audio-visual media and proves opportunities for collaboration.
- *AI tutors*—they support students with customized instructions/resources, provide prompt answers to questions and feedback, and does not mind repeated questions.
- *Augmented reality*—AR enables learning through combining real and virtual worlds.
- *Virtual reality*—VR enables learning through providing virtual scenarios.
- *Simulation*—it mimics complex activities/scenarios in the real world.
- *Big data systems*—they provide actionable insights about students and learning activities/strategies.

Our primary aim is to present a framework for instructor-AI collaboration in a student-centered entrepreneur education environment (Fig. 7.1) where feedback is provided to students to support their learning. This framework can be used as a decision support tool for the use of AI in teaching and learning.

The framework provides insights into how to overcome the following limitations associated with traditional teaching and learning approaches used in entrepreneurship education:

- Teacher-centered didactic pedagogy (mainly focuses on theoretical and factual knowledge);
- Tendency to cover a large number of materials in the class;

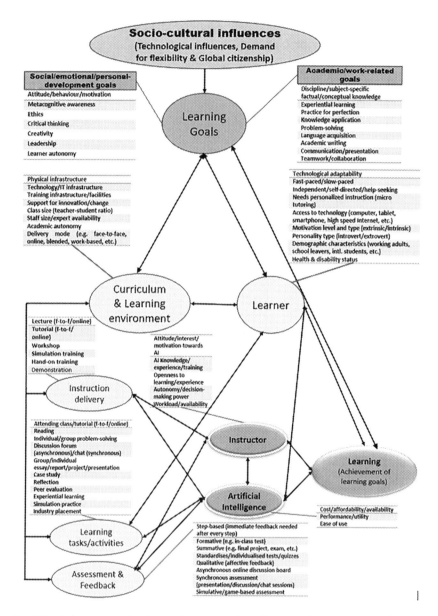

Fig. 7.1 A framework for instructor-AI collaboration in a student-centered entrepreneurship education

- Learners adopt a passive and compliant role (e.g. listening to lectures, memorizing facts/details, reading textbooks, completing homework, quizzes);
- Limited encouragement for asking questions and thinking critically;
- Excessive stress on competition and grades (turn the class into a group of disconnected individuals rather than a community of learners); and
- Ignorance of individual learner differences (students are considered as a homogenous group).

Figure 7.1 indicates how socio-cultural influences (e.g. technological changes, demand for flexibility, and global citizenship) shape the learning goals. While education can be seen through different perspectives, as a socio-cultural phenomenon (Rogoff, 1990; Vygotsky, 1978), education paves the way to social interactions that can take place between learners themselves or among learners and facilitators. Social interaction leads to a richer experience from a learner's point of view, as emphasized by Brown et al. (1989). A few of the (potential) driving factors include feelings of inclusion from shared experiences with peers; opportunities to reinforce learning through engaging in the discussion of learning materials; exposure to different points of view; and development of skills that lead to the establishment of robust argumentation. Education is also shaped by the way that society creates and adapts itself to changes in culture and norms; personal development is an act of enculturation (John-Steiner & Mahn, 1996). For instance, the advent of online learning can be traced back to technological innovations (mainly the Internet) that enabled the consumption of education through (and on) different devices, which itself can be deemed as a cultural change. Not only in terms of the way that one has access to education but also the contents of education depend on developments in the cultural dimension. It is important then to understand the main drivers of socio-cultural changes that impact how education takes place. It is out of the scope of this chapter to digress on all the possible agents and actors; however, we can reasonably select a few that are important insofar as understanding socio-cultural changes are concerned such as *technological changes*, *demand for flexibility*, and *global citizenship* (Palmer, 2011; Summit, 2013).

Technological changes are viewed as innovations that create the possibility for (potential) consumers to engage with products and services that otherwise not be possible. For example, Fintech—financial technology—enables access to financial services to those who have a mobile device but who, nonetheless, resides in a location not serviced by traditional banks. In terms of education, innovation would be the access and use of different platforms that could, for example, substitute traditional classroom instruction—think of different forms of online learning, consumed through a laptop, mobile, and so on and how these might vary to the extent that all learning was online or partially enabled or supported through online platforms. It is clear that technological changes affect culture—traditional ways of doing things are replaced, including in education. As for *demand for flexibility*, society is heading toward a direction where people are constantly moving, and constant change is rather the norm. We live in a more integrated world where parents share more responsibilities in the upbringing of their children, companies accept employees working remotely, and most of the society is endowed with devices that would allow professional objectives to be achieved in non-traditional ways, at a time that suits people's other commitments. By the same token, learners don't need to have a fixed schedule (e.g. classes on Mondays at 10 a.m.) to work toward a degree: flexibility is required, and technological changes allow for that. On the other hand, *global citizenship* refers to the fact that now we all live in a global village where information is ubiquitous and easily accessible. Most likely, we work/study with people that are native speakers of a language different than ours; our clothing is manufactured by different companies with supply chains in different parts of the globe; our customers are from abroad, and so are our students. Being in this global village requires us to stay attuned to what is happening elsewhere, which in itself demands flexibility (how and when can you communicate with your international customers?). This demands technological advances, allowing us to consume what we want, when we want, and how we want to receive it.

Our proposed framework (Fig. 7.1) is in line with the 'backward design' approach of curriculum design as the learning goals are foregrounded and used to guide decisions about instructional methods and assessment rather than outcomes which are driven by the selection and sequencing of content or a preferred instructional approach (Wiggins & McTighe, 2006). Backward design is in contrast with the textbook-dependent curriculum; it is shaped by constructivism and social constructivism and emphases that learners should be provided with opportunities to connect their previous knowledge, understanding, and experiences with new information obtained through interaction with others (e.g. instructors and peers) and the environment (Wiggins & McTighe, 2006; Childre et al., 2009).

Figure 7.1 lists two types of learning goals: (1) *academic goals* such as discipline/subject-specific factual knowledge/concept, experiential learning, practice for perfection, knowledge application, problem-solving, language acquisition, academic writing, communication/presentation and teamwork/collaboration and (2) *social, emotional, and self-development* goals such as attitude/behavior/motivation, metacognitive awareness, ethics, critical thinking, creativity, leadership, and learner autonomy. The framework also indicates that curriculum and learning environments differ in terms of physical infrastructure, technology/IT infrastructure, training infrastructure/facilities, support for innovation/change, class size (teacher-student ratio), staff size/expert availability, academic autonomy, and delivery mode (e.g. face-to-face, online, blended, and work-based) (Jara & Mohamad, 2007; Bates, 2015).

A student-centered curriculum and learning environment should take account of the characteristics of learners (Baeten et al., 2010; Struyven et al., 2010). Accordingly, to determine the scope and extent of AI that can be integrated into instruction delivery, learning tasks/activities, and assessment and feedback, Fig. 7.1 includes a list of learner characteristics such as technological adaptability, fast-paced/slow-paced, independent/self-directed/help-seeking, needs personalized instruction (micro-tutoring), access to technology (e.g. computer, tablet, smartphone, and high-speed Internet), motivation level and type (extrinsic/intrinsic), personality type (introvert/extrovert), demographic characteristics (e.g. working adults, school leavers, and international students), and health and disability status (Boyer et al., 2007; Davies & West, 2014; Kim et al., 2013; Vandewaetere & Clarebout, 2014; Vandewaetere et al., 2011; Truong, 2016). The framework also includes five types of instructor characteristics, namely attitude/interest/motivation toward AI, AI knowledge/experience/training, openness to learning/experience, autonomy/decision-making power, and workload/availability (Kim & Baylor, 2008; Schofield et al., 1990; Timms, 2016).

Next, to identify the context for using instructor-AI collaboration possibilities and approaches, three elements of the curriculum and learning environment need to be examined keeping in mind the learning goals such as (1) *instruction delivery modes* (e.g. lecture/tutorial (f-to-f/online), workshop, simulation training, hands-on training and demonstration); (2) *learning tasks/activities* (e.g. class/tutorial (f-to-f/online), reading, individual/group problem-solving, discussion forum (asynchronous)/chat (synchronous), group/individual essay/report/project/presentation, case study, reflection, peer evaluation, experiential learning, simulation practice, and industry placement); and (3) *assessment and feedback* (e.g. step-based—immediate feedback needed after every step), formative (e.g. in-class test), summative (e.g. final project and exam), standardized/individualized tests/quizzes, qualitative (e.g. affective feedback), asynchronous online discussion board, synchronous assessment (e.g. presentation/discussion/chat session), and simulative assessment/game-based assessment. Essentially, the choice of AI will depend on three factors such as cost/affordability/availability, performance/utility, and ease of use (McArthur et al., 2005; Roll & Wylie, 2016).

In the framework, 'Learning (Achievement of learning goals)' has been positioned at the end and also connected to the 'Learning goals' node, as there need to be feedback mechanisms to understand if the learning goals have been achieved and the necessary modification in learning goals, curriculum, and learning environment have not been achieved. Drawing from Kansanen and Meri (1999), it can be restated that learning is invisible as it takes place in the learner's mind; the teacher and the instructional processes can influence and facilitate learning, but the control of learning remains in the minds of the students.

To sum up, the best learning environment should not be completely controlled by instructors, students, or AI, rather there should be a purpose-based optimal mix of instruction by the teacher and the use of AI. For example, as suggested by McArthur et al. (2005), AI (e.g. ITS) can offer micro-tutoring and enables faster learning in subjects like mathematics through providing richer feedback such as accurate and detailed diagnosis of errors. This is particularly important when skills are embedded. In a large classroom, when teachers provide feedback only in the form of grades or marks, students might find it difficult at what point the error is made and what could have been done. On the other hand, AI cannot help students' higher-order thinking skills.

Conclusion

In this chapter, we have discussed in the context of entrepreneurship education that learning goals should go beyond just productivity, but include technological changes, demand for flexibility, and global citizenship. Also, it is inappropriate to think that AI's role is to reconceptualize education and replace instructors. Rather AI will challenge the contemporary teaching practices so that we can continuously improve. It will suggest what new things can be learned and the optimal ways to learn them. Therefore, we should allow AI to challenge us instead of resistance so that we can fine-tune current approaches and practices in teaching and learning. Essentially, the effective instructor-AI collaboration will require changes in curricula and new goals for teaching and learning. New materials should be added so that teachers can explore new methods of teaching and students can explore new methods of learning, new skills, and new outcomes. Accordingly, there is a need for new teaching practices and professional standards, and new ways to measure the skills and outcome. Importantly also, cooperation and coordination are needed among various actors including teachers, students, administrators, curricula experts, technology developers, teacher trainers, and educational standards authority.

References

Adekiya, A. A., & Ibrahim, F. (2016). Entrepreneurship intention among students. The antecedent role of culture and entrepreneurship training and development. *The International Journal of Management Education, 14*(2), 116–132. https://doi.org/10.1016/j.ijme.2016.03.001

Ahmed, T., Chandran, V., Klobas, J. E., Liñán, F., & Kokkalis, P. (2020). Entrepreneurship education programmes: How learning, inspiration, and resources affect intentions for new venture creation in a developing economy. *The International Journal of Management Education, 18*(1), 100327.

Alvarez, S. A., & Barney, J. B. (2000). Entrepreneurial capabilities: A resource-based view. In G. Meyer & K. Heppard (Eds.), *Entrepreneurship as strategy: Competing on the entrepreneurial edge* (pp. 63–81). Sage Publications.

Anggadwita, G., Luturlean, B. S., Ramadani, V., & Ratten, V. (2017). Sociocultural environments and emerging economy entrepreneurship. *Journal of Entrepreneurship in Emerging Economies, 9*(1), 85–96.

Bacq, S., & Lumpkin, G. (2020). Social entrepreneurship and COVID-19. *Journal of Management Studies, 58*, 285–288.

Baeten, M., Kyndt, E., Struyven, K., & Dochy, F. (2010). Using student-centred learning environments to stimulate deep approaches to learning: Factors encouraging or discouraging their effectiveness. *Educational Research Review, 5*(3), 243–260.

Bates, A. W. (2015). *Teaching in a digital age: Guidelines for designing teaching and learning*. Tony Bates Associates Ltd.

Billhardt, B. (2004). The promise of online simulations. *Chief Learning Officer, 3*(2), 38–41.

Boyer, K. E., Vouk, M. A., & Lester, J. C. (2007). The influence of learner characteristics on task-oriented tutorial dialogue. *Frontiers in Artificial Intelligence and Applications, 158*, 365.

Brown, J. S., Collins, A., & Duguid, P. (1989). Situated cognition and the culture of learning. *Educational Researcher, 18*(1), 32–42.

Buchanan, B. G. (2005). A (very) brief history of artificial intelligence. *AI Magazine, 26*(4), 53–53.

Byrne, J., Alain, F., & Toutain, O. (2014). Entrepreneurship education: What we know and what we need to know. In E. Chell & M. Karatas-ozkan (Eds.), *Handbook of research in small business and entrepreneurship*. Edward Elgar.

Castro, M. P., & Zermeño, M. G. G. (2020). Being an entrepreneur post-COVID-19–resilience in times of crisis: A systematic literature review. *Journal of Entrepreneurship in Emerging Economies, 13*(4), 721–746.

Chaturvedi, A. (2021). The dynamism of entrepreneurship education: The evolving role of an entrepreneurship educator in an emerging economy. In *Innovation in global entrepreneurship education*. Edward Elgar Publishing.

Childre, A., Sands, J. R., & Pope, S. T. (2009). Backward design: Targeting depth of understanding for all learners. *Teaching Exceptional Children, 41*(5), 6–14.

Davies, R. S., & West, R. E. (2014). Technology integration in schools. In *Handbook of research on educational communications and technology* (pp. 841–853). Springer.

Delanoë-Gueguen, S., & Fayolle, A. (2019). Crossing the entrepreneurial Rubicon: A longitudinal investigation. *Journal of Small Business Management, 57*(3), 1044–1065.

Dreyfus, H. L. (2007). Why Heideggerian AI failed and how fixing it would require making it more Heideggerian. *Philosophical Psychology, 20*(2), 247–268.

Fayolle, A. (2013). Personal views on the future of entrepreneurship education. *Entrepreneurship and Regional Development, 25*(7–8), 692–701.

Fayolle, A. (2018). Personal views on the future of entrepreneurship education. In *A research agenda for entrepreneurship education*. Edward Elgar Publishing.

Fayolle, A., & Gailly, B. (2015). The impact of entrepreneurship education on entrepreneurial attitudes and intention: Hysteresis and persistence. *Journal of Small Business Management, 53*(1), 75–93.

Feinstein, A. H., & Cannon, H. M. (2002). Constructs of simulation evaluation. *Simulation and Gaming, 33*(4), 425–440.

Fiore, E., Sansone, G., & Paolucci, E. (2019). Entrepreneurship education in a multidisciplinary environment: Evidence from an entrepreneurship programme held in Turin. *Administrative Sciences, 9*(1), 28.

Foster, J., & Lin, A. (2003). Individual differences in learning entrepreneurship and their implications for web-based instruction in e-business and e-commerce. *British Journal of Educational Technology, 34*(4), 455–465. https://doi.org/10.1111/1467-8535.00342

Fox, J., Pittaway, L., & Uzuegbunam, I. (2018). Simulations in entrepreneurship education: Serious games and learning through play. *Entrepreneurship Education and Pedagogy, 1*, 61–89.

Hägg, G., & Gabrielsson, J. (2019). A systematic literature review of the evolution of pedagogy in entrepreneurial education research. *International Journal of Entrepreneurial Behavior and Research, 26*(5), 829–861. https://doi.org/10.1108/IJEBR-04-2018-0272

Harmeling, S. S., & Sarasvathy, S. D. (2013). When contingency is a resource: Educating entrepreneurs in the Balkans, the Bronx, and beyond. *Entrepreneurship Theory and Practice, 37*(4), 713–744.

Higgins, D., Refai, D., Klapper, R., & Fayolle, A. (2018). *Promoting authentic learners through 'withness' Entrepreneurship Education.* Paper presented at ISBE Conference, November 2018, Birmingham, UK.

Hindle, K. (2002). A grounded theory for teaching entrepreneurship using simulation games. *Simulation and Gaming, 33*(2), 236–241.

Hoppe, M., Westerberg, M., & Leffler, E. (2017). Educational approaches to entrepreneurship in higher education. *Education + Training, 59*(7/8), 751–767. https://doi.org/10.1108/ET-12-2016-0177

Ibrahim, G., & Vyakarnam, S. (2003). Defining the role of the entrepreneur in economic thought: Limitations of mainstream economics. *Nottingham Business School Working Paper.*

Jamieson, I. (1984). Education for enterprise. In A. G. Watts & P. Moran (Eds.), *Schools and enterprise* (pp. 19–27). CRAC, Bellilnger.

Jara, M., & Mohamad, F. (2007). Pedagogical templates for e-learning. *WLE Centre Occasional Papers in Work-based Learning 2.* https://core.ac.uk/download/pdf/82439.pdf

Jarrahi, M. H. (2018). Artificial intelligence and the future of work: Human-AI symbiosis in organizational decision making. *Business Horizons, 61*(4), 577–586.

John-Steiner, V., & Mahn, H. (1996). Sociocultural approaches to learning and development: a Vygotskian framework. *Educational Psychologist, 31*(3–4), 191–206.

Jones, C., & English, J. (2004). A contemporary approach to entrepreneurship education. *Education and Training, 46*(8/9), 416–423.

Jones, C., Penaluna, K., & Penaluna, A. (2020). Value creation in entrepreneurial education: Towards a unified approach. *Education + Training, 63*(1), 101–113. https://doi.org/10.1108/ET-06-2020-0165

Jones, P., Pickernell, D., Fisher, R., & Netana, C. (2017). A tale of two universities: graduates perceived value of entrepreneurship education. *Education + Training, 59*, 689–705.

Kansanen, P., & Meri, M. (1999). The didactic relation in the teaching-studying-learning process. *Didaktik/Fachdidaktik as Science (-s) of the Teaching Profession, 2*(1), 107–116.

Kim, C., & Baylor, A. L. (2008). A virtual change agent: Motivating pre-service teachers to integrate technology in their future classrooms. *Journal of Educational Technology and Society, 11*(2), 309–321.

Kim, J., Lee, A., & Ryu, H. (2013). Personality and its effects on learning performance: Design guidelines for an adaptive e-learning system based on a user model. *International Journal of Industrial Ergonomics, 43*(5), 450–461.

Kirby, D. A. (2004). Entrepreneurship education: Can business schools meet the challenge? *Education + Training, 46*, 510–519.

Krishnamurthy, S. (2020). The future of business education: A commentary in the shadow of the Covid-19 pandemic. *Journal of Business Research, 117*, 1–5. https://doi.org/10.1016/j.jbusres.2020.05.034

Kuratko, D. F. (2005). The emergence of entrepreneurship education: Development, trends, and challenges. *Entrepreneurship Theory and Practice, 29*(5), 577–597.

Kyrö, P. (2018). The conceptual contribution of education to research on entrepreneurship education. In *A research agenda for entrepreneurship education*. Edward Elgar Publishing.

Lemaignan, S., Warnier, M., Sisbot, E. A., Clodic, A., & Alami, R. (2017). Artificial cognition for social human–robot interaction: An implementation. *Artificial Intelligence, 247*, 45–69.

Lewis, K., & Henry, C. (2018). A review of entrepreneurship education research. *Education + Training, 60*(3), 263–286. https://doi.org/10.1108/ET-12-2017-0189

Liguori, E., & Winkler, C. (2020). *From offline to online: Challenges and opportunities for entrepreneurship education following the COVID-19 pandemic*. SAGE Publications.

Low, M., Venkataraman, S., & Srivatsan, V. (1994). Developing an entrepreneurship game for teaching and research. *Simulation and Gaming, 25*(3), 383–401.

Makridakis, S. (2017). The forthcoming artificial intelligence (AI) revolution: Its impact on society and firms. *Futures, 90*, 46–60.

Maritz, A., Perenyi, A., de Waal, G., & Buck, C. (2020). Entrepreneurship as the unsung hero during the current COVID-19 economic crisis: Australian perspectives. *Sustainability, 12*(11), 4612.

Matlay, H., Bridge, S., Hegarty, C., & Porter, S. (2010). Rediscovering enterprise: Developing appropriate university entrepreneurship education. *Education + Training, 52*, 722–734.

McArthur, D., Lewis, M., & Bishary, M. (2005). The roles of artificial intelligence in education: Current progress and future prospects. *Journal of Educational Technology, 1*(4), 42–80.

McMullen, J. S., & Shepherd, D. A. (2006). Entrepreneurial action and the role of uncertainty in the theory of the entrepreneur. *Academy of Management Review, 31*(1), 132–152.

Mwasalwiba, E. S. (2010). Entrepreneurship education: A review of its objectives, teaching methods, and impact indicators. *Education + Training, 52*, 20–47.

Nabi, G., Liñán, F., Fayolle, A., Krueger, N., & Walmsley, A. (2017). The impact of entrepreneurship education in higher education: A systematic review and research agenda. *Academy of Management Learning and Education, 16*(2), 277–299.

Neck, H. M., & Corbett, A. C. (2018). The scholarship of teaching and learning entrepreneurship. *Entrepreneurship Education and Pedagogy, 1*(1), 8–41.

Newbery, R., Lean, J., Moizer, J., & Haddoud, M. (2018). Entrepreneurial identity formation during the initial entrepreneurial experience: The influence of simulation feedback and existing identity. *Journal of Business Research, 85*, 51–59.

Nuseir, M. T., Basheer, M. F., & Aljumah, A. (2020). Antecedents of entrepreneurial intentions in smart city of Neom Saudi Arabia: Does the entrepreneurial education on artificial intelligence matter? *Cogent Business and Management, 7*(1), 1825041.

Oftedal, E. M., Iakovleva, T. A., & Foss, L. (2018). University context matter. *Education+ Training, 60*, 873–890.

Oosterbeek, H., van Praag, M., & Ijsselstein, A. (2010). The impact of entrepreneurship education on entrepreneurship skills and motivation. *European Economic Review, 54*(3), 442–454. https://doi.org/10.1016/j.euroecorev.2009.08.002

Palmer, S. R. (2011). The lived experience of flexible education—theory, policy and practice. *Journal of University Teaching and Learning Practice, 8*(3), 1–16.

Pegden, C. D., Sadowski, R. P., & Shannon, R. E. (1995). *Introduction to simulation using SIMAN*. McGraw-Hill, Inc.

Piperopoulos, P., & Dimov, D. (2015). Burst bubbles or build steam? Entrepreneurship education, entrepreneurial self-efficacy, and entrepreneurial intentions. *Journal of Small Business Management, 53*(4), 970–985.

Pittaway, L., & Cope, J. (2007). Entrepreneurship education: A systematic review of the evidence. *International Small Business Journal, 25*(5), 479–510.

Prensky, M. (2001). Fun, play and games: What makes games engaging. *Digital Game-Based Learning, 5*(1), 5–31.

Ratten, V. (2020a). Coronavirus (covid-19) and entrepreneurship: Changing life and work landscape. *Journal of Small Business and Entrepreneurship, 32*(5), 503–516.

Ratten, V. (2020b). Coronavirus (Covid-19) and the entrepreneurship education community. *Journal of Enterprising Communities: People and Places in the Global Economy, 14*(5), 753–764. https://doi.org/10.1108/JEC-06-2020-0121

Ratten, V., & Jones, P. (2021a). Covid-19 and entrepreneurship education: Implications for advancing research and practice. *The International Journal of Management Education, 19*(1), 100432. https://doi.org/10.1016/j.ijme.2020.100432

Ratten, V., & Jones, P. (2021b). Entrepreneurship and management education: Exploring trends and gaps. *The International Journal of Management Education, 19*(1), 100431. https://doi.org/10.1016/j.ijme.2020.100431

Rauch, A., & Hulsink, W. (2015). Putting entrepreneurship education where the intention to act lies: An investigation into the impact of entrepreneurship education on entrepreneurial behavior. *Academy of Management Learning and Education, 14*(2), 187–204.

Rideout, E. C., & Gray, D. O. (2013). Does entrepreneurship education really work? A review and methodological critique of the empirical literature on the effects of university-based entrepreneurship education. *Journal of Small Business Management, 51*(3), 329–351.

Rogoff, B. (1990). *Apprenticeship in thinking.* Oxford University Press.

Roll, I., & Wylie, R. (2016). Evolution and revolution in artificial intelligence in education. *International Journal of Artificial Intelligence in Education, 26*(2), 582–599.

Russell, S. J. (1997). Rationality and intelligence. *Artificial Intelligence, 94*(1-2), 57–77.

Santos, S. C., Neumeyer, X., & Morris, M. H. (2019). Entrepreneurship education in a poverty context: An empowerment perspective. *Journal of Small Business Management, 57*, 6–32.

Schofield, J. W., Evans-Rhodes, D., & Huber, B. R. (1990). Artificial intelligence in the classroom: The impact of a computer-based tutor on teachers and students. *Social Science Computer Review, 8*(1), 24–41.

Schumpeter, J. A. (1934). *The theory of economic development.* Harvard University Press.

Secundo, G., Mele, G., Vecchio, P. D., Elia, G., Margherita, A., & Ndou, V. (2021). Threat or opportunity? A case study of digital-enabled redesign of entrepreneurship education in the COVID-19 emergency. *Technological Forecasting and Social Change, 166,* 120565. https://doi.org/10.1016/j.techfore.2020.120565

Struyven, K., Dochy, F., & Janssens, S. (2010). 'Teach as you preach': The effects of student-centred versus lecture-based teaching on student teachers' approaches to teaching. *European Journal of Teacher Education, 33*(1), 43–64.

Summit, J. (2013). Global citizenship demands new approaches to teaching and learning: AASCU's global challenges initiative. *Change, 45*(6), 51–57.

Timms, M. J. (2016). Letting artificial intelligence in education out of the box: Educational cobots and smart classrooms. *International Journal of Artificial Intelligence in Education, 26*(2), 701–712.

Tkachenko, V., Kuzior, A., & Kwilinski, A. (2019). Introduction of artificial intelligence tools into the training methods of entrepreneurship activities. *Journal of Entrepreneurship Education, 22*(6), 1–10.

Truong, H. M. (2016). Integrating learning styles and adaptive e-learning system: Current developments, problems and opportunities. *Computers in Human Behavior, 55,* 1185–1193.

Vandewaetere, M., & Clarebout, G. (2014). Advanced technologies for personalized learning, instruction, and performance. In *Handbook of research on educational communications and technology* (pp. 425–437). Springer.

Vandewaetere, M., Desmet, P., & Clarebout, G. (2011). The contribution of learner characteristics in the development of computer-based adaptive learning environments. *Computers in Human Behavior, 7*(1), 118–130.

Vogel, J. J., Vogel, D. S., Cannon-Bowers, J., Bowers, C. A., Muse, K., & Wright, M. (2006). Computer gaming and interactive simulations for learning: A meta-analysis. *Journal of Educational Computing Research, 34*(3), 229–243.

Von Graevenitz, G., Harhoff, D., & Weber, R. (2010). The effects of entrepreneurship education. *Journal of Economic Behavior and Organization, 76*(1), 90–112.

Vygotsky, L. S. (1978). *Mind in society: The development of higher psychological processes.* The MIT Press.

Wang, B., Liu, H., An, P., Li, Q., Li, K., Chen, L., Zhang, Q., Zhang, X., & Gu, S. (2018). Artificial intelligence and education. In D. Jin (Ed.), *Reconstructing our orders* (pp. 129–161). Springer.

Wiggins, G., & McTighe, J. (2006). *Understanding by design* (2nd ed.). Prentice Hall.

Wu, Y.-C. J., Wu, T., & Li, Y. (2019). Impact of using classroom response systems on students' entrepreneurship learning experience. *Computers in Human Behavior, 92*, 634–645.

8

Massive Open Online Courses and Entrepreneurship Education in Higher Education Institutions

Shamsa Al Shaqsi and Raihan Taqui Syed

Introduction

Entrepreneurship as a paradigm has received immense academic and political attention due to the various associated benefits, namely, that of stimulating innovation, invention, economic and socio-economic development. It has been a strong economic driving force in developing and developed nations—acting as a means of economic diversification, contributing to a nation's output and catalyzing the overall development of a country (Resei et al., 2018). From a socio-economic standpoint, it has become a solution to generating wealth, creating jobs, and enhancing the quality of life (Matlay, 2005). Joseph Schumpeter introduced the notion of Innovation

S. Al Shaqsi (✉) • R. T. Syed
Modern College of Business & Science, Muscat, Oman
e-mail: raihan@mcbs.edu.om

Economics in 1942 which adds to classic economic theory and even goes as far as to argue that entrepreneurship and innovation are at the heart of economic growth (Kuratko, 2005). This notion was further developed and drew greater attention in the 1980s by Paul Romer, stressing the importance of knowledge and investing in human capital—his theory specifically considered technological change and how this was brought about by entrepreneurs and researchers who responded to economic incentives. He theorized that anything which influences entrepreneurial effort such as that of fiscal and monetary policy, research findings, and particularly education would have a major and long-term effect on economic prospects (Jones, 2019). Due to the growing understanding of the economic contribution and significance of Entrepreneurship, the topic of it has been in common parlance with academics and policymakers globally (Stoica et al., 2020).

Entrepreneurship teaching programs have proliferated and Entrepreneurship Education (EE) has become a standard practice in secondary and higher education institutions globally (Kuratko, 2005). Although there have been studies that indicate a positive relationship between EE and entrepreneurial activity (Aparicio et al., 2019), EE holds notable complexities-if it is not pedagogically approached effectively it could cause substantial consequential dichotomy between pedagogy and practice. The question of whether entrepreneurship can be taught is obsolete; the more relevant question would rather be what and how it should be taught (Kuratko, 2005). In terms of *what* is to be taught, curricula varies. However, there are common skills to be acquired/competencies to be developed for the entrepreneur to apply theoretical knowledge gained into practice. Other than general management knowledge and competencies in areas such as that of general management, operations, finance, human resources, and marketing administration, among others, there are more specific entrepreneurial skills. These skills include developing a capacity for lateral thinking, creativity, and innovation; interpersonal skills/communication skills to deal with people as well as network effectively; and resilience, flexibility, and adaptability (Azim & Al-Kahtani, 2014).

The World Economic Forum report published in 2009, titled 'Educating the Next Wave of Entrepreneurs—Unlocking Entrepreneurial Capabilities to Meet the Global Challenges of the 21st Century', highlights that for effective pedagogy to take place, entrepreneurship education should focus on developing higher-order thinking skills, hands-on, project-based, multidisciplinary, and non-linear approaches. In terms of *how* entrepreneurship should be taught, the report mentions that the most effective curricula for entrepreneurship programs include activities that often take place outside the classroom setting alongside clear objectives tied to textbook topics with reflective and evaluative sessions. Activities can include but are not limited to stimulating games; interactive teamwork and group activities; action-oriented market research; creating business plans; and exposure to successful entrepreneurs. There was a specific emphasis on the use of technology in leveraging the experience through providing greater accessibility and scalability (Wilson et al., 2009). Therefore, the objective of this study is to determine the value and benefit of integrating different technological tools, specifically Massive Open Online Courses (MOOCs), into EE and provide evidence of successful integration within Higher Education Institutions (HEIs). The following sections of this chapter cover literature published on the integration of MOOCs into entrepreneurship education programs in HEIs, illustrate the present status, and propose future directions.

Digital Technology: Integration into Entrepreneurship Education

Online learning and the integration of technology in education was a response to the need and demand for a democratized education (Blayone et al., 2017). It has created an overall efficiency through time flexibility, scalability across geographical boundaries, accessibility, and an overall reduction in long-term costs/prices (Mondal et al., 2015). In doing so it provides access to a large pool of professionals as well as students. Within EE, the integration of technology has transformed the nature of academic and entrepreneurial processes as well as outcomes (Nambisan, 2017). Classrooms are moving toward blended learning where technology is used alongside brick-and-mortar education, thus providing instructors and students with easier, faster, and more affordable access to high-quality information, resources, and peers for learning and teaching (Vorbach et al., 2019). A study by Chen et al. (2013) stresses that EE cannot be taught through traditional linear teaching methods where the instructor dictates what is to be learned and the students follow/obey. Löbler (2006) states that the most effective way to teach and learn entrepreneurship is through student-directed learning where students develop their own learning goals; content to be covered should be derived from the problems and learning goals identified by the students. Emergent education technologies that can support this approach have proliferated rapidly such as that of the Internet of Things, game-based learning, and MOOCs.

Integration of MOOCs into Entrepreneurship Education

MOOCs have increased in popularity within EE providing a means to meet the high demand for entrepreneurship and business knowledge. It has improved the effectiveness of the innovative student-centered education required to transform theoretical entrepreneurs into practice (Akhmetshin et al., 2019). Online courses facilitate the development of entrepreneurial skills in ways that traditional teaching cannot—through having access to superlative material created by leading professionals, universities, and successful entrepreneurs globally as well as a platform to share experiences and exchange ideas (Resei et al., 2018). Traditional classroom approaches can now be replaced with modern digital learning methodologies using various media formats, such as videos, podcasts, webinars, recorded online presentations, interactive content, or online tutorials, and are effective in sharing large amounts of conceptual content (O'Flaherty & Phillips, 2015). MOOCs are an opportunity for broader collaboration and networking on a global scale, thus enriching the experience of EE which requires such exposure to develop the necessary skills and apply them. This is increasingly beneficial in the context of developing countries where EE is not often available or tuition fees are high: providing them with opportunities that they may not have received

8 Massive Open Online Courses and Entrepreneurship Education…

otherwise; this can also be an opportunity to collaborate and start-up businesses cross-nationally (Welsh & Dragusin, 2013).

MOOCs have been a more recent phenomenon emerging in the early 2000s as a disruptive educational technology providing a means of large-scale interactive participation and open access to courses online (Resei et al., 2018). MOOCs have been described as a successor to educational radio, with the ability for extended reach, being ubiquitous, and eliminating the sense of distance (Dousay & Janak, 2018). This idea was developed to address global education problems of access and affordability (Askeroth & Richardson, 2019). The emergence of MOOCs as a concept can be traced back to the early 2000s, where the idea was developed by Stephen Downes and George Siemens. They aimed to explore the possibility of creating a platform for mass interaction between a wide variety of participants through the use of online tools to attempt to uncap the potential traditional tools allowed (MUAT, 2021; Stevens, 2013). They developed the earliest official MOOC experience through the University of Manitoba, providing access to 25 students on campus and thousands more participated online (MUAT, 2021). Soon after, Peter Norvig and Sebastian Thrun of Stanford University offered an Artificial Intelligence (AI) course online which was successful in enrolling over 160,000 students (Rodriguez, 2012). Their success led to a partnership between them and Google birthing Udacity as a MOOC platform. Months later Stanford University launched its own MOOC Coursera. Within the following years, many more MOOCs were established; the number of online learners totaled 81 million students across 800 universities in 2018 (Shah, 2018) and has been growing since. Many of the Ivy League and Russell Group universities, such as Harvard, Oxford, and Massachusetts Institute of Technology (MIT), have capitalized by launching their MOOC platforms or providing courses on MOOCs. Successful known MOOC platforms include Coursera, Udacity, and edX of Harvard and MIT (Resei et al., 2018). MOOCs, in their varied formats, provide an 'opportunity to achieve educational objectives among a massive number of participants in informal contexts such as entrepreneurial culture' (Vorbach et al., 2019, p. 103).

The early and generic characteristics of MOOCs were identified as (1) being open to everyone (no entry requirements), (2) having no restriction in terms of the number of participants, and finally (3) being offered free of charge (Schulmeister, 2013). However, different branches of MOOCs have been developed which do not always match all three characteristics but are rather tailored to suit the context in which it is being used. The main two branches are that of xMOOCs and cMOOCs (Caulfield & Collier, 2013):

* xMOOCs: the 'x' stands for extended—extended traditional university courses. This format emphasizes broadcasting content with the traditional top-down/centralized/linear pedagogical approach (Dousay & Janak, 2018) where the instructor is the main provider of all information, goals are predefined, resources are chosen by the instructor, and there are focused set of topics (Yousef, 2015).
* cMOOCs: the 'c' stands for connectivism, reflected in its approach. This format—much like social constructivist approaches—prioritizes social interaction, collaboration, and peer influence while directly engaging with content (Rodriguez, 2012). Therefore, students become both teachers and learners (Dousay & Janak, 2018) where they can collaboratively create and share knowledge. Unlike xMOOCs, cMOOCs give students autonomy and control over their learning: learning is self-directed, in a decentralized approach where resources are open, goals are self-made, and topics are up for exploration (Yousef, 2015).

There are multiple variations of x and c MOOCs. Much like non-online/face-to-face learning, there are different ways to organize and structure learning within different approaches depending on the context in which the learning takes place (Brown, 2018, p. 136). Some of which go alongside brick-and-mortar education in the form of blended learning which can be described as bMOOCs (Mohsen, 2016) or that which take elements from both, revise and adapt approaches—such as aMOOCs (McCallum et al., 2013). There are also MOOCs being combined into larger programs such as nanodegrees and Micro Masters to act as a gateway into respective brick-and-mortar education—so only part of the learning occurs online and further education can take place in brick-and-mortar institutions which are not always free of charge (Read et al., 2018). This demonstrates how varied MOOC formats are, which are limited to not only the general overarching benefit of affordability and accessibility but also the flexibility that can meet the high demand for entrepreneurship and business knowledge suited to the context it is being taught in.

MOOCs and Their Utilization in Higher Education Institutions

Since the emergence of MOOCs in HEIs in the 2000s, the utilization and purposes have shifted. Brown (2018, p. 136) described the shift of utilization in HEI in three waves; starting with being used for marketing purposes to boost the institution's visibility and student enrolment. The next wave was used to provide and promote lifelong learning leveraged by the scalability of MOOCs on a local, international, and cross-institutional level. Finally, the third wave is to 'use MOOCs for credit recognition and continuing professional development pathways' (Brown, 2018, p. 136). Read et al. (2018) add that there are multiple uses for MOOCs other than institutional branding and marketing. Erasmus of the EU, UNESCO, and other institutions have targeted and invested in education projects that utilize MOOCs for this purpose such as that of the 'Moonliteproject'. Their goal was to provide training and higher education needed for social inclusion such as building language competencies and entrepreneurial skills (Moonliteproject, 2021). Although all of the aforementioned are important and beneficial utilization of MOOCs in higher education, one of the key takeaways of MOOCs is in creating an interface for all participants involved in teaching and learning to interact, receive feedback, and more importantly be observed to gain a better understanding of how to better conduct education. Thille (2017) states that great power can come from technology in education 'if we design technology-mediated learning environments properly, then every interaction a student makes is a

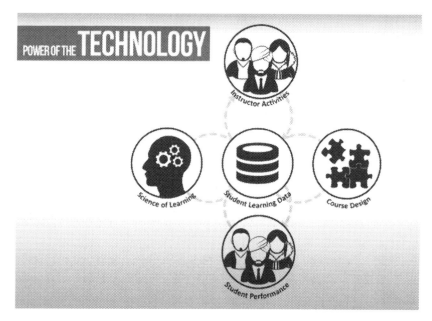

Fig. 8.1 Power of technology. (Source: (Thille, 2017) From Stanford Micro Lecture made available on YouTube)

piece of evidence about their learning [data analytics can be used] to provide critical feedback to the human actors in the education system' (See Fig. 8.1), thus creating a virtuous feedback loop that can refine learning and theory models (see Fig. 8.2). She stresses the importance of utilizing data collection as she described it as a means of finding ways to not only enhance and refine but revolutionize education.

Integration of MOOCs into HEIs

There are numerous approaches to integrate MOOCs into HEI which have been broken down by Brown (2018, p. 136) into three types which include the following:

- *Integration into formal learning*: Structured with an explicit goal to earn credit/certificates

8 Massive Open Online Courses and Entrepreneurship Education... 195

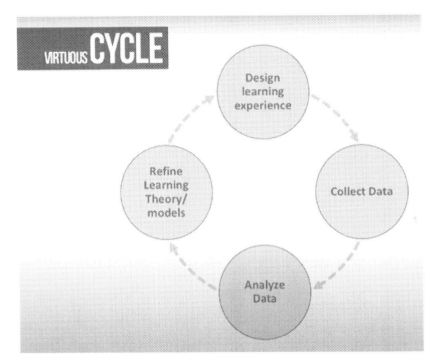

Fig. 8.2 Virtuous cycle of using data collection in education. (Source: (Thille, 2017) From Stanford Micro Lecture made available on YouTube)

- *Integration into formal blended learning*: Used alongside brick-and-mortar education with partial face-to-face interaction—this is used to supplement parts of formal courses
- *Integration into informal learning*: No intention of earning credits or certificates and therefore unnecessary to reach completion of the course

From a learner's perspective, the third type has been shown to elicit higher enrolment as it alleviates pressure and expectation of achievement and completion (Belanger & Thornton, 2012). From a teaching and learning perspective, online learning has enabled a push further away from the traditional didactic teaching approach where the instructor/teacher is the main source of information (Austin, 2013, p. 947). It moves closer to student-centered learning where the students, for the most part (especially in type 3 MOOCs), have the autonomy of choice and direction. This enables more time devoted to higher-order cognitive thinking skills in replacement of time spent transmitting content information and knowledge (Kuhn, 2007). Researchers and academics have noted better student participation and learning outcomes using open online course material (Wang & Zhu, 2019). Therefore, boosting enrolment rates and participation outcomes could also be the reasons and benefits of integrating MOOCs in HEIs.

There are various common generic challenges faced by MOOCs such as lack of support, lack of frequent feedback, and high dropout rates (Ejreaw & Drus, 2017; Read et al., 2018; Resei et al., 2018; Al Aljaraideh, 2019; Zulkifli et al., 2020). Finger and Capan (2014) also add the challenge of difficulties in assessing learning outcomes due to assessment design and lack of reliability in heavily relied upon peer assessment. Kinash (2013) found that 'a high proportion of surveyed employers have indicated that they would not consider graduates from university programs offered via MOOC…MOOCs often have no criteria and poorly developed prerequisites for student enrolment'. Although these challenges are valid in some cases, Brown (2018) argues against MOOCs being perceived as a single entity as it is overly simplistic. He compares it to perceiving all face-to-face teaching as the same in design quality, benefits, drawbacks, and outcomes. He cautions against narrow binary debates that make sweeping generalizations about the boon and bane of MOOCs. He implores that MOOCs ought to be studied and 'understood as a multi-faceted phenomenon'. Considering this argument, when referring to challenges, this chapter will specifically explore sustainability and monetization challenges that are faced by MOOCs. MOOCs have emerged as a disruptive technology with no initial or clear business model (Finger & Capan, 2014); it was introduced as open and free to learners. Read et al. (2018) fittingly remind their readers of the common dictum that nothing is free; 'there is no such thing as free, since someone, somewhere, somehow is paying the costs of whatever we do,' MOOCs included. They add that the initial focus of MOOCs was on developing the technology for open access and refining pedagogical factors, not financial ones. Substantial investment goes into constructing and delivering MOOCs—although the students faced no costs, the investors and donors do. This presented a long-term sustainability challenge which led many MOOCs to consider business models and how to monetize operations while still providing widespread access to education. This was done through paid certification, nanodegrees, and pathway courses. Certain MOOCs, for instance, Udacity, generate income from selling educational content and data to organizations, charging monthly or one-time fees for attending certain courses or freemiums, 'free access to introductory courses or proportions of their nanodegree' (Vicktor, 2021). Another consideration for MOOC providers is the justifications for funding or costs to replace others, such as raising brand awareness and marketing which could offset the investment cost of MOOCs and meeting social needs—which would attract governmental funding agencies (Read et al., 2018). Many MOOCs have been funded by governments/large non-profit organizations such as the Bill and Melinda Gates Foundation, the MacArthur Foundation, the National Science Foundation, and the American Council on Education (Kim, 2016).

Successful Integration of Entrepreneurship Education into MOOCs

This section will detail how the following HEIs have offered Entrepreneurship Education and integrated it onto MOOC platforms. The HEI examples will include Stanford University, MIT, and Harvard University.

MIT and Entrepreneurship Education

The following information about MIT entrepreneurship education was sourced from the report 'Entrepreneurship and Innovation at MIT Continuing Global Growth and Impact' (Roberts et al., 2015) as well as the MIT and edX websites. MIT initiated an entrepreneurship development program in the late 1990s which came with the launch of their MIT Entrepreneurship Center (Martin Trust Center for MIT Entrepreneurship). The program is based on three main principles: '(1)

Mens et Manus, (2) teams, no individuals, and (3) cross-disciplinary collaboration'. *Mens et Manus* is a Latin MIT motto that translates to Mind in Hand; this motto promotes an educational approach that connects theory to practice which is reflected in their entrepreneurship curricula that aim to transform entrepreneurial ideas into innovations/inventions in the marketplace. Instructors as well as leading professionals and successful entrepreneurs deliver content based on their research findings and experience. Due to their research that found teams were more likely to create successful businesses over solo entrepreneurship and complimentary cross-disciplinary teams set a foundation for greater achievement, MIT heavily enforced a constructivist approach where there is a focus on team-based learning with students from all five MIT schools working together on projects. The university also heavily invested in global initiatives for entrepreneurship education including their executive education course for starting up and developing companies. Their Regional Entrepreneurship Acceleration Program is a two-year education and training program that organizes and assembles global teams from different regions in cohorts that work together with the end goal of forming an enterprise that catalyzes their regions' economic growth. MIT has created a global network to establish open communication between all bodies involved in the program called 'MIT Reap Global Innovation Network (GIN)' (MIT REAP, 2021).

One of MIT's major global initiatives is the MITx 'Entrepreneurship 101' course offered on their MOOC platform edX. edX was founded in 2012 as a partnership between MIT and Harvard. Their platform and the course have enabled them to reach and access 100,000 entrepreneurs globally (the ones excelling are often invited to a boot camp on campus to further develop their ideas). This would be considered a type 3 MOOC experience, as previously defined by Brown (2018), where earning credit is an option but unnecessary to get access. However, it shifts into a type 1 MOOC where more formal learning takes place with an explicit goal to earn credit/certificates. This option is made available by opting to pay for Micro Masters. Due to the more formal nature of the credit courses, they are structured differently, where there is a more rigorous assessment with required evidence of identification, limited question attempts, and virtual proctoring (edX, 2020). The MOOC shifts to type 2 when the course enables learners to choose to use their Micro Masters as a pathway into a full master's program at MIT. This is where MOOCs would then be used as formal blended learning. Through MIT's combined entrepreneurship education initiatives, it was reported that MIT alumni have successfully started '30,000 active companies, creating 4.6 million jobs and generating $1.9 trillion in annual revenue' (Roberts et al., 2015). The universities have also been able to sustain edX through contributions, grants, and self-generated revenue from the credit and certificate pathways amounting to over $37 million in 2018 (Shah, 2020) which was a 48% increase in revenue from the previous year.

MIT also has *MIT Open Courseware* which makes all open course material available online to everyone. It has material from over 2500 courses with 500 million visitors (Open Courseware, 2021). This portal is completely free of charge and has ample material from various entrepreneurship courses taught over the years. Material ranges from lecture notes to assignment examples.

Harvard University Entrepreneurship Education

In 2003, a donation of $25 million by alumnus and venture capitalist Arthur Rock was invested in creating an Entrepreneurship Management program at Harvard University. The donation was used to create not only the program but also the Arthur Rock Center for Entrepreneurship. The Rock Center was the root of all Harvard Business School's entrepreneurial initiatives. The center provides education for entrepreneurship as well as having accelerator programs for early-stage startups which have the opportunity to pitch their ideas to investors on an organized Demo Day. Through their entrepreneurial initiatives, it was reported that Harvard has over 50% of its graduate startup businesses (Arthur Rock Accelerator, 2021).

Harvard University introduced its Entrepreneurship courses on MOOCs through HarvardX on edX as well as on their own independent MOOC platform Harvard Online. Their courses, for the most part, are structured like the MIT courses; however, they are less dynamic as they do not have as many options for students to choose from. Although free classes are made available with an option to pay for a certificate, pathway courses such as that of Micro Masters are unavailable. Therefore, in the case of Harvard University, there is no gateway into their institution through MOOCs or access to the accelerator through their platforms. The accelerator is only open to graduate students or alumni. They are making revenue and learners are benefitting from the online courses. However, access, in this case, is somewhat limited.

Stanford University and Entrepreneurship Education

Stanford University founded the Center for Entrepreneurship Studies (CES) in 1996 in response to the need for a greater understanding of challenges faced in the entrepreneurial environment. An integral component of Stanford Business School's ethos is to cultivate an 'entrepreneurial mindset that makes innovation and transformation possible' (GBS, 2021). This is reflected in the variety and volume of options made available to learn about entrepreneurship. The university has traditional face-to-face entrepreneurship programs and courses; online courses are provided through Stanford Online as well as other MOOC platforms and free resources as well as learning material openly accessible to the public about entrepreneurship. Furthermore, they have a Launchpad which is an accelerator and incubator program that runs in spring, launching businesses in 10 weeks. It was reported that since 2010, '60% of the Launchpad ventures are in business, $500 million has been raised in venture capital funding and thousands of new jobs have been created' (Launchpad, 2021). Launchpad is only made available internally (for Stanford University students and alumni). Although Stanford University found Coursera in 2012, which has since been monetized through providing paid certification options, many of their courses and programs, specifically that of entrepreneurship, are offered through Stanford Online (a platform to access all of Stanford University's online education opportunities). Unlike edX, Stanford Online has bifurcated the online experience into courses that require payment and provide a certification of achievement upon completion and free education. Under those two branches there are professional education opportunities that require payment and prerequisites and provide a certificate of achievement upon completion; Graduate Education which provides access to Stanford classes for payment; Master's Degrees which allow an individual to enroll in programs and courses that are both online and on-campus or fully online which again require payment and often prerequisites and graduates receive a degree; Custom Programs that are tailored for organizations and their needs where a group of 5–20 people can take the same courses and finally they have free open access courses which require no prerequisites. While MITx on edX built off the same course by either certification or pathway options and HarvardX provided options for certification, Stanford completely separated certified degree programs from free programs (they are different courses with different material). Most of their certified programs have two payment access plans: (1) Individual Plan, each course to be taken individually with 60-day access to all material or (2) an All-Access Plan, a package of all courses with 365-day access to all material. For instance, their Professional Program 'Stanford Innovation and Entrepreneurship Certificate' requires 10 courses to be completed for a certificate. The university has numerous separate free courses which are open to the public with no prerequisite requirements. It should be noted that Stanford has a *Nanodegree* but does not have pathway courses such as the MIT Micro Masters. There is also no connection or gateway between the MOOCs and accelerator/incubator programs. Another free entrepreneurship education initiative by Stanford is the Stanford eCorner which is a platform open to the public with free resources and learning material such as videos, podcasts, articles, and live online interviews with leading professionals and entrepreneurs on entrepreneurship. This platform is funded by Cisco as well as other donors.

Conclusion

This chapter encapsulates the plethora of value added to EE, students, and HEIs by using digital technology-specifically MOOCs. It enables larger scalability with broader access for students to be exposed to a talent pool of professionals and quality learning material. Due to this, MOOCS not only contribute to the democratization of education but also the overall improvement of the quality of education. More importantly MOOCS provide opportunity (an alternative route to the conventional brick-and-mortar education). For instance, it provided the opportunity to re-integrate school dropouts and push learners toward entrepreneurship (Welsh & Dragusin, 2013). Lower-priced and higher quality education provides those who may have otherwise not had access due to geographical location financial constraints or otherwise. Moreover, the creation of newly recognised certifications such as nanodegrees and Micro Masters can be used to not only secure job opportunities but also further advance their career growth. These opportunities cause a domino effect reducing unemployment and poverty levels, improving general quality of life and stimulating economic growth. The value-added from the HEIs perspective is that of scalability—having wider access to students from diverse backgrounds and creating new revenue streams from monetization of features. Furthermore, MOOCs are being used for marketing purposes to boost the institution's visibility and student enrolment (Brown, 2018). Although there are challenges highlighted in this chapter with regards to usage of MOOCS such as that of sustainability and engagement, it provides exemplars of successful cases in which the solution to those challenges have also been highlighted. Solutions such as monetization of features, providing more flexibility, and facilitating student-centered learning. On the research front, this study lays a foundation for further in-depth, primary research studies which could be carried out across different geographic regions to develop an inclusive understanding of MOOCs and Entrepreneurship Education in HEIs. Furthermore, this chapter and examples of success stories illustrated could be utilized as a reference by educators, policymakers, institutional heads, and governmental agencies.

References

Akhmetshin, E., Mueller, J., Chikunov, S., Fedchenko, E., & Pronskaya, O. (2019). Innovative technologies in entrepreneurship education: The case of European and Asian countries. *Journal of Entrepreneurship Education, 22*(1), 1–15.

Aljaraideh, Y. (2019). Massive open online learning (MOOC) benefits and challenges: A case study in Jordanian context. *International Journal of Instruction, 12*(4), 65–78.

Aparicio, G., Iturralde, T., & Maseda, A. (2019). Conceptual structure and perspectives on entrepreneurship education research: A bibliometric review. *European Research on Management and Business Economics, 25*(3), 105–113.

Arthur Rock Accelerator. (2021). Rock accelerator—entrepreneurship—Harvard Business School. Retrieved 25 March 2021, from https://entrepreneurship.hbs.edu/programs/mba/Pages/rock-accelerator.aspx

Askeroth, J., & Richardson, J. (2019). Instructor perceptions of quality learning in MOOCs they teach. *Online Learning, 23*(4), 135–159.

Austin, S. (2013). Didactic approaches. In *Encyclopedia of autism spectrum disorders* (p. 947). Springer.

Azim, M., & Al-Kahtani, A. (2014). Entrepreneurship education and training: A survey of literature. *Life Science Journal, 11*(1), 127–135.

Belanger, Y., & Thornton, J. (2012). Bioelectricity: A quantitative approach. Retrieved 28 March 2021, from https://dukespace.lib.duke.edu/dspace/bitstream/handle/10161/6216/Duke_Bioelectricity_MOOC_Fall2012.pdf

Blayone, T., van Oostveen, R., Barber, W., DiGiuseppe, M., & Childs, E. (2017). Democratizing digital learning: Theorizing the fully online learning community model. *International Journal of Educational Technology in Higher Education, 14*(1), 13.

Brown, M. (2018). *Why invest in MOOCs? Strategic institutional drivers* (pp. 6–9). EDATU.

Caulfield, M., & Collier, A. (2013). Rethinking Online Community in MOOCs Used for Blended Learning. Retrieved 24 March 2021, from https://er.educause.edu/articles/2013/10/rethinking-online-community-in-moocs-used-for-blended-learning

Chen, S., Hsiao, H., Chang, J., Chou, C., Chen, C., & Shen, C. (2013). Can the entrepreneurship course improve the entrepreneurial intentions of students? *International Entrepreneurship and Management Journal, 11*(3), 557–569.

Dousay, T., & Janak, E. (2018). All things considered: Educational radio as the first MOOCs. *Techtrends, 62*(6), 555–562.

edX. (2020). *2020 Impact Report*. Portland: edX. Retrieved from https://www.edx.org/assets/2020-impact-report-en.pdf

Ejreaw, A., & Drus, S. (2017). The challenges of massive open online courses (MOOC)—A preliminary review. *6th International Conference on Computing and Informatics*. Universiti Utara Malaysia, pp. 473–479.

Finger, G., & Capan, L. (2014). MOOCs and quality issues: A student perspective. In *ACEC 2014: Now it's personal* (pp. 1–12). Communique.
GBS. (2021). Center for Entrepreneurial Studies. Retrieved 23 March 2021, from https://www.gsb.stanford.edu/experience/about/centers-institutes/ces
Jones, C. (2019). Paul Romer: Ideas, Nonrivalry, and endogenous growth. *The Scandinavian Journal of Economics, 121*(3), 859–883.
Kim, S. (2016). MOOCs in Higher Education. *Virtual Learning, 1*(1), 1–17. https://doi.org/10.5772/66137
Kinash, S. (2013). MOOCing about MOOCs. *Educational Technology Solutions, 57*, 56–58.
Kuhn, D. (2007). Is direct instruction an answer to the right question? *Educational Psychologist, 42*(2), 109–113.
Kuratko, D. (2005). The emergence of entrepreneurship education: Development, trends, and challenges. *Entrepreneurship Theory and Practice, 29*(5), 577–597.
Launchpad. (2021). Launchpad. Retrieved 23 March 2021, from https://www.launchpad.stanford.edu/
Löbler, H. (2006). Learning entrepreneurship from a constructivist perspective. *Technology Analysis & Strategic Management, 18*(1), 19–38. https://doi.org/10.1080/09537320500520460
Matlay, H. (2005). Researching entrepreneurship and education: Part 1: What is entrepreneurship, and does it matter? *Education + Training, 47*(8), 665–677.
McCallum, C., Thomas, S., & Libarkin, J. (2013). *The AlphaMOOC: Building a massive open online course one graduate student at a time [Ebook]* (3rd ed., pp. 1–9). eLearning Papers.
MIT REAP. (2021). Accelerating inclusive economic growth and social progress. Retrieved 16 March 2021, from https://reap.mit.edu/
Mohsen, A. (2016). MOOCs integration in the formal education. *International Journal for Infonomics, 9*(3), 1–7.
Mondal, M., Bose, B., & Kumar, A. (2015). Entrepreneurship education through MOOCs for accelerated economic growth. *2015 IEEE 3Rd International Conference on MOOCs, Innovation and Technology in Education (MITE).*
Moonliteproject. (2021). MOONLITE—MOOCs for social inclusion and employability. Retrieved 20 March 2021 from, https://multinclude.eu/wp-content/uploads/sites/30/2019/08/MOONLITE-O5-Report.pdf
MUAT. (2021). A brief history of MOOCs. Retrieved 23 March 2021 from, shorturl.at/fiIEN

Nambisan, S. (2017). Digital entrepreneurship: Toward a digital technology perspective of entrepreneurship. *Entrepreneurship Theory and Practice, 41*(6), 1029–1055.

O'Flaherty, J., & Phillips, C. (2015). The use of flipped classrooms in higher education: A scoping review☆. *The Internet and Higher Education, 25*, 85–95.

OpenCourseWare. (2021). MIT OpenCourseWare. Retrieved 25 March 2021, from https://ocw.mit.edu/index.htm

Read, T., Barcena, E., & Sedano, B. (2018). *Current trends in MOOC research and applications* (pp. 10–14). EDATU.

Resei, C., Friedl, C., & Żur, A. (2018). MOOCs and entrepreneurship education-contributions, opportunities, and gaps. In *5th AIB-CEE Chapter Annual Conference* (pp. 151–166). Academy of AIB International Business.

Roberts, E., Murray, F., & Kim, D. (2015). *Entrepreneurship and innovation at MIT continuing global growth and impact.* Massachusetts Institute of Technology.

Rodriguez, O. (2012). MOOCS and the AI-Stanford like courses: Two successful and distinct course formats for massive open online courses. *European Journal of Open Communication.* Retrieved 23 March 2021 from, https://eric.ed.gov/?id=EJ982976

Schulmeister, R. (2013). *MOOCs, massive open online courses* (1st ed.). Waxman.

Shah, D. (2018). By The Numbers: MOOCS in 2017. Retrieved 20 March 2021, from https://www.classcentral.com/report/mooc-stats-2017/

Shah, D. (2020). EdX's 2020: Year in review-in 2020, edX attracted 10 million new users and became one of the world's top-1000 websites. Retrieved 23 March 2021 from, https://www.classcentral.com/report/edx-2020-review/

Stanford Center for Entrepreneurial Studies. (2021). About Center for Entrepreneurial Studies.

Stanford eCorner. (2021). Where entrepreneurs find inspiration ideas and research from Stanford University.

Stevens, V. (2013). What's with the MOOCs? *The Electronic Journal for English as a Second Language, 16*(4), 1–14.

Stoica, O., Roman, A., & Rusu, V. (2020). The Nexus between entrepreneurship and economic growth: A comparative analysis on groups of countries. *Sustainability, 12*(3), 1186.

Thille, C. (2017). *Stanford micro lecture: Online education with Candace Thille [Video].* YouTube.

Vicktor, S. (2021). The Udacity business model—How does Udacity work & make money? Retrieved 23 March 2021 from, shorturl.at/itOQU

Vorbach, S., Poandl, E., & Korajman, I. (2019). Digital entrepreneurship education—The role of MOOCs. *International Journal Of Engineering Pedagogy (IJEP), 9*(3), 99.

Wang, K., & Zhu, C. (2019). MOOC-based flipped learning in higher education: Students' participation, experience and learning performance. *International Journal of Educational Technology in Higher Education, 16*(1), 33.

Welsh, D., & Dragusin, M. (2013). The new generation of massive open online course (MOOCS) and entrepreneurship education. *Small Business Institute® Journal, 9*(1), 51–56.

Wilson, K., Vyakarnam, S., Volkmann, C., Mariotti, S., & Rabuzzi, D. (2009). Educating the next wave of entrepreneurs: Unlocking entrepreneurial capabilities to meet the global challenges of the 21st century. Retrieved 25 March 2021 from, http://ssrn.com/abstract=1392369. Electronic copy available at: http://ssrn.com/abstract=13923

Yousef, A. (2015). *Effective design of blended MOOC environments in higher education (MA)*. RWTH Aachen University.

Zulkifli, N., Hamzah, M., & Bashah, N. (2020). Challenges to teaching and learning using MOOC. *Creative Education, 11*(3), 197–205.

9

A Case-based Transformative Framework for Online Collaborative and International Entrepreneurship Education

Anne M. J. Smith, Julie Roberts, Mindy S. Kole, and Sonya Campbell-Perry

Introduction

Entrepreneurship education across continents using online technologies is indeed a pedagogical challenge, particularly since there is little evidence available to inform our understanding of how to design an entrepreneurial learning environment that effectively combines cultural diversity with online communication technologies (Jones, 2019).

Delivering entrepreneurship education in a turbulent world remains essential in the drive to support global entrepreneurship and cross-border

---

A. M. J. Smith (✉) • J. Roberts • S. Campbell-Perry
Glasgow Caledonian University, Glasgow, UK
e-mail: anne.smith@gcu.ac.uk; Julie.Roberts@gcu.ac.uk; sonya.campbellperry@gcu.ac.uk

M. S. Kole
SUNY Ulster, New York, NY, USA
e-mail: kolem@sunyulster.edu

© The Author(s), under exclusive license to Springer Nature Switzerland AG 2022
D. Hyams-Ssekasi, N. Yasin (eds.), *Technology and Entrepreneurship Education*,
https://doi.org/10.1007/978-3-030-84292-5_9

trade, with the development of entrepreneurial talent fundamental to growing and developing economies (Smith & Paton, 2011; Stadler & Smith, 2017; Liguori et al., 2018). Student exchange, internships and mentoring schemes are often ways of educating future talent, but in times of high costs, closed borders, low-level mobility and pandemics, how do we create an online international entrepreneurial learning environment that offers a global, inclusive and credible student experience? An online framework of entrepreneurial learning needs to be cost-effective and enabling; any framework must engage with cultural diversity, provide a mediating function and be inclusive; the framework should offer the experience of entrepreneurship and support learning and the framework should enable learning through activity. Kraus et al. (2018) emphasize the need for entrepreneurs to acquire advanced communication technologies, claiming they are a must for the twenty-first-century entrepreneur.

This chapter discusses an online entrepreneurial learning framework that utilizes a partner-based initiative called COIL, Collaborative Online International Learning (www.COIL.SUNY.edu), which enables students to engage in collaborative projects involving students in other countries. The learning design is informed by a tested and trialed project, presented in this chapter as a case study, detailing how entrepreneurship students embark on 'live' trade by importing and exporting products to partner teams in UK and USA that are then sold on campus. Students are required to research the overseas market opportunities; navigate logistics, Customs, and Excise; and then finally, sell the products at a profit. Underpinning project activity is students' ability to compare and contrast the process for importing/exporting goods in Scotland, the UK, and the USA; analyze what this comparison teaches them about conducting business with other nations; articulate factors for success in working with people from other cultures; adapt their plans and finally, learn to collaborate and communicate with peers from diverse cultures using various digital technologies including Web 2.0, that support dynamic and time-bound project activities (García-Morales et al., 2020; Kraus et al., 2018; Kalinowski et al., 2019). Our pedagogy was applied to a Module titled 'Employability, Enterprise and Entrepreneurship'; Learning Outcome 1 (LO1) required students to research a business opportunity. Students were encouraged to investigate many sources, collect and create data sets from market research and online reports. Learning Outcome 2 (LO2) required students to analyze data and determine venture viability and then prepare a trading plan. Thereafter Learning Outcome 3 (LO3) required business applications which in our case included collaborative efforts, negotiating business laws and regulations associated with exporting and importing goods for sale and then costing and pricing using different exchange rates.

Our case study informs a cost-effective, inclusive and transformative learning framework which explains how to engage in online and collaborative entrepreneurship with international partners. We continue by acknowledging the challenges and solutions facing international entrepreneurship education before presenting our case study. Thereafter, we analyze our pedagogical principles and examine the higher-level learning processes through a framework of transformative learning using digital communications.

International Entrepreneurship Education as a Solution to Global Challenges

In current and unpredictable times, it becomes less clear as to how we can collaborate with others across the globe. Pandemics, war and natural catastrophe can make it almost impossible for some to connect and thrive through entrepreneurship, despite the continued advancement in digital communications (García-Morales et al., 2020). Digitization is therefore not the answer on its own as the existence of other barriers to entrepreneurship remains equally problematic, such as the increasing challenges of cross-border movement caused by the Covid-19 pandemic, which is as important to economic sustainability, social development and the ability to evolve as an inclusive society sustainably and fairly (Smith et al., 2017). Of course, not all barriers are of governmental or natural design, with many difficulties created by individual paralysis, for example, time, money and perhaps even trepidation or lack of confidence to travel overseas. Finding solutions, ways of tackling these barriers are now of the utmost importance, as a global pandemic has demonstrated that despite limitations in physical travel and mobility, we can continue to do business as usual. Digitization and communication technologies have the potential to provide solutions to support international entrepreneurial education at a global level. However, we need to ascertain what we can do with these technologies, what we can design, what we can deliver and importantly we need to understand what students need to learn to become global entrepreneurs. In our case, technologies were specifically chosen, introduced at particular intervals, and selected for the facilitation of social and formal learning processes in international collaboration. In the first instance, we used Facebook as a social platform (a private page), because students were familiar with FB technology and the primary requirement was to make friends and build social relationships; second is a more formal and operational stage where Apps including Slack were used as planning and collaboration tools; and finally, an online secure Wiki in a Higher Educational Institution VLE enabled assessment. Students need time to socially develop, before launching a formal business team and then working under assessment. Ramos et al. (2018) acknowledge that students are social learners as well as visual thinkers and that technologies are now a rich classroom for innovation; therefore, we must go beyond any one educational design component and understand fully the dynamic of learning entrepreneurship online. Our work is based on combining technology with an inclusive approach to engaging with cultural differences, which creates an entrepreneurial learning environment for students to experience behavioral transformation around the phenomenon of *being* entrepreneurial (Fayolle & Kyro, 2008; Holcomb et al., 2009). This means considering entrepreneurial learning theory overlaid on educational processes, therefore integrating some entrepreneurial learning with the educational instructional design. Our instructional design harnesses digital communications, processes, groups design and cultural sensitivity.

Case Study

Context: Our Collaborative Online International Learning project (COIL) was embedded in a third-year university Entrepreneurship module at Glasgow Caledonian University (GCU), UK and an

Entrepreneurship module in SUNY Ulster, USA (Slimp et al. 2018). Entrepreneurship students from Glasgow Caledonian University (GCU) collaborated with students from SUNY Ulster University, part of the State University of New York. GCU is a Higher Education Institution in Glasgow, UK. SUNY Ulster is located in the Hudson Valley region of New York State in the USA. Both institutions serve local education markets, with many students never having traveled beyond their own country. Five teams were formed in each institution and then coupled, forming five cross-border collaboration groups with students from different backgrounds and cultures. Each coupling was tasked to collaborate and undertake a venturing project. We learned from a past COIL project, Kyoto University, Japan, (see McKinnon et al., 2015) the importance of both university partners assessing student performance. Module learning outcomes were embedded into the project and subsequently assessed.

- LO1: Demonstrate a developed understanding of opportunity recognition and market orientations in selected countries using complex and incomplete data from a range of sources.
- LO2: Develop and implement a viable and ethical business plan for a live trading venture.
- LO3: Apply and evaluate a range of venturing and business applications and processes.

Project Activity: Students were challenged to participate in a six-week 'live' transatlantic trading venture, which involved each team importing and exporting products to their partners between the USA and Scotland, UK, with partners' products being sold at the respective campus. To do this, students had to engage in direct communication, research types of products that would be desirable in each market, the USA and the UK. Operationally, they were required to learn and understand Customs and Excise and legal processes as well as gain insight into markets and consumer preferences. Students were then required to compare and contrast the process for importing/exporting goods in Scotland and the USA. Finally, students exported/imported the agreed products and sold them on campus.

Technologies: To enable the trading process, online technologies were harnessed; all had a different purpose and application. The project involved live synchronous Skype interactions at the start and end of the project.

Technology	Purpose
Skype	Collective and safe participation. Tutor-led, semi-formal
Facebook	Group-based, social and informal space, little tutor involvement
Slack	Project management, collaboration platform and communication tool, formal and group-based with tutor access and support
Google Docs	Collaboration semi-formal and a document exchange space not tutor monitored
VLE Wiki	Assessed, secure, tutor managed and group-based

Social learning and the degree to which students overcame initial participation fears were notable. Tensions between groups or individuals appeared on Facebook rather than Slack suggesting students harbored perceptions about formal and non-formal spaces, technology types and purposes. Facebook was utilized for asynchronous interactions to take place, enabling the students from each nation to work together at different times; there was a five-hour time zone difference. A Private group called 'Globalizing Entrepreneurship' meant students could arrange to connect in FB Messenger and the main class group to post photos, information and stories about their lives and communities, learn about each other. As the project unfolded, students moved away from Facebook and towards Slack for communication and collaboration. Channels were set up for each team, enabling students to share files within their conversations, although some did prefer Google Docs.

Cultural Diversity: At the start of the project, the initial exposure to diversity and culture was through live Skype to find out more about each other, the UK/US economy, the business community, family life, religion and geography of their respective countries. At the time of the project, there was big news, a new president was elected in the USA and the UK had just voted to leave the European Union in the Brexit vote. Students, therefore, had a lot of questions for each other. Despite being 'news aware', the lack of international travel by both student groups became clear; students had pre-conceived notions of national stereotypes.

Primarily based on media portrayal in films and news stories, questions on wearing a skirt (kilt), the Loch Ness Monster posed by SUNY Ulster students and questions on junk food and the use of legal use of firearms posed by GCU students were most common. Students had the opportunity to briefly introduce themselves on camera; most students appeared shy, perhaps awkward saying hello to the screen and their teams, with a few big characters shining through and receiving a round of applause from their peers.

Critical Incidents: Several critical incidents happened during the project. Students suggested posting their products from all the teams together, a form of cooperative business model, demonstrating responsible business community spirit by the students. However, it also meant some teams did not send all of their products—a lack of organization and poor collaboration. Products were tracked through Customs; GCU students had their package from the USA held in Customs for over a week and were required to pay additional Duty. During the project, students from both nations complained that their team members were not communicating frequently enough, with the main issue cited as being a lack of response to communications. Some 'influencers' did try different ways to engage their teammates, but a few students felt embarrassed to speak to someone they did not know. The result meant that some groups were not aware of the products their team was sending, so they set up a stand to sell a few 'surprise items'.

Mediation and Communication: A new 'Feedback Feedforward; communication record' for this COIL project was implemented. Learning from past projects informed a process where tutors proactively asked students to reflect each week on effective team communication. Unfortunately, high levels of frustration were often reported during this process. Each week the academic tutors provided feedback in a flip classroom intervention, and allowed each group to discuss their latest research, ideas and challenges and then receive feedback on continued progress. Tutor mediation involved supporting and advising students on the trading process then coaching students on ways to unpack and reframe their use of stereotypes. Additional interventions were required when written communications were misinterpreted, although it was noted that increased maturity and more developed non-cognitive skills enabled better cultural sensitivity (Opengart, 2018).

Learning Dynamics and Reflection: While the project's aim was for students to sell partners' products on campus for a profit, it did create a *buzz* and group competitiveness. However, resulting sales were not of the utmost importance for assessment, albeit students could have improved their creative selling strategies. Primary importance was *what students learned* and *how students captured their journey* including logging activities that took place, research and findings, analysis of information and minutes of the team meetings. GCU students were required to contribute to an online Wiki that was assessed using the three learning outcomes and was subsequently marked.

At the end of the project, a final live synchronous interaction using FB FaceTime brought the project to a close (Skype failed to connect). All students were issued with a voluntary, ethically approved, pre and post-project survey to collect feedback on their understanding before and after the project. This reflection captured what worked well or could be improved and detailed students' global perspectives, and their thoughts on newly acquired intercultural competencies. We built in a reflective component into our project specifically to trigger critical thinking about such interactions and articulate success factors for cross-cultural entrepreneurship.

The following section unpacks and analyses our pedagogical rationale and project design delivery; we continue by explaining how the sociopsychology of learning is coupled with cultural group behavior theory to create a pedagogical learning design that supports and enables a very complex learning environment—a Transformative Learning Framework for Online Collaborative Global Entrepreneurship Projects combining technology, culture and inclusiveness.

Pedagogical Rationale and Analysis

For our work, our approach to the delivery of entrepreneurial and enterprise education was essentially combining components of social learning theory and communication technologies (Bandura, 1977; Lewin,

1997; Franz & Nunn, 2009; Hyysalo, 2009; Smith & Campbell, 2012), with cultural sensitivity to create entrepreneurial learning experiences through online experiential and action research projects (Dickens & Watkins, 1999; Raelin, 1999: Grisoni, 2002: Kolb, 1984; Pittaway & Cope, 2007). With few exceptions, entrepreneurial learning is considered emergent and highly relevant to the understanding of entrepreneurial processes and opportunity recognition (Cope & Watts, 2000; Cope, 2005; Harrison & Leitch, 2005; Politis, 2005; Corbett, 2005; Erdélyi, 2010; Cope & Down, 2010). Processes and interactions dominate studies in entrepreneurial learning over time (Voudouris et al., 2011; Erdélyi, 2010, Jones, 2019). Yet, entrepreneurial learning is considered as a social process (Cope & Down, 2010), or in relation to knowledge and situated in the entrepreneurial process and opportunity recognition (Politis, 2005; Corbett, 2005; Ardichvili et al., 2003), all perspectives continue to attract interest with an extensive research agenda.

As part of our contribution to entrepreneurial education through entrepreneurial learning, we consider the higher-level processes associated with skills and behavioral development which are socio-psychological. These higher-level processes are transformative and stimulate individuals to reshape what they do, how they do it and why they take a particular action. Pedagogical design is through a social constructivist lens and the works of Vygotsky (1978). Essentially, Vygotsky (1978) considered that a teacher would provide architecture or scaffolding that guided and facilitated learning and that once the learning had progressed to the required place, there would be a fading of support. The teacher is seen as the *more knowledgeable other*, with this phenomenon referred to as *the Zone of Proximal Development* (ZPD); the space where others learn from more knowledgeable others (Vygotsky, 1978). In our case study, everyone had an opportunity to be the more *knowledgeable other* depending on what questions were being asked. Piaget's (1972) view differed from the idea that more cognitive awareness was required to learn, whereby prior knowledge is required, with cognitive development based on assimilations and information processing around existing known schemas and frameworks involving stages of development. In our case study, we can see that the cultural groups brought prior knowledge in the form of their cultural norms which they were able to share with the other groups. This led to the sharing of experiences from different cultures and learning through social communications using a variety of online Apps and platforms.

Vygotsky's (1978) and Piaget's (1972) work were conducted with study groups in childhood. Yet, together the contributions create the very platform of what is understood to be social constructivism. To create applicability across adult learning, further contributions in terms of socio-cultural learning concerning workplace learning was developed by Cox (2005), but most notably it was developed by Knowles et al. (2012) and Lave and Wenger (1991). We learn from Knowles et al. (2012) the significance of prior knowledge which shapes meaning and sense-making processes; why they have learned and what they have learned. Knowles et al. (2012) in addition, identify six principles relating to adult learning. These include a need to or a reason for learning; experience as a basis for learning; positioning 'self' in the management of learning; very importantly, relevance of learning; problem-centered learning; and finally, intrinsic motivations for learning; these principles were woven into our project through assessment. In a contrasting viewpoint, Piaget (1972) considers development in terms of static and transformational periods, suggesting that adaptive development is an underpinning that is capable of shifting mindsets, cultural and institutional. Transformational periods as Piaget (1972) describes are notable changes in knowledge and are therefore fundamental to moving from one state of knowledge to another state of knowing. Transformative learning is a high-level process that we attempt to create through an entrepreneurial learning environment and online projects, and it became evident during our reflective process when students could unpack the journey, good experiences, and challenging experiences.

Cope and Down (2010) integrated three specific domains of practice, identity and knowledge in their study to acknowledge the part played by social learning processes in the creation of transformative experiences. They recognize the centrality of practice and argue that a theory of entrepreneurial practice has not as yet been fully developed. Cope and Down (2010) stress the real-world element of entrepreneurial activity and look to their conceptual integrated framework as a way of depicting the process. They argue their integrative thinking demonstrates that cognition and social practice are inextricably linked. Furthermore, that inextricable linkage has become ever more complex through social media and ideas of online identity, an online persona transmitted and conferred through a plethora of online technologies that challenge the socio-psychological make-up of relationships and our real-world identity (Ramos et al., 2018). In this regard, students struggled with their online identity at the beginning; combined with a lack of confidence, they were reluctant to share any information as to who they were. However, as time went on they began to reveal themselves to their teammates, and the social process involved in learning became critical to pursue the project activities.

In summary, the higher-level processes and the concept of an online space where there are more *knowledgeable others* with prior knowledge *create* our learning environment. The nexus of culture, technology and inclusivity is a ZPD and is a socio-psychological melting pot of identity, culture, knowledge and learning as well as difference, shyness, conflict and disruption. We demonstrate and explain the construction of the learning environment through our framework in Fig. 9.1.

We consider technology, culture and inclusivity to be our main pedagogical pillars: culture because we are integrating national culture with communications and trade etiquette; technology because that is our means of communication and the act and process of doing business; and finally, inclusivity because students find ways through socialization to learn about each other, experience different identities, experience different thinking around etiquettes and explore socio-cultural engagement that enables cognitive and non-cognitive skill sets to be tested and stretched (Kurmanov et al., 2020). Social learning processes are a very significant feature of an online entrepreneurial learning environment, and to facilitate and manage the entrepreneurial learning space, it is relevant to consider the nature of collaboration, collaborators and group behavior (Curseu et al., 2018). This chapter continues with an examination of the three pillars—before considering the collaborative, group and social processes in detail and relation to the student experiences in the case study.

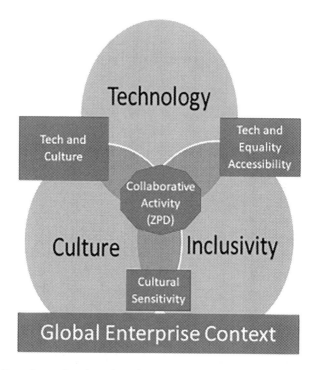

Fig. 9.1 Transformative learning framework for online collaborative global entrepreneurship projects

Communication Technologies, Cultural Sensitivity and Inclusivity

Next, to understand our design pillars in more depth, we examine the role of digital communications, culture in terms of interpretation before addressing the concept of educational inclusivity through accessibility.

The emergence of the digital business is, according to Kalinowski et al. (2019), notable, and they argue that business relies on digital skills more than ever before, as business growth requires a developed communication technology capability. In preparing entrepreneurship students our design presented them with an array of Apps and platforms to experience, test and trial: FB for social communication, Slack for project management capability and development and a Wiki platform for collaborative document production. García-Morales et al. (2020) note the use of Web 2 technologies as essential in supporting a pedagogical advancement for students. The Glasgow students were introduced to the idea of collaborative working in groups, encouraging contribution from all members which in turn encouraged an inclusive approach to their work, and the collaborative output was assessed. We harnessed the Wiki not only as a tool to reduce cultural barriers but also as one that created the opportunity for accessibility by all students, furthermore an effective method for increasing digital capability (Halcro & Smith, 2011). Through discovery from each other, the more knowlegdeable other—Vygotsky's (1978) Zone of Proximal Development—students learned how to use the raft of digital technologies, thus enhancing their digital competencies.

In their study, Kurmanov et al. (2020, p1.) examined digital competency development and suggest *an approach to developing digital entrepreneurship competencies model in the form of an ordered list of four groups: entrepreneurial competencies; digital competencies; communication, interpersonal and intercultural interaction; self-development and security competencies*. It holds that exposure to digital technologies will drive up competency levels and therefore capability. However, Kurmanov et al. (2020) note that communications, and more specifically effective communication, relies on an individual's ability to process information through application and self-awareness of non-cognitive and cognitive skills. Non-cognitive awareness includes emotions associated with frustrations often experienced while working in diverse and heterogeneous groups while cognitive skills support the student's capability to process information, understand and organize the task, solve the problem, and mediate—essential skills for collaborative group work. Collaborative groups are a highly effective method of learning according to Curseu et al. (2018) and use social learning theory to construct and design tasks (Bandura, 1977). We adopted Wiki as our collaboration tool and harnessed social interactions as part of the learning process. In essence, we increased cognitive self-awareness and social interaction during classroom sessions, encouraged awareness of difference as a feature of diversity, and encouraged groups to accommodate differences through mediation and resolution. Tutors were sensitive to students' non-cognitive (emotional) state. Stereotypes, learning about identity and mediation, fairness and inclusion featured in reflective discussions. At the undergraduate level, there are limitations to supporting student self-awareness in terms of non-cognitive and cognitive skills development; therefore, we are dealing with complex group behaviors which require reflective periods and in-class management from tutors. Diversity management in-class during projects of this nature requires transparency, an in-class task set up, task reflection again in-class, and a monitoring system of social interaction establishing a mediating role for culture and sub-cultures in the real world of the entrepreneurial venture (Dahanayake et al., 2018). We arrive full circle and our socio-psychological learning design which provides the vehicle for entrepreneurship education, students learn how to trade across cultures, import-export, market, and sell products in an inclusive and accessible environment.

In summary, we created an online international entrepreneurial learning environment that offers a global, inclusive and credible student experience. The project design was complex and conceived from socio-psychological principles. Three pillars of the learning framework *culture –technology –inclusivity* form a nexus creating a situated collaborative learning space, a Zone of Proximal Development, requiring in-class diversity management and a nurturing approach to cognitive and non-cognitive skills development.

Conclusion

Creating an online international entrepreneurial learning environment that offers a global, inclusive, and credible student experience is challenging but possible. With decades of knowledge around experiential learning (Dickens & Watkins, 1999; Raelin, 1999: Grisoni, 2002; Kolb, 1984; Pittaway & Cope, 2007), combined with recent developments in digital communications and cultural learning (García-Morales et al., 2020; Kraus et al., 2018; Kalinowski et al., 2019), the team conceived an approach providing an online international entrepreneurial learning environment. A low-cost solution, accessible and inclusive, with a method that enabled the basics of importing and exporting traded goods, was experienced, providing a situated environment, a nexus of *culture –technology –inclusivity*. Involving an overseas partner through the partner-based initiative called COIL, Collaborative Online International Learning (www.COIL.SUNY.edu), our transatlantic team designed and implemented learning for third-year entrepreneurship students. Our pedagogical rationale was validated using the fundamental philosophy of social constructivism and Vygotsky's (1978) *more knowledgeable other*, the Zone of Proximal Development. This project created a ZPD in the nexus space, in-class and online students learned from each other (and tutors) about how to trade, how to work and manage the technologies; they learned about frustration; they learned about mediation; and they experienced social interaction forming friendships across cultures. Simultaneously, module learning outcomes were achieved, notably LO1 through exposure to opportunities across nations, different sources of information, and different consumer behavior across multi-national markets. Meeting LO2 became exciting, in real-time, when Customs provided a real-world intervention with delays and duty payments, and finally, LO3 was met through enhanced insights, differences, and similarities, and how international venture creation must navigate laws and business regulation as well as interact through the lens of multi-national cultures.

Collaboration presents multiple challenges; it is a socio-psychological learning environment where diversity management is required. What is exciting are the many possibilities for application of this learning design, for example, different groups using multi-cultural teams, deeper analysis of the development of non-cognitive and cognitive skills, and there is scope to work with disadvantaged groups. It follows that further research into the transferability of COIL-based teaching-learning and learning processes would benefit groups of students who have experienced financial and physical barriers preventing them from connecting and collaborating with students from different cultures and global nations. The global environment is extraordinary, and in post-pandemic times, digital capability, cultural sensitivity, and accessibility are the enablers to allow an entrepreneurial business to flourish in the online world.

References

Ardichvili, A., Cardozo, R., & Ray, S. (2003). A theory of entrepreneurial opportunity identification and development. *Journal of Business Venturing, [Online] 18*(1), 105–123. https://doi.org/10.1016/s0883-9026(01)00068-4

Bandura, A. (1977). *Social learning theory.* Prentice-Hall.

Cope, J. (2005). Toward a dynamic learning perspective of entrepreneurship. *Entrepreneurship: Theory and Practice, 29*(4), 373–397.

Cope, J., & Down, S. (2010). *I think therefore I learn? Entrepreneurial cognition, learning and knowing in practice.* Presented at Babson College Entrepreneurship Research Conference, Lausanne, Switzerland, June 9–12. https://ssrn.com/abstract=2478694

Cope, J., & Watts, G. (2000). Learning by doing – An exploration of experience, critical incidents and reflection in entrepreneurial learning. *International Journal of Entrepreneurial Behaviour and Research, 6*(3), 104–124.

Corbett, A. C. (2005). Experiential learning within the process of opportunity identification and exploitation. *Entrepreneurship Theory and Practice, 29*(4), 473–491.

Cox, R. (2005). Adult learners learning from experience: Using a reflective practice model to support work-based learning. *Reflective Practice, 6*(4), 459–472.

Curseu, P. L., Chappin, M. M. H., & Jansen, R. J. G. (2018). Gender diversity and motivation in collaborative learning groups: The mediating role of group discussion quality. *Social Psychology of Education, 21*(2), 289–302. https://doi.org/10.1007/s11218-017-9419-5

Dahanayake, P., Rajendran, D., Selvarajah, C., & Ballantyne, G. (2018). Justice and fairness in the workplace: A trajectory for managing diversity. *Equality, Diversity and Inclusion: An International Journal, 37*(5), 470–490. https://doi.org/10.1108/EDI-11-2016-0105

Dickens, L., & Watkins, K. (1999). Action research: Rethinking Lewin. *Management Learning, 30*(2), 127–140.

Erdélyi, P. (2010). *The matter of entrepreneurial learning: A literature review.* In OLKC (International Conference on Organisational Learning, Knowledge and Capabilities), Northeastern University, Boston, MA, 3–6 June 2010.

Fayolle, A., & Kyro, P. (2008). *The dynamics between entrepreneurship, environment and education: European research in education.* Edward Elgar.

Franz, M., & Nunn, C. L. (2009). Rapid evolution of social learning. *Journal of Evolutionary Biology, 22*(9), 1914–1922.

García-Morales, V. J., Martín-Rojas, R., & Garde-Sánchez, R. (2020). How to encourage social entrepreneurship action? Using web 2.0 technologies in higher education institutions. *Journal of Business Ethics, 161*(2), 329–350.

Grisoni, L. (2002). Theory and practice in experiential learning in higher education. *International Journal of Management Education, 2*(2), 40–52.

Halcro, K., & Smith, A. M. J. (2011). Wikis: Building learning experiences between academe and businesses. *Reflective Practice, 12*(5), 679–693.

Harrison, R. T., & Leitch, C. M. (2005). Entrepreneurial learning: Researching the interface between learning and the entrepreneurial context. *Entrepreneurship Theory and Practice, 29*(4), 351–371.

Holcomb, T. R., Ireland, R. A., Holmes, R. M., Jr., & Hitt, M. A. (2009). Architecture of entrepreneurial learning: Exploring the link among heuristics, knowledge, and action. *Entrepreneurship Theory and Practice, 33*(1), 167–192.

Hyysalo, S. (2009). Learning for learning: Economy and social learning. *Research Policy, 38*(5), 726–735.

Jones, C. (2019). A signature pedagogy for entrepreneurship education. *Journal of Small Business and Enterprise Development, 26*(2), 243–254. https://doi.org/10.1108/JSBED-03-2018-0080

Kalinowski, T. B., Głodek, P., Valls, M. P., Solomon, A., Fornaci, M. L., Limonta, T., Atanasovska, I., UribeToril, J., & Real, J. R. (2019). *Building next generation of globally responsible digital entrepreneurs*. DIGI-GRENT.

Knowles, M. S., Holton, E. F., & Swanson, R. A. (2012). *The adult learner: The definitive classic in adult education and human resource development* (6th ed.). Elsevier.

Kolb, D. A. (1984). *Experiential learning: Experience as the sources of learning and development*. Prentice-Hall.

Kraus, S., Palmer, C., Kailer, N., Kallinger, F. L., & Spitzer, J. (2018). Digital entrepreneurship: A research agenda on new business models for the twenty-first century. *International Journal of Entrepreneurial Behavior & Research*.

Kurmanov, N., Aliyeva, Z., Kabdullina, G., & Mutaliyeva, L. (2020). Digital entrepreneurship competencies among students: Methodological aspects of the maturity level and development program making. *Journal of Entrepreneurship Education, 23*(2), 1–11.

Lave, J., & Wenger, E. (1991). *Situated learning*. Cambridge University Press.

Lewin, K. (1997). *Resolving social conflicts: Field theory in social science*. American Psychological Association.

Liguori, E., Winkler, C., Winkel, D., van Gelderen, M. W., Marvel, M., Keels, K., & Noyes, E. (2018). The entrepreneurship education imperative: Introducing EE&P. *Entrepreneurship Education & Pedagogy, 1*(1), 5–7. https://doi.org/10.1177/2515127417737290

McKinnon, S., Smith, A. M. J., & Thomson, J. (2015). Window to the world: Using technology to internationalise entrepreneurship education. *Journal of Perspectives in Applied Academic Practice, 3*(3), 15–23.

Opengart, R. (2018). Short-term study abroad and the development of intercultural maturity. *Journal of International Education in Business, 11*(2), 241–255.

Piaget, J. (1972). *Psychology and epistemology: Towards a theory of knowledge.* Penguin Press.

Pittaway, L., & Cope, J. (2007). Simulating experiential learning: Integrating experiential and collaborative approaches to learning. *Management Learning, 38*(2), 211–233.

Politis, D. (2005). The process of entrepreneurial learning: A conceptual model. *Entrepreneurship Theory and Practice, 29*(4), 399–424.

Raelin, J. A. (1999). The design of the action project in work–based learning. *Human Resource Planning, 22*(3), 12–28.

Ramos, J. L., de Jong, F., Maaike, V., Espadeiro, R., Cattaneo, A., Leijen, A., Laiten-Vaananen, S., Burns, E., Bent, M., Tiebosh, N., & Bel, H. (2018). *The video supported collaborative learning knowledge alliance Erasmus+ (EU)-project.* Knowledge Building Summer Institute.

Slimp, M., Smith, A. M. J., Thomson, J., Windle, H., & Kole, M. (2018). *Case study: SUNY Ulster and Glasgow Caledonian University COIL published in how the internet of things is changing higher education, our classrooms, and our students.* Rowman & Littlefield Publishers.

Smith, A. M. J., & Campbell, S. (2012). Exploring a 'middle ground': Engagement with students in a social learning environment. *Electronic Journal of e-learning, 10*(3), 342–350.

Smith, A. M. J., Jones, D., Scott, B., & Stadler, A. (2017). Designing and delivering inclusive and accessible entrepreneurship education. In P. Jones, G. Maas, & L. Pittaway (Eds.), *Entrepreneurship education: New perspectives on research, policy & practice.* Emerald Publishing.

Smith, A. M. J., & Paton, R. (2011). Delivering global enterprise: International and collaborative entrepreneurship in education. *International Journal of Entrepreneurial Behaviour & Research, 17*(1), 104–118.

Stadler, A., & Smith, A. M. J. (2017). Entrepreneurship in vocational education: A case study of the Brazilian context in Industry and Higher Education. *Industry and Higher Education, 29*(3), 185–196.

Vygotsky, L. S. (1978). *Mind in society: The development of higher psychological processes*. Ed. M. Cole, V. John-Steiner, S. Scribner, & E. Souberman. : Harvard University Press.

10

Digital Tools and Experiential Learning in Science-Based Entrepreneurship Education

Marlous Blankesteijn and Jorick Houtkamp

Introduction

This chapter assesses the use of digital tools in experiential learning in entrepreneurship education, namely science-based entrepreneurship education (SBEE) (Blankesteijn et al., 2020). SBEE refers to entrepreneurship education in science faculties, whereby fundamental scientific research in physics and chemistry is a vantage point to develop entrepreneurial activities for and with students. SBEE requires students to learn how to cross the valley of death between fundamental,

---

M. Blankesteijn (✉)
Faculty of Science, Section Science, Business & Innovation, Vrije Universiteit Amsterdam, Amsterdam, The Netherlands
e-mail: m.l.blankesteijn@vu.nl

J. Houtkamp
Department of Chemistry, Section Science, Business & Innovation and Section Innovations in Human Health & Life Sciences, Vrije Universiteit Amsterdam, Amsterdam, The Netherlands
e-mail: J.Houtkamp@vu.nl

© The Author(s), under exclusive license to Springer Nature Switzerland AG 2022
D. Hyams-Ssekasi, N. Yasin (eds.), *Technology and Entrepreneurship Education*,
https://doi.org/10.1007/978-3-030-84292-5_10

natural science, and application on the one, and commercialization on the other hand (Retra et al., 2016). A crucial component in teaching SBEE is that students experience the challenges in transferring science to the market and society, in order to create commercial and social value. These challenges are referred to by the "the valley of death" between science and innovation. The valley of death is a metaphor developed by Barr et al. (2017) in order to conceptually capture the gap between research and commercialization of research, between researchers and entrepreneurs and investors.

The main task of academic education has for a long time been conceptualized as a preparation for students for a research career only. SBEE recognizes that the "first mission" of a university is providing a training in scientific research. However, especially with regard to entrepreneurship education, permanent interaction with professionals outside academia is important as well. Entrepreneurial action needs to be grounded on scientific evidence that contributes to building support for upscaling the technology and to cross the valley of death, thus combining the research task with the aims of entrepreneurship education. To achieve these aims SBEE programs draw upon experiential learning to facilitate entrepreneurial engagement and to enable meaningful student development, while acknowledging also the rich potential of such experiences to be translated into academic contributions on how to cross the valley of death, such as scientific publications.

Experiential learning on how to cross the valley of death is thus an essential element of SBEE. Experiential learning is a form of learning whereby real-worldness, ill-defined problems, execution and reflection are essential design principles in transferring real-life experience into academic education (Perusso et al., 2020, 2021). In science-based entrepreneurship education, students need to gain experience with the process of transferring scientific knowledge and subsequent innovation to contexts of application and commercialization.

A SBEE program recognizes that crossing the valley of the death, through starting a new firm or by commercializing science in an existing firm, requires engagement with different types of professionals such as scientists, engineers, business developers, innovation managers, clients and consumers. By incorporating engagement in their educational programs, students are enabled to play a more active, co-producing and co-creating role in their higher education experience (Dollinger et al., 2018). This experience is mediated by digital tools and potentially enriches the learning experience—such as Canvas, online communication platforms and online guest lectures. How do these digital tools enable and enrich experiential learning in science-based entrepreneurship education?

By drawing upon the work of Perusso et al. (2020, 2021) a set of design principles for effective experiential learning is formulated. It is analyzed how digital tools contribute to experiential learning projects in the SBEE program. Digital tools enable students to replicate the real-world experience in science-based entrepreneurship education, at least to a certain extent. One question is to what extent digital tools enable students to experience the difficulties in transferring science to business. To assess this, these design principles are used.

First, this chapter puts science-based entrepreneurship education in the broader context of challenges that have been identified with regard to the innovation ecosystem in The Netherlands and presents the two educational programs as a response to these challenges. Secondly, a theoretical background on experiential learning is presented and four analytical categories are developed based on the scientific literature on experiential learning in management education. Thirdly, the contribution of digital tools to convey the "real experience" of entrepreneurial action based in science will be critically assessed. Their contribution of digital tools to experiential learning is assessed in the context of the bachelor's and master's program Science Business Innovation (SBI) at VU University Amsterdam. In these programs, aspects of the real world are simulated by using digital tools in order to convey the experience of science-based entrepreneurship to students. How this is done is evaluated in the next section. By way of conclusion, lessons are drawn on how digital tools may further enhance science-based entrepreneurship education.

Entrepreneurship Education in a Science Context

Traditionally universities produce disciplinary-based knowledge. Their position is shifting to include interdisciplinary research (Blankesteijn et al., 2019) in which managerial complexity of application of science through innovation is fully acknowledged. This type of research helps to close the "relevance gap" in management education (Perusso et al., 2020)—that is, the extent to which management education prepares students for real life, "wicked" management problems for which a traditional theory-based management education program does not prepare them sufficiently. One driver of this development at universities is the idea that economic progress can be achieved by innovation from science. However, despite increasing scientific knowledge the commercialization from new scientific findings remains limited.

A SBEE program incorporates involvement with both type of market actors and their real life challenges. The challenge is to connect market actors to newly developed, early-stage technologies (Meadowcroft, 2009). Incumbent market actors often experience creative limitations andreluctance to experiment, adopt and scale-up alternative science and technology-based business models. New market actors (e.g. entrepreneurs) might be less hindered by these constraints but are confronted by gaining legitimacy such that their innovative products and services are accepted by the market.

The SBI master's program at the Vrije Universiteit Amsterdam is an SBEE program that approaches commercialization from new scientific findings as an knowledge production process with organizations in the broader regional network in order to stimulate university-industry technology transfer. Important is the development of soft skills through interaction with industry experts. These interactions help students in practicing with pitching entrepreneurial opportunities and gaining resources to enable entrepreneurial experimentation. Within the walls of the academy students are stimulated to develop a solid understanding of natural sciences. In addition, students are trained to use business and innovation theories to analyze and develop business practice based on evidence drawn from these theories. This combination enables them to make and elaborate on smart, strategic choices. All steps are mediated by digital technology in the classroom. Also due to the current COVID-pandemic, there currently is ample experience with using digital tools to replicate aspects of the experience of science-based entrepreneurship. This chapter uses these experiences to explore the value of digital tools in bringing in the experience of science-based entrepreneurship in its full managerial complexity into the classroom.

Finding the balance between the exact sciences and managerial and entrepreneurial realities is a unique challenge for each technological innvation, because the application context is always different. This also requires to develop digital didactics unique for each course and level of the group of students. As the student's experience and knowledge increases, more freedom can be offered and more responsibility can be demanded to demarcate research into relevant subjects.

Students first need a generic understanding of the innovation process. The innovation process in which students are taught to develop entrepreneurial actions is conceptualized in the program as the innovation chain (Berkhout et al., 2010). Explanations of this chain are repeated throughout the program as the backbone of the understanding of innovation trajectories and opportunities to become entrepreneurial.

Students choose a real-life case and position it in the innovation chain. The innovation chain conceptualizes the process of converting science to business through innovation. New knowledge is created at universities and in science-based organizations, providing the science base. In between universities and R&D intensive industries, enabling technologies are developed that are brought one step further, into prototypes, at technology platforms. Then new products and services are developed, appealing to existing market needs or creating new markets. This needs to be combined with the creation of new consumer needs, or the alteration of existing ones.

Figure 10.1 exemplifies the "mental movement" students need to make in order to develop an analytical understanding of the case they are researching. Students start with identifying drivers and barriers, existent in the process from moving from left to right in the innovation chain. They then choose a particular set of drivers and/or barriers, and thus

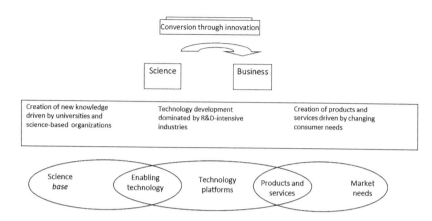

Fig. 10.1 The innovation chain (Berkhout et al., 2010)

position their case study in the innovation chain. This is a purely conceptual exercise, not involving the use of digital technology yet (Fig. 10.2).

They then choose a real-life case of science-based innovation. They interogate scientists, experts and other stakeholders involved in order to develop a preliminary idea of what is the main type of problems they face in moving from left to right in the innovation. They also do research whereby they use databases on the web, helping them to develop digital literacy in science and scientific research. Problems might for example be grounded in collaboration with external parties. Then they conceptualize that problem, using theories from the management of innovation literature, again drawn from digital databases. If the main problem is related to collaborating with external parties, for example, a suitable theoretical approach to analytically understand the case is "open innovation" (Chesbrough, 2004). They then choose that theory to further dive into and apply it to the case, to get a better sense of the underlying mechanisms at work in the innovation chain, either driving or hampering a movement in the process from left to right.

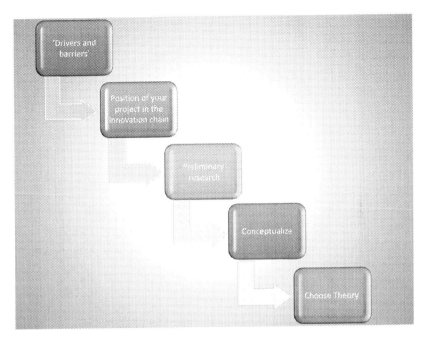

Fig. 10.2 Conceptualization of the underlying mechanisms in a case based on theory

Experiential Learning: Design Principles

In order to assess and thus develop recommendations on how to further optimize the learning effect of experiential learning in SBEE via digital tools, experiential learning theory is operationalized here and four design principles of experiential learning are presented. Perusso et al. (2020) suggest that the experiential learning environment should consist of a real-world context, with ill-defined problems, and require student execution, followed by an element of reflection.

Real-Worldness

The first design principle of experiential learning is real-worldness (RW) because students should learn to deal with elements of uncertainty, pressure, moral judgments and risk while working on university-industry technology transfer. An authentic work environment allows learners to acquire the dynamic and "culture of the practice". Sharing such insights with the class while conducting case-study research could unlock discussion of both broad and specific implications of theory for practice of university-industry technology transfer.

Ill-Defined Problems

The second design principle is that cases should consist of an ill-defined problem (IDP). Students need to learn how to identify and frame university-industry technology transfer. Traditionally, cases have clear (learning) goals to help students learn, understand and synthesize theory. Information and answers can be clearly be found in the learning materials. However, the nature of a experience in the real world is often complex, unstructured and might disrupt current logic; therefore, it might benefit learning if cases are ill-defined.

Execution

The third design principle is execution (E) because students should learn how to deal with adaptation. By testing potential technology transfer approaches or even going as far as to work on university-industry technology transfer in real life, students are confronted with adapting to new information. Researching a case might enable students to incorporate a broad range of information sources and feedback loops. Thereby proposed solutions and recommendations might be evaluated with practitioners, experts but also documentation, questionnaires and observations. Solutions should be the result of an in-depth study which often requires a process of adaptation.

Reflection

The fourth design principle is structured reflection (R) because students should learn that the process that leads to the solution requires stepping back from experience even while still being amidst the cognitive processes. Although every case on university-industry technology transfer might be unique to some degree, similarities might be found that might transform experience into learning.

Table 10.1 provides some relevant background material and gives an overview of the four general design principles, namely problem definition, real-worldness, execution and reflection. One of the most important aspects of coaching and giving feedback is that it is the input to stimulate reflection.

Perusso et al. (2020) show that three types of reflection can be distinguished, namely reflection-in-action, reflection-on-action and critical reflection. Reflection-in-action requires students to re-think the rules, facts and theories and invent and experiment their new understanding during the experiential learning project. The coaching teacher might raise inconsistencies during the interaction and suggest new directions thereby creating an active learning situation that stimulates reflection and development of competencies. Reflection-on-action considers what happened during the execution but discusses the experiences after it happened. The coaching teacher helps students to move beyond the intuitive actions that have been taken and develop competencies by understanding the behavior and considering alternative behaviors that might be more effective. Finally, critical reflection focusses student's attention on personal and hidden assumptions and aims to stimulate thinking how personal influences shape experiences. These forms of reflection and learning require input. Feedback and coaching are something that a teacher can directly control and can take into consideration while designing the educational context. In addition, we recognize three general design principles while considering an experiential learning environment aimed at thinking about university-industry technology transfer.

These denominators are derived from the literature on experiential learning (Table 10.1). They represent a set of design principles that can be followed in educational programs to help the student (re)construct a business problem in experiential learning settings. These design principles enable the students to develop a particular way of understanding university-industry technology transfer. The design principles have been used in the exploration of digital tools and their contribution to learning from experience.

Table 10.1 Summary of design principle to enable implementation of university-industry technology transfer education

Design principle	Implications for case-study education on university-industry technology transfer	Relevant background
1. Real-world context (RW)	Cases need to reflect real scientific, entrepreneurial, corporate and governmental challenges and therefore case-driven research projects must allow and even enable interaction with scientists, entrepreneurs, corporations and governmental agencies. Such a context facilitates students in observation of practitioners' daily routines, strategies and manners enabling insights about the influence of elements such as uncertainty, pressure, moral judgments and risk. Thereby the case discussion with the class allows to take the workplace dynamics into the discussion.	Carriger (2015)
2. Determination of the problem boundaries (often ill-defined) (IDP)	The real world situation of university-industry technology transfer is complex, unstructured and the boundaries of science, business and innovation are often unclear, therefore case-driven research projects must allow students to practice with demarcating case-driven projects into concepts that are relevant and can be "tested." Such a context stimulates active learning by students because clear conceptual demarcation, consistency and accurate measurement with relevant data require more than a straightforward application of theoretical models.	Kilbane et al. (2004) and Gosling and Mintzberg (2006)

(continued)

Table 10.1 (continued)

Design principle	Implications for case-study education on university-industry technology transfer	Relevant background
3. Execution (E)	Execution of university-industry technology transfer is often hindered by lack or abundance of data, therefore case-driven research projects must allow students to become acquainted with using and organizing feedback loops. Such an interaction context with teachers, industry experts and fellow students stimulates incorporation of criteria for the (proposed) solutions that meet all actors perspectives thereby stimulating design thinking and perspective taking. In addition, through dialogue students are confronted with validity of the criteria and generalizability of their outcomes.	Farashahi and Tajeddin (2018)
4. Reflection (R)	The results of execution in a complex, ill-defined real-world context impacts multiple aspects of university-industry technology transfer therefore reflection is an important competency. Case-driven research projects must allow and even enable practicing the use and development of structured reflection mechanisms for example stimulated through embedment of in-action, on-action and critical reflection. Including such generic reflection mechanisms extends learning beyond the (re)solution of the case and enables professional development of group and individuals	Grey (2004 and Gosling and Mintzberg (2006)

Experiential Learning in SBI Bachelor's and Master's Programs

Many of the SBI bachelor's and master's programs at the VU are based on experiential learning. Table 10.2 shows an analysis of the four elements in courses in the bachelor's and master's programs involving real-world cases and how they facilitate experiential learning. In the following paragraph, the table will be discussed per analytical category of real-worldness, ill-defined problems, execution and reflection. In this context, the use of digital tools will be explained and evaluated.

Real-World Context

Students choose cases based on real-world innovations and problems with valorization. Teachers make sure the cases are embedded in the real world. In the innovation projects in the bachelor's program, for example, guest lectures with professionals are organized. Students interview potential customers. Students both in the bachelor's and in the master's programs do internships in R&D departments of companies in order to gain first-hand experience with the conversion of science into commercial application through innovation. Real-worldness is an aspect of cases chosen in the more advanced courses, toward the end of the bachelor's program and in the master's program. The didactical choice here is that the further the students get into the program, the more they need to be prepared for the world of work. Especially in the innovation projects, this becomes manifest.

Real-worldness is a crucial element of these projects. For example, in the Innovation Project Energy, students work on a problem from a large-scale commercial company in the energy sector and develop, in close consultation with a professional, recommendations related to smart grid solutions. In the innovation project health and diagnostics students work on a case provided by an early-stage academic entrepreneur. Such entrepreneurs often ran into challenges with the business side of the idea. Students collaborate with the entrepreneur to understand the fundamental scientific knowledge and work to develop the business side of the idea,

Table 10.2 Design principles of experiential learning in SBI bachelor's and master's program courses

	Course name (bachelor or master, year, period)	Short course description	RW?	IDP?	E?	R?
Bachelor's program	Essentials of Science, Business and innovation (B-Y1-P1)	General theoretical introduction of natural science driven innovation, and application of on self-defined "innovation X project"			✓	
	Innovation project medicine (B-Y1-P3)	Acquiring knowledge and insight into the development process of new medicines by working on the drug development trajectory for a predefined illness			✓	✓
	Entrepreneurship and innovation (B-Y1-P5)	Basic knowledge about entrepreneurship by comparing four cases that analyze the opportunity, entrepreneur, development process and the role of resources and environment.			✓	✓
	Innovation project energy (B-Y1-P6)	Work as an *intrapreneurial* team developing criteria for science-based opportunities by talking to the innovation manager of an energy company, then evaluating and developing ideas and finally pitching the idea to the innovation manager.	✓		✓	✓
	Innovation project health and diagnostics (B-Y2-P3)	Work as an entrepreneurial team on a natural-science-based idea, developing SB-criteria for evaluating elements of the project context and finally poster pitching the best idea.			✓	✓

(continued)

Table 10.2 (continued)

Course name (bachelor or master, year, period)	Short course description	RW?	IDP?	E?	R?
Innovation project alternative fuels (B-Y2-P6)	Explore an alternative fuels and related technologies in relation to economic, business and innovation context by analysing specific transition context, conducting scenario planning assignments and presenting value chains with entrepreneurial opportunities.	✓	✓		✓
SBI bachelor's project (B-Y3-P4, P5 and P6)	Students conduct an independent small research project within a company including *defining* the value of the project context in relation to the relevant SBI elements, *designing* the project to reach academically valid research results and *executing* project consisting of data acquisition and pitching the results.	✓	✓	✓	✓
Master's program	Science project (M-Y1-P4 and P5)	Methodological design and execution of a research project on R&D from both a science, business and innovation perspective.		✓	✓	✓
	SBI Project & master thesis (M-Y2-P3, P4, P5, and P6)	Independent research project consisting of an internship in an organization, the formulation of an SBI-related problem, an analysis of this problem and written and oral reporting of the problem and analysis.	✓	✓	✓	✓

consisting amongst others of interviewing potential customers. In the Project Alternative Fuels they for the first time are challenged to take a more conceptual approach to a problem of science to business conversion via innovation, meaning that the students start from the abstract conceptual stage of the experiential learning cycle. This real-worldness in this context is that students have to gain knowledge about the alternative fuel in the real world before being able to start on the project. Digital tools play an essential role to facilitate real-worldness in the innovation projects, by, for example, enabling students to conduct interviews or to watch guest lectures. Moreover, the possibility of digitally providing lectures lowers the threshold for guest lectures. This is mainly because digital lectures do not put a time strain on the schedule due to travel requirements, whereas real-life lectures do.

Finally, the SBI bachelor's project is an internship of four months through which students experience first-hand and in actual work situation the drivers and barriers in moving from left to right in the innovation chain.

In the master's program, the science project and the SBI master's project, in which respectively internships are optional and obligatory, a real-world context is crucial for approval and successful development of the project. The level of these courses is advanced, and the ultimate goal is to have students develop a scientific research paper that is relevant for industry as well.

Whereas both bachelor's and master's students before did an internship to gain the real experience, they now take part in digital Teams and Zoom meetings. They go through a different, but valuable trajectory—developing more autonomy, self-confidence and a way to relate to people via digital means—which is a wholly different skill than the usual personal encounters and networking within a real-life internship context. At the same time, less personal encounters also mean that students are limited in the extent to develop interpersonal competencies such professional communications. The didactic implication is that a balance needs to be struck between solely digital and real-life context in order to create a meaningful learning experience.

Ill-Defined Problems

Management problems are not clear-cut. Reality is messy and unstructured. To carve out a case in a particular stage of the innovation chain, the problem first needs to be defined. What is the topic? Here especially the relevance of experiential learning becomes clear. A case is based on IDP but needs to be defined based on the SBI approach to decrease the extent to which it is "ill defined". The case needs to be defined based on searches on the web, enhancing the digital literacy of students.

Then the research topic and research question need to be defined. This is different from direct questions of professionals. It needs a translation to a topic related to known problems in the translation from science to business through innovation. In the innovation projects, the case concerns technology. The Innovation Project Energy can be considered in terms of an intrapreneurship context. The company in question has a technological base focused on charging electronic cars and work on balancing the electric grid. Students are stimulated to think like business developers. They are provided with insights and data about the products, services and company and can interview the innovation manager about their opportunities. The interview contributes to the demarcation of criteria and subsequently, students make an analysis and provided substantiation with documents and calculations. The process is linear. The context of Innovation Project Diagnostics and Health is that of the early-stage academic entrepreneur. To guide the process, students use a weekly action research methodology formulating hypotheses, gathering data and testing them. The process starts with a fundamental science idea but subsequently moves iteratively between awareness of problems and developing potential solutions, toward advice.

During the project, students conduct at least five interviews and further substantiation takes place with documents and calculations. The entrepreneurs often mention that both the interaction and the advice provide ample inspiration to move in new directions. In both the Innovation Project Energy and the Innovation Project Diagnostics and Health students start with experiences and input from an expert and subsequently need to reflect, conceptualize and experiment. In other words, students can ask expert advice about the problem boundaries. The Innovation Project Alternative Fuels however requires a higher degree of independence in defining the case itself. Students first work on understanding the transition toward alternative fuels by, among others, analyzing science and market dynamics and in the final stage develop and evaluate opportunities. What we observe is that an experiential, case-driven project can start at different stages of the learning cycle.

At a master's level, the case is defined in a broader sense. The case can be how a certain decision-making process works, for example. That decision-making process needs to be conceptualized based on what we know from the scientific literature on decision-making. This is a core element of both the science as well as the master's project in the master's SBI.

Defining the problems requires interaction and instead of real-life interactions, students now use digital tools to facilitate the interaction for example through digital Teams and Zoom meetings. However, digital communications are mentally straining therefore students are more often required to provide small summaries or questions in advance. This approach enables short and meaningful conversations about ill-defined problems, for example, with coaches, entrepreneurs and industry experts. In didactical terms, it requires students to be more active in defining the problem before an interaction can lead to a meaningful conversation and creates a learning experience that helps students move beyond the ill-defined boundaries of the problem.

Execution

From the bachelor's to the master's program the independent execution of case-driven research projects and incorporation of information from industry experts slowly increases. The early bachelor courses (Essentials of Science, Business & Innovation (ESBI), Innovation Project Medicines (IPG), and Entrepreneurship & Innovation (O&I)) focus on developing an active learning attitude and collaboration competencies through the execution of group assignments. For example, in the course Essentials of Science, Business, Innovation students choose a case to research on a very rudimentary level the extent to which technology has commercial viability, thereby stimulating an active learning attitude. This is followed by the Innovation Project Medicine which aims to develop collaboration competencies. SBI students are required to collaborate with pharmaceutical science students in the group assignment. Group coaching focuses on tasks and supporting collaboration. Lectures treat the topics that should be addressed in the assignments and contain relevant knowledge to carry out the assignments. The interaction with industry experts has only limited consequences for the assignments. They mostly function as a source of inspiration. Information to substantiate evaluations and conclusions is mainly based on websites and documents. During these projects students get acquainted with moving through the four stages of the experiential learning cycle.

In the next courses (Innovation Project Energy (IPE), Innovation Project Diagnostics & Health (IDG) and Innovation Project Alternative Fuels (IAF)) a homogeneous group of SBI students works on assignments that require more independence in defining the project criteria. Lectures support the execution of the assignments by highlighting the topics that should be addressed. However, the amount of knowledge provided decreases per lecture. The data gathered via interviews should be included to support evaluations and conclusions by the students. In part, this is possible because students have had a research methodology course that introduces terms such as validity. Students have more freedom to experiment with what type of experiences they find meaningful to learn from. Group coaching shifts from tasks and support for collaboration toward a focus on process suggestions and creative problem-solution feedback. However, the support during execution is still mandatory and follows a week-by-week schedule. The goal of these meetings is to support the reflection and support in formulating potential learning goals.

Analyzing the execution with digital tools highlights the importance of body language (or lack thereof) and improvization. For example, the process of group coaching requires that the teacher takes more control over and directs the conversation because otherwise, students are hesitant to participate. Another example is the online defense. Seeing mostly faces only makes it more difficult to assess the use of other non-verbal communication. Students however improvise quite easily with the use of digital tools, thereby creating experiences upon which they can draw in their professional work—for example, on how to work together online, as a team. Moreover, the students also learn how collaboration can be facilitated with digital tools thereby preparing them to some extent in becoming "digital nomads".

The bachelor's, science and master's projects do not contain mandatory meetings that provide room to discuss feedback and process on an individual level. This contrasts with courses like the Innovation Project Energy, the Innovation Project Diagnostics & Health and the Innovation Project Alternative Fuels. Students have a high degree of independence and responsibility in the execution of these research projects. Assignments are still used to create an opportunity for providing feedback and there are some supporting lectures. However, the main goal of the lectures is to introduce a moment for questions about the assignments, share insights into research projects and support each other in creative problem-solving. Especially in the master's project the development of a professional skillset is important and tested.

An interesting point in the innovation projects in the bachelor's and master's program is the group composition. In the innovation projects, the group composition is mixed with students from different study programs. The goal is to develop collaboration competencies while executing a project, while in other courses, mostly on the master's level, the different disciplinary backgrounds are used to guide the approach of the group for example via the division of tasks among the students. Both projects provide students with experience in working with people from different disciplines. Especially at the master's level, this creates an experience wherein SBI students learn that they are able and perhaps responsible for leveraging the multi-disciplinary backgrounds from all team members to produce viable advice.

A red thread throughout the bachelor's and master's courses is that increasingly, the autonomy of students is stimulated. Students need to find a balance between the wishes of companies on the one side, and academic requirements on the other. On an increasing practice- and theory-informed basis, students practice with developing evidence-based recommendations and entrepreneurial strategies and thus develop a personal toolkit of knowledge, skills and attitude on the level of execution.

Reflection

Both in the bachelor's and the master's programs, the three forms of reflection discussed are implemented. Reflection is fundamental to learn from the experience. During the innovation projects, reflection-in-action happens during the coaching session with the teacher. Especially in the beginning of the bachelor's and master's, students seem to require an acquaintance period to familiarize themselves with re-thinking the rules, facts and theories. Getting familiar with and actively drawing upon the topics is a first step toward conducting, inventing and experimenting with case-driven research projects. In part actively reflecting in-action could be considered an exercise of creativity, because it draws upon the fundamental knowledge of the learner. This does not mean that at a later stage inconsistencies and suggestions for new directions can be raised by the teacher.

Beyond this first stage, reflection-on-action becomes more important as the interaction with the teacher shifts from specific tasks topics initiated by the teacher toward process and execution challenges that draw upon teachers' execution experience. Reflection-on-action is implemented and stimulated through coaching by the teacher, a review by peer feedback or a business pitch. This happens for example in the innovation projects, in which, through weekly group meetings, it is considered if the goals have been achieved and to what extent a different strategy might be used. Another stimulus to activate reflection-on-action is peer feedback. Receiving feedback from other groups raises questions about the criteria used and the sources that substantiate them. The same reflection could be achieved through a business pitch. Reflection-on-action during the bachelor's project, science project, and master's project are facilitated—but only when students ask. Often teachers consider such meetings as an exercise of creativity. By highlighting some alternative paths, students are stimulated to rethink their basic assumptions.

Critical reflection is embedded in several courses via writing assignments and interactions. For example the Innovation Projects students first give and receive feedback from other students on a competencies level. Then they analyze the peer feedback and present a summary to the group under supervision of a teacher. Group members have the possibility to provide additional explanation or suggestions. The teacher can suggest alternative interpretations of the feedback and support in the reflection by highlighting alternative competency developments approaches. After the meeting students write a short reflection report which provides an action plan for further development. Critical reflection is also part of the bachelor's and master's project. Reflection is on the internship experience is the last step before graduating. Reflection is an important part of the work execution grade in the SBI master's project.

Digital tools play an important facilitating and supporting role in several of the innovation projects. Digital tools facilitate engagement by (1) providing short pre-recorded lectures enabling critical thinking and preparation before the lectures and (2) support students in peer-review of group assignments. Especially peer-review is important because it supports and stimulates students to understand and learn other cases by reviewing other students work. Furthermore, digital tools support meaningful student development through (1) individual group member evaluation on entrepreneurial competences which subsequently (2) facilitates a group discussion supervised by a teacher. This two-step reflection eventually stimulates a more critical reflection enabling the creation of a thoughtful plan of action. Didactic implication is that digital tools enable *individual* students to think actively about their entrepreneurial competences. The tools also enable *social* embeddedness of the learning activity.

Through the bachelor's and master's program, reflection is fundamental activity in learning from the experience and for guiding further experimentation. As students become more acquainted with the steps from the experiential learning cycle the implemented forms of reflection shift to more advanced levels, providing a higher degree of independence. Digital tools facilitate and mediate this process via activating students and making them aware of the social context in which they perform such reflection.

Conclusion

All four elements of experiential learning come back in both the bachelor's and master's programs. Real-worldness is stimulated by interaction with professionals, guest lectures and real consultancy assignments. Students translate ill-defined problems into cases that they can research, thus transgressing from ill-defined to defined "SBI" problems. Execution is part of their assignments, mostly during their internships. Reflection is mostly included as a means for the development of entrepreneurial skills and attitudes.

The use of experiential learning techniques, enhanced by digital technology, stimulates critical thinking on the relation between theoretical concepts and real management problems in SBEE. At the same time, it offers students some and an increasing degree of freedom, for example in choosing the theoretical approach. It helps them to define the problem and make use of the scientific literature in order to act evidence-based as entrepreneurs. This enables students to consult with companies on the chosen research approach, such as to ensure that the results provide relevant and useful outcomes. Methodology should support students, business and academics to co-create a relevant and meaningful research project. Experiential learning via digital technology is a form of learning that activates students to actively re-think and to help them build the bridge between university and industry.

This chapter shows that digital tools can be used to play a role in facilitating engagement and meaningful student development, thereby enabling students to move through the steps of the experiential learning cycle both a case content level and an individual competences level. Via digital tools the real-world experience can be at least partly replicated. Further research is needed on how digital tools may more effectively used in order to convey the real-world experience in such a way that the learning effect in this type of education, in which experiential learning is key, is optimized.

Learning Points

1. Experiential learning can be facilitated by taking into account the four building blocks: 1. real-worldness, 2. ill-defined problems, 3. execution, 4. reflection.
2. Building blocks in the courses that make up for the program in a balanced and sophisticated manner (and thus: not randomly).
3. When implemented as a learning tool in science- and technology-based entrepreneurship education programs, digital tools assist in conveying the real-world experience to students via guest lectures, interviews and interactions with representatives from industries.
4. And enables students to draw lessons from these experiences that are relevant to practice, while at the same time containing academic relevance as well.

References

Barr, S. H., et al. (2017). Bridging the valley of death: Lessonss learned from 14 years of commercialization of technology education. *Academy of Management Learning & Education, 8*(3), 370–388.

Berkhout, G., et al. (2010). Connecting technological capabilities with market needs using a cyclic innovation model. *R&D Management, 40*(5), 474–490.

Blankesteijn, M., et al. (2019). Entrepreneurial universities and knowledge circulation: Challenges to university-industry interaction. In N. Caseiro & D. S. Hershey (Eds.), *Smart specialization strategies and the role of entrepreneurial universities* (pp. 81–98). IGI-Global.

Blankesteijn, M., et al. (2020). Science-based entrepreneurship education as a means for university-industry technology transfer. *International Journal for Entrepreneurship and Management, 17*, 779–808.

Carriger, M. S. (2015). Problem-based learning and management development—Empirical and theoretical considerations. *The International Journal of Management Education, 13*(3), 249–259.

Chesbrough, H. (2004). Managing open innovation. *Research-Technology Management, 47*(1), 23–26.

Dollinger, M., et al. (2018). Co-creation in higher education: Towards a conceptual model. *Journal of Marketing for Higher Education, 28*(2), 210–231.

Farashahi, M., & Tajeddin, M. (2018). Effectiveness of teaching methods in business education: A comparison study on the learning outcomes of lectures, case studies and simulations. *The International Journal of Management Education, 16*(1), 131–142.

Gosling, J., & Mintzberg, H. (2006). Management education as if both matter. *Management Learning, 37*(4), 419–428.

Grey, C. (2004). Reinventing business schools: The contribution of critical management education. *Academy of Management Learning & Education, 3*(2), 178–186.

Kilbane, C., et al. (2004). The real-time case method: Description and analysis of the first implementation. *Innovative Higher Education, 29*(2), 121–135.

Meadowcroft, J. (2009). What about the politics? Sustainable development, transition management, and long term energy transitions. *Policy Sciences, 42*(4), 323.

Perusso, A., et al. (2020). The contribution of reflective learning to experiential learning in business education. *Assessment & Evaluation in Higher Education, 45*(7), 1001–1015.

Perusso, A., et al. (2021). The effectiveness and impact of action learning on business graduates' professional practice. *Journal of Management Education, 45*(2), 177–205.

Retra, K., et al. (2016). Educating the science–business professional. *Industry and Higher Education, 30*(4), 302–309.

11

The Future of Enterprise and Entrepreneurship Education in Relation to Technology

Denis Hyams-Ssekasi and Naveed Yasin

Introduction

Entrepreneurship and enterprise is a multifaceted term and often used interchangeably. As such, there is a considerable interest for both entrepreneurs and entrepreneurship, respectively. Entrepreneurship is never taken for granted, and as such, governments are playing an important role to ensure that it is taught at a higher level with a view to developing future entrepreneurs. Higher education institutions (HEIs) worldwide are strengthening entrepreneurship education to enable students to acquire knowledge and practical skills, develop interests, and become entrepreneurs. In fact, the need to increase the supply of entrepreneurs

D. Hyams-Ssekasi (✉)
Institute of Management, University of Bolton, Bolton, UK
e-mail: dh4@bolton.ac.uk

N. Yasin
Faculty of Management, Canadian University Dubai, Dubai, United Arab Emirates
e-mail: naveed.yasin@cud.ac.ae

has been argued by Burns (2016, p. 7) to be "probably one of the major challenges facing business schools in the 21st century". The general overview is that entrepreneurship as a discipline is not new, but how it is taught differs from one educational institution to another. What seems to be a common denominator is that entrepreneurial knowledge and skills are still needed. Undoubtedly, the idea of acquiring business skills and the ability to implement these align with entrepreneurship education. It becomes a process for knowledge acquisition, skills development, and decision making. Lorz et al. (2011) concur to the effectiveness of entrepreneurship education on entrepreneurship skill development whilst Liñán (2004) perceives entrepreneurship education as a well-known approach for innovation.

According to Scott (2004), 15 years ago, only a handful of schools were offering entrepreneurship courses. Nowadays, there are more colleges and universities inculcating entrepreneurship to inspire students to become entrepreneurs. Entrepreneurship embedded into education gears to make students entrepreneurs, to have a business mindset, and to develop the relevant skills and competencies with a view to exploiting entrepreneurship and new ventures (Liñán, 2005). In their analysis, Muofhe and Du Toit (2011) argue that the degree to which entrepreneurship education impacts the choice for individuals to become entrepreneurs is progressing steadily, and positive influences have been noticed as more HEIs continue to provide courses as well as attracting more students to study enterprise and entrepreneurship. Current literature indicates that entrepreneurship education creates self-sufficient, motivated, and enterprising individuals who leave the education system with skills and knowledge to start their businesses. Vestergaard et al. (2012) found that former students who were fully engaged in entrepreneurship education started their businesses. This is echoed by Matlay (2008) and Stokes et al. (2010) who argue that the choices to become an entrepreneur and subsequent entrepreneurial careers are linked to entrepreneurship education. Gerba's (2012) research on undergraduate studying business and engineering courses concluded that business students who partake in entrepreneurship education tend to have defined entrepreneurial intentions as compared to engineering students who had not undertaken the programme. Based on this notion, it can be noted that education can influence students' attitudes towards entrepreneurship and their entrepreneurial competence in varied contexts (Yasin et al., 2020, 2021a).

Despite the growing interest in entrepreneurship education, there is a demand for adopting digital technologies in the delivery and assessment of enterprise education. Numerous strategies and methods in teaching and learning have been devised, but as we move forward into the future, there is a need to embrace more advanced and disruptive technologies. The use of educational technology in this present climate becomes a lifeline for the efficacy of entrepreneurship and enterprise education.

A Theoretical Perspective

There is a tendency to confuse entrepreneurship education with enterprise education. While the similarity between the two terms is theoretically the same, contextually, these are different. The definition of Brown (1999) and Béchard and Toulouse (1998) focuses on the skills taught and characteristics engendered in students through formalized structures delivery for purposes of developing new and innovative skills and mindset shifting (Wilson, 2008) to enable one to start up a new business. In simple terms, entrepreneurship education is formalized teaching programmes in an educational establishment. Furthermore, entrepreneurship education continues to pave the way to make it a worthwhile discipline especially in higher education institution worldwide. While contemplating educational provisions, it is worth noting the challenges HEIs are experiencing in relation to entrepreneurship education. Hannon (2005) proposed three important questions to be considered in entrepreneurship education:

1. Is entrepreneurship education management or business related?
2. Is entrepreneurship education a part of a learner's life capabilities?
3. Is entrepreneurship education a process of identifying organizational opportunities?

Hannon stated that an "underpinning philosophy of an educational programme will partially determine the outcomes of the educational process and influence the educational experience" (Hannon, 2005).

The consensus for the future of entrepreneurship education is as follows:

1. Entrepreneurship education would contribute to the development and prosperity of enterprising economies.
2. Entrepreneurship education will enhance an individual's ability to become self-sufficient.
3. Entrepreneurship education will improve an individual's knowledge of enterprise and business ventures.
4. Entrepreneurship education will cultivate unique skills and enable individuals to think outside the box.
5. Entrepreneurship education will allow the individual to recognize commercial opportunities.
6. Entrepreneurship will prepare an individual for an uncertain future.

How technology will be used in the future in enterprise education and entrepreneurship education?

Although there are advancements to be made in the delivery of enterprise and entrepreneurship education, such goals for higher education institutions and their enterprise educators emphasize the need to incorporate a wider range of stakeholders in the development, delivery, and assessment of entrepreneurship projects. In an article published by the *Higher Education Digest*, Yasin (2020) emphasizes the importance of "not only research-informed teaching", but also, "teaching informed research", where he proposed eight strategies for the effective delivery and assessment of enterprise and entrepreneurship education:

1. Gamification and simulations
2. Digital technology and CPU-aided quizzes
3. Measuring the effectiveness of enterprise education
4. Reflective practices
5. No closed book examinations
6. Collaborative and interdisciplinary approaches

7. Gearing up for the real world of entrepreneurship
8. Knowledge co-creation

There is growing consensus on the ability to teach entrepreneurship and support from many stakeholders, including policymakers (and related support agencies), academics, and learners. Based on the contributions of each chapter, there is also a consensus that the role of technology in teaching and learning, and in entrepreneurship itself, cannot be undermined as we move towards pedagogical advancement in the field. Thus, engaging students using technology is important to develop their enterprise and entrepreneurial skills (Yasin & Khansari, 2021) whilst exploring not only the students' experiences (E) but the preferences (P), recommendations (R), and impressions (I) (Yasin et al., 2021a).

The crucial role of emerging technologies in entrepreneurship requires further adoption and emphasis in enterprise education. The rise of modern technologies such as virtual reality (VR), artificial intelligence (AI), augmented reality (AR), and robotics is meant to support enterprise and entrepreneurship students learning. The adoption of such technologies in enterprise education provides students to learn through experiential learning, thus bridging the gap between scientific knowledge and business education with an explicit purpose to address the market needs.

General Discussion

Gamification, as it currently stands in education, is being utilized differently in various disciplines. However, social sciences have traditionally lagged behind, unable to fully engage with learners. As technology is deeply rooted into the existing generation of students and the trend set to continue, gamification of the curriculum becomes vital and should not be ignored. Higher education institutions have a role to play in creating an environment which embraces student's skill set that stimulates creative thinking and problem solving, and enables students to become industry employment ready. This type of pedagogy requires planning and some element of innovation, but more importantly, the instructors to be able to adapt to the future of the changing environment blended with this approach.

As technology changes at an exponential rate, the ability to embed gamification and the technology multiplies so do the modes of communication. The idea to link multiple devices is the new present to inculcate entrepreneurial education for the future generation of learners' and for a contemporary curriculum. Many successful multinational corporations (MNCs) have embraced technology to improve processes and in some cases reacted to the omni-channels of communication lines with their customers. The current changes as well as the expansion of higher education have unlocked the full potential towards using technology to improve delivery. The need for the curriculum hinges upon a continuum of multiple modes of communications to collaborate holistically; otherwise, it becomes a vicious circle. Rather than traditional learning through individual piece of technology in isolation, the significance of the ability to gamify learning through multiple modes will determine engagement, increase the competitiveness of the department, and ensure students are ready to harness their inert learnt skills.

The future of gamification in entrepreneurship education is here to stay and any new encounter within the learning environment will need to revisit this approach continually to evolve with the generation advancement. The ability for student to access information that is readily available has significantly changed the pedagogy; however, the adaption of gamification stretches and challenges the students much further which cannot be achieved by traditional teaching methods, per se.

Based on the various learning points that are presented by each chapter, we propose the following directions for enterprise and entrepreneurship education:

1. Adoption of computer-based simulation games at undergraduate and postgraduate levels of learning to enhance the technical, communication, and cognitive skills of the learner.
2. Recognizing the importance of digital marketing in enterprise education by focusing on digital advertising, digital marketing, and e-commerce. Other factors such as teaching style, teaching model,

and classroom climate influence the effectiveness of the teaching delivery of the digital marketing course.
3. Fostering entrepreneurship attitudes and intentions. Aligning entrepreneurship courses to be student-oriented, experimental-oriented, and curiosity-based. Teaching pedagogy should adopt techniques such as gamification and simulations, design-based thinking, reflective learning, practice-based case study and lectures by entrepreneurs, starting start-up activities, real-world experience, action, and reflective process; it should encourage participants to start their ventures, learn from the experience of others.
4. Incorporating emerging technologies such as AI, AU, and VR for effective instructor-AI collaboration in entrepreneurship education as key dimensions of teaching and learning including curriculum design, instruction, assessment, and feedback.
5. Recognizing the importance of MOOCs in terms of the educational contexts and emphasizing its scalability, enhanced coverage, and democratization of enterprise education.
6. Learning from international case studies to engaging in collaborative projects involving students in other countries.
7. Optimizing digital tools for learning in enterprise education.

Conclusion

In this chapter, it is evident that the future of enterprise and entrepreneurship education will start from developing the overarching theoretical and practical discourse for advancing pedagogies and moving towards the adoption and embeddedness of technology, creative approaches to teaching, and learning student-centric and flipped classroom approaches, creative methods of learning and assessment of learners, engaging with real-life entrepreneurs and real-life scenarios for new product and service development (i.e. incubator projects). The pertinence of technological advancement in entrepreneurship as well as in the teaching and learning of entrepreneurship and enterprise education should not be undermined. Using gamification approaches in education will not only increase students' motivation and engagement but also make the learning more interesting and interactive. Students' creative talents need to be nurtured by the development of university-based business incubators (UBIs). Therefore, the way forward is to embrace new technologies in entrepreneurship education and to integrate gamification and game-based learning to motivate, engage, and unlease the entrepreneurial talents of university students'.

References

Béchard, J. P., & Toulouse, J. M. (1998). Validation of a didactic model for the analysis of training objectives in entrepreneurship. *Journal of Business Venturing, 13*, 317–332.
Brown, C. (1999). Teaching new dogs new tricks: The rise of entrepreneurship education in graduate schools of business. *Digital Geographic Information Working Group, 99*(2), 1–4.
Burns, P. (2016). *Small business and entrepreneurship: Start-up, growth and maturity* (4th ed.). Palgrave Macmillan.
Gerba, D. T. (2012). Impact of entrepreneurship education on entrepreneurial intentions of business and engineering students in Ethiopia. *African Journal of Economic and Management Studies, 3*(2), 258–277.
Hannon, P. D. (2005). The journey from student to entrepreneur: A review of the existing research into graduate entrepreneurship. *Proceedings of the International Entrepreneurship Conference*, Guildford, UK
Liñán, F. (2004). Intention-based models of entrepreneurship education. *Piccolla Impresa/Small Business, 3*, 11–35.
Liñán, F. (2005, 10–13 July). Development and validation of an entrepreneurial intention questionnaire (EIQ). *IntEnt05 Conference*, Guildford, UK.
Lorz, M., Müller, S., & Volery, T. (2011). Entrepreneurship education: A meta-analysis of impact studies and applied methodologies. *Conference Paper, FGF G-Forum 2011*, Zurich.
Matlay, H. (2008). The impact of entrepreneurship education on entrepreneurial outcomes. *Journal of Small Business and Enterprise Development, 15*(2), 382–396.
Muofhe, N. J., & Du Toit, W. F. (2011). Entrepreneurial education's and entrepreneurial role models' influence on career choice. *South African Journal of Human Resource, 9*(1), 1–15.

Scott, R. S. (2004). The growth and advancement of entrepreneurship in higher education: An environmental can by "Kauffman Center for Entrepreneurial Leadership Staff"; "The Contribution or Entrepreneurship Education: An analysis of the Berger Program". *Academy of Management Learning and Education, 3*(3), 340–342.

Stokes, D., Wilson, N., & Mador, M. (2010). *Entrepreneurship*. Cengage Learning EMEA, Andover.

Vestergaard, L., Moberg, K., & Jorgensen, C. (2012). *Impact of entrepreneurship education in Denmark—2011*. The Danish Foundation for Entrepreneurship.

Wilson, K. (2008). Chapter 5: Entrepreneurship education in Europe. In J. Potter (Ed.), *Entrepreneurship and higher education*. OECD Publications.

Yasin, N. (2020). Not only research-informed teaching but teaching-informed research. Higher Education Digest, Middle East Special Issue.

Yasin, N., & Khansari, Z. (2021). Evaluating the impact of social enterprise education on students' enterprising characteristics in the United Arab Emirates. *Education+ Training, 63*(6), 827–905.

Yasin, N., Khansari, Z., & Sharif, T. (2020). Assessing the Enterprising Tendencies of Arab Female Undergraduate Engineering Students in the Sultanate of Oman. *Industry and Higher Education, 35*(6), 429–439.

Yasin, N., Gilani, S. A. M., & Nair, G. (2021a). "Dump the Paper Quiz" The 'PERI' Model for Exploring Gamification in Student Learning in the United Arab Emirates. *Industry and Higher Education, 0*(0), 1–15.

Index

A

Adopting, 163, 164, 253
Adult learning, 216
Artificial intelligence (AI), vi, vii, 61, 69, 70, 72, 106, 159–177, 191, 255, 257
Assessment, vi, 30, 31, 56, 64, 70, 71, 81, 85, 97, 111, 161, 174–176, 196, 198, 210, 214, 216, 253, 254, 257

B

Bibliometric, 133–151
Blended learning, brick-and-mortar education, 189, 192, 195
Business, v, 3, 25–46, 54, 77, 105, 134, 159, 189, 208, 229, 252

C

Challenge, 3, 11, 25, 27, 53–55, 65, 68, 78, 81, 82, 85, 108, 134, 149, 167–169, 177, 196, 197, 200, 202, 207, 209, 213, 217, 221, 229–231, 238, 246, 252, 253, 256
Classroom, vii, 15, 27, 54, 56, 59, 61, 74, 80, 109–114, 116–117, 119, 120, 122–124, 163, 167, 171, 174, 177, 189, 190, 210, 213, 219, 257
Communication, 28, 30, 54, 63, 70, 73, 74, 79–81, 85–87, 89, 94–97, 106, 136, 167, 175, 188, 198, 207–214, 216–220, 229, 241, 243, 244, 256
Culture, 6, 53, 162, 169, 173, 174, 191, 208, 211, 212, 214, 216–218, 220, 221, 234

D

DBA, 77–97
Digital
  communication, 209, 210, 218, 220, 243
  marketing, vii, 105–124, 256, 257
  technology, 53–74, 106–108, 167, 189–190, 202, 208, 219, 231, 232, 248, 253, 254
  tools, 227–249, 257
Digitalization, 107, 161, 166, 167
Diversity, 207, 208, 212, 219–221

E

Economic, vii, 3–6, 15, 53, 54, 79, 160, 166, 187, 188, 198, 202, 209, 230
Education entrepreneurship, v, 3–16, 25–46, 53–74, 78, 133–151, 159–177, 207–221, 227–249, 251–258
Engagement, vi, 7, 10, 14, 15, 27, 28, 30, 71, 81, 110, 111, 117, 122, 148, 150, 161, 167, 170, 202, 217, 228, 229, 247, 248, 256, 257
Enterprise, 5, 9, 26–28, 31–32, 45, 53–74, 97, 169, 198, 208, 214, 251–258
Entrepreneur, 5, 6, 8, 33, 74, 95, 108, 133, 144, 160, 164, 171, 188, 208, 238, 242, 252
Entrepreneurial, vii, 4, 27, 54, 77–97, 108, 133, 149, 159, 188, 207, 227, 252
Exchange, 190, 208, 209
Experience, 10, 13, 15, 26–30, 58, 60, 64, 65, 71–73, 78, 79, 81, 82, 88, 106, 108, 109, 112, 113, 148, 150, 161, 166, 167, 173, 175, 176, 189–191, 198, 200, 208, 210, 215–218, 220, 228–231, 235, 238, 241–249, 254, 255, 257
Experiential, vi, vii, 9, 26, 29, 31, 45, 72, 79, 81, 115, 134, 135, 164, 166, 167, 169, 170, 175, 176, 215, 220, 227–249, 255
future, 4, 6, 251, 254, 256, 257

G

Games, 10–16, 25–46, 59, 60, 134–138, 147–151, 168–170, 176, 189, 190, 256, 258
Gamification, vi, vii, 3–16, 45, 136, 254–258
Global challenges, 188, 209–210
Graduate, v, vi, 5, 6, 57, 61, 63, 74, 78, 107, 108, 160, 196, 199–201

H

Higher Education, 4, 8, 9, 16, 25–46, 62, 65, 69–70, 78, 108, 133, 187–202, 229, 251, 254–256

I

Industry, vi, 4, 29, 30, 58, 62, 96, 106–108, 160, 162, 168, 176, 230, 231, 234–237, 241, 243, 244, 248, 249, 255
Information, 5, 14, 27, 45, 55, 57, 58, 66, 68, 73, 80–82, 86, 96, 97, 105, 114, 115, 123, 148,

159, 169, 174, 175, 190, 192, 195–197, 199, 200, 202, 212, 214, 215, 217, 219, 221, 234, 243, 244, 256
Innovation, vi, 3, 9, 56, 58, 67, 69, 71, 74, 86, 93–95, 106, 108, 144, 160, 162, 168, 173–175, 187, 188, 198, 200, 210, 228–232, 238, 241–247, 252, 255
International student, 175
Internet, 11, 62, 106, 173, 175
Internships, 208, 238, 241, 247, 248

K

Knowledge, 4–11, 14, 15, 27, 30, 54–57, 59, 62, 65, 71, 81, 82, 86, 87, 96, 107–109, 112–115, 122, 123, 133, 136, 137, 160–164, 168, 169, 171, 175, 176, 188, 190, 192, 193, 196, 215–217, 219, 220, 228, 230, 231, 238, 241, 244–246, 251, 252, 254, 255

L

Learner, vi, 5, 6, 10–13, 26, 27, 29, 30, 58, 65, 71, 72, 80–82, 86, 114, 161, 164, 166, 168–170, 173–176, 191, 192, 195, 196, 199, 200, 202, 210, 234, 246, 253, 255–257
Learning, vi, 3–16, 25–46, 54, 78, 107, 134, 160, 189, 207, 227–249, 253
Learning styles, 28, 114, 121

M

MBA, v, 77–97
Motivation, 5, 7, 10, 11, 14, 16, 27, 81, 82, 87, 109, 111, 114, 136, 160, 161, 175, 216, 257

N

Network, 82, 95, 139, 143, 145, 188, 198, 230

O

Online, vi, vii, 14, 27, 32, 46, 70, 89, 105–107, 117, 121, 167, 173–176, 187–202, 207–221, 229, 244, 245
Organization, 4, 54, 58, 77, 78, 81, 86, 87, 95, 96, 107, 139, 160, 166, 197, 201, 213, 230, 231

P

Pedagogy, vi, 16, 45, 58, 64, 73, 109, 133–151, 160, 165, 171, 188, 208, 255–257
Program, v–vii, 4, 6, 8, 9, 15, 16, 32, 46, 56, 57, 60, 63, 67, 78, 80, 81, 88, 94, 95, 162, 163, 168, 188, 189, 192, 196–201, 228–231, 238–249, 253
Progress, 10, 14, 31, 70–71, 109, 161, 168, 213, 230
Project, 7, 28, 57, 60, 61, 67, 68, 74, 111–113, 115, 176, 189, 193, 198, 208, 211–218, 220, 221, 229, 235, 238–248, 254, 257

Q
Quality, 31, 57, 74, 106, 109, 112, 160, 187, 196, 202

R
Reflection (R), 164, 176, 214, 220, 228, 233–236, 238, 244, 246–249

S
Science-based, 227–249
Simulation, vi, vii, 14, 25–46, 56–59, 69, 77–97, 133–151, 168–171, 176, 254, 256, 257
Skills, vi, vii, 4–11, 14, 26, 30, 54, 55, 57–63, 65–69, 71–74, 77–97, 106–108, 112–115, 123, 134, 136, 149, 160, 162, 163, 166, 169, 170, 173, 177, 188–190, 193, 196, 214, 215, 217–221, 230, 241, 245, 248, 251–256
Student, v, 5, 25, 54, 77–97, 107, 133, 159, 189, 208, 227, 251

T
Teaching, vii, 4–7, 9–12, 14, 16, 25–29, 32, 33, 44, 45, 54–56, 63, 64, 72, 73, 77–97, 107–124, 133–151, 161–164, 166–168, 171, 177, 188, 190, 195, 196, 228, 235, 253–257
Teams, 12, 31, 60, 62, 68, 71, 95, 198, 208, 210–214, 220, 221, 241, 243, 245

Techniques, 10, 16, 27, 54, 56, 78–81, 94–97, 135, 136, 138, 139, 150, 248, 257
Technology, vi–viii, 14–16, 28–30, 45, 53–74, 80, 105–108, 114, 115, 117, 136, 148, 160, 167–171, 174, 175, 177, 189–191, 193, 194, 196, 202, 207, 208, 210, 212, 214, 217–221, 228, 230–232, 234–237, 242, 243, 248, 249, 251–258

U
United Kingdom (UK), 4, 109, 142, 150, 208, 210–212
University, v–vii, 5, 8, 15, 28, 55, 58, 70, 73, 78–80, 105–124, 142, 190–192, 196, 198–201, 210, 211, 228, 230, 231, 248, 252
Unlocking, 188

V
Values, 5, 7, 45, 62, 71–73, 78, 89–93, 95, 96, 119–122, 137, 160, 162–164, 189, 202, 228
Virtual learning, 28, 29, 136

W
Workload, 176

Printed in the United States
by Baker & Taylor Publisher Services